Colloquial
Spanish of
Latin America

The Colloquial Series

Series adviser: Gary King

The following languages are available in the Colloquial series:

	Afrikaans		Japanese
	Albanian		Korean
	Amharic		Latvian
	Arabic (Levantine)		Lithuanian
	Arabic of Egypt		Malay
	Arabic of the Gulf and Saudi Arabia		Mongolian
	Basque		Norwegian
	Bulgarian		Panjabi
*	Cambodian		Persian
*	Cantonese		Polish
*	Chinese		Portuguese
	Croatian and Serbian		Portuguese of Brazil
	Czech		Romanian
	Danish	*	Russian
	Dutch		Scottish Gaelic
	Estonian		Slovak
	Finnish		Slovene
	French		Somali
	German	*	Spanish
	Greek		Spanish of Latin America
	Gujarati		Swedish
	Hindi	*	Thai
	Hungarian		Turkish
*	Icelandic		Ukrainian
	Indonesian		Urdu
	Italian	*	Vietnamese
			Welsh

Accompanying cassette(s) (*and CDs) are available for the above titles. They can be ordered through your bookseller, or send payment with order to Taylor & Francis/Routledge Ltd, ITPS, Cheriton House, North Way, Andover, Hants SP10 5BE, UK, or to Routledge Inc, 29 West 35th Street, New York NY 10001, USA.

COLLOQUIAL CD-ROMs
Multimedia Language Courses
Available in: Chinese, French, Portuguese and Spanish

Colloquial
Spanish of
Latin
America

Roberto Rodríguez-Saona

Senior Lecturer in Spanish,
Trinity and All Saints College,
of the University of Leeds

London and New York

First published 1994
by Routledge
11 New Fetter Lane, London EC4P 4EE

Simultaneously published in the USA and Canada
by Routledge
29 West 35th Street, New York, NY 10001

Reprinted 1995, 1996, 1998 (twice), 1999, 2000

Second edition first published 2002

Routledge is an imprint of the Taylor & Francis Group

© 1994, 2002 Roberto Rodríguez-Saona

Typeset in Times Ten by Florence Production, Stoodleigh, Devon

Printed and bound in Great Britain by
St Edmundsbury Press, Bury St Edmunds, Suffolk

British Library Cataloguing in Publication Data
A catalogue record for this book is available from the British
Library

Library of Congress Cataloguing in Publication Data
A catalogue record for this book is available from the Library of
Congress

ISBN 0–415–23786–6 (book)
ISBN 0–415–23787–4 (cassettes)
ISBN 0–415–23788–2 (book and cassettes course)

To Hazel, Emma and David

Contents

Introduction

Spanish in Latin America developed independently of, but at the same time in parallel to, that in Spain. There are lexical and some grammatical differences between the two main varieties of the language, but they share the same basic structure. Within Latin America regional accents have developed due to a number of factors, which include the influence of the language of Southern Spain and the Canaries, the language of the indigenous people of Latin America, African languages brought by the slaves and in recent times, American English. However, by acquiring the basic functions, notions, grammar and vocabulary of Spanish the learner should be able to communicate effectively in situations likely to be encountered as a visitor to one of the Spanish-speaking countries of Latin America. The aim of this book is to help you achieve this level of fluency.

This book is intended for learners with little or no knowledge of Spanish. The language in the book includes the kind of Spanish used in everyday life by native speakers in Latin America, especially in oral communication. In some Language Points sections an explanation is given regarding the use of an alternative form in Peninsular Spanish, i.e. that used in Spain. In the glossary at the back of the book you will find additional words with different uses in Latin America and in Spain.

In each chapter – with the exception of the last one, which is a revision chapter – the language presented to the learner is focused on some specific functions, notions and grammar points. These concepts are explained in the Language Points section which usually appears after a dialogue. At the beginning of each chapter you will find a list of the main objectives expected to be achieved by the learner. The book deals with a number of situations in which you are likely to use Spanish, e.g. using the phone, booking a hotel room, eating in a restaurant, routine at work, etc. There are also a number of functions that will be learned in each chapter, e.g.

greeting people, apologizing, telling the time, expressing likes and dislikes, describing objects, and others.

The Language points are illustrated in examples that follow each explanation. It is essential to read these examples carefully before proceeding to the exercises. It is advisable that you write all answers to the exercises in a notebook to keep a systematic record of your progress.

There is a variety of exercises; some require completion of a sentence with a word, others involve rewriting sentences in different words, changing the word order or matching questions with answers, etc. With the exception of open exercises, i.e. those in which there is more than one possible answer, you will find answers to the exercises at the end of the book. It is advisable to consult these answers only after you have provided your own.

The glossary at the end of the book lists, in alphabetical order, all the vocabulary introduced throughout the chapters. In some cases it provides a comparison between current terminology in Latin America which is different from that used in everyday Peninsular Spanish.

The Grammar section at the end of the book gives a brief description of the main points of the Spanish language. It is not intended to be a comprehensive grammar but a quick, essential reference section.

The recorded material for this book is optional, but you are advised to have access to it in order to improve your listening and understanding skills.

The author would like to thank Katia Valdeos Ardiles, Carolina Alegre Bellasai, Lena Gazey, Juliet Wood, Penny Levene and Genista Horsley for their help in the preparation of this book.

Pronunciation

The following section on pronunciation is intended as a guide, comparing the sounds of Spanish to the closest equivalent in English. You would also find it useful to listen to the recorded material which accompanies this book.

Vowels

Vowels in Spanish are clearer than in English, and all are considered of the same quality, that is, they are pronounced whether they are stressed or unstressed. There are five vowels in Spanish:

a	similar to the **a** in 'father', but shorter	**casa**
e	similar to the first **e** in 'elephant'	**elegir**
i	similar to the **i** in 'clean', but shorter	**mirar**
o	similar to the **o** in 'cot', but shorter	**moto**
u	similar to the **oo** in 'boot'	**cuna**

Consonants

b	similar to the English **b** but less explosive	**baño, ambos**
c	preceding **e** or **i** it is pronounced like the **s** in 'simple'	**ceder, hacer**
	preceding **a**, **o** or **u**, it is pronounced like the **c** in 'cat'	**carga, coro**
ch	like the **ch** in 'chair'	**chico, rancho**
d	in initial position it is pronounced like the English **d** but not aspirated. The tip of the tongue is placed lower than in the production of the English **d**. When it is not in initial position it is practically imperceptible to English speakers	**dar, cada**
f	like the English **f**	**feria, garrafa**
g	preceding **a**, **o**, **u**, like the **g** in 'god'	**ganar, gol**
	preceding **e** or **i**, like the **h** in 'hen'	**general, ágil**
h	silent	**hacer, ahora**
j	like the **h** in 'hen'	**jefe, caja**
k	like the English **k**	**kilo, káiser**
l	like the **l** in 'live'	**libro, papel**
ll	like the **y** in 'young', but a bit stronger; in Argentina and Uruguay it is pronounced like the **s** in the English word 'vision'	**llamar, pollo**
m	like the English **m**, but with the lips not firmly closed when it is not in initial position	**mar, América**
n	like the English **n**	**nada, pena**
ñ	like the **n** in 'onion'	**caña, niño**
p	like the English **p** but not aspirated	**papa, tapa**
q	like the unaspirated English **k**; found only in the groups **que** and **qui** in a word	**quince, porque**
r	more rolled than in English; in initial position it is trilled twice	**rosa, ramo**
	between vowels it is rolled once	**coro, pero**

rr	strongly trilled	**carro, perro**
s	like the **s** in 'sample'	**santa, suero**
t	less aspirated than in English; the tip of the tongue is placed against the back of the upper front teeth	**tomar, gato**
v	the same as the sound **b** described above	**vaca, cueva**
w	like the English **w**; only found in a few words of foreign origin	**whisky, Walter**
x	softer than the English **x**	**éxito, sexto**
y	the same as the sound **ll** described above	**mayo, yo**
z	the same as the sound **s** described above	**zona, zapato**

1 Saludos

Greetings

By the end of this chapter you should be able to:

- Use some greetings
- Use numbers up to 100
- Make simple enquiries
- Use personal pronouns (I, you, etc.)
- Use some verbs in the present tense indicative
  (e.g. I live in Mexico)

Dialogue 1 🔲

En la agencia de viajes

Miguel is trying to find out the travel agent's fax number over the phone. He talks to a member of the staff called Cecilia

CECILIA: Aló, buenos días. Agencia de Viajes El Sol.
MIGUEL: Buenos días, señorita. ¿Tienen fax?
CECILIA: Sí, señor.
MIGUEL: ¿Qué número es?
CECILIA: Es el dos, noventa y dos, treinta y cinco, setenta y seis, noventa y ocho (292–357698).
MIGUEL: ¿Y página Web?
CECILIA: Sí, claro. el sol, punto, com (*elsol.com*)
MIGUEL: Gracias.
CECILIA: De nada.
CECILIA: *Hello, good morning. El Sol Travel Agent.*
MIGUEL: *Good morning. Do you have a fax?*
CECILIA: *Yes, sir.*
MIGUEL: *What's the number, please?*

CECILIA: *It's 292–357698.*
MIGUEL: *What about a Web page?*
CECILIA: *Yes, of course. Elsol.com*
MIGUEL: *Thank you.*
CECILIA: *That's all right.*

Language points

Números de teléfono

When reading aloud telephone or fax numbers it is usual in Spanish to say them in pairs: e.g. 356791, **treinta y cinco, sesenta y siete, noventa y uno**; 031–705466, **cero, treinta y uno, setenta, cincuenta y cuatro, sesenta y seis**.

Correo electrónico

Two words are key to understand and/or provide e-mail addresses in Spanish:
arroba = @   **punto** = . (a dot)
For example, **alberto@portal.com** is read out: **alberto, arroba, portal, punto, com**.

Por favor

The use of **por favor** 'please' in requests is not as common in Spanish as it is in English.

De nada/No hay de qué

When somebody thanks you, apart from the usual response **De nada**, you can use the expression **No hay de qué**, although it sounds slightly more formal. Both mean 'You're welcome'.

Números

As in English, a number precedes the noun it refers to:

dos boletos	two tickets
diez alumnos	ten students

Uno becomes **un** before a masculine noun and **una** before a feminine noun (see Chapter 3 for information on masculine and feminine nouns):

un diccionario	one dictionary
una lección	one lesson

1	**uno**	11	**once**
2	**dos**	12	**doce**
3	**tres**	13	**trece**
4	**cuatro**	14	**catorce**
5	**cinco**	15	**quince**
6	**seis**	16	**dieciseis**
7	**siete**	17	**diecisiete**
8	**ocho**	18	**dieciocho**
9	**nueve**	19	**diecinueve**
10	**diez**	20	**veinte**

¡Más números!

Note: in Spanish, an exclamation mark is used at the beginning as well as at the end of a sentence. The same rule applies to question marks.

21	**veintiuno**	60	**sesenta**
22	**veintidos**	63	**sesenta y tres**
25	**veinticinco**	70	**setenta**
30	**treinta**	77	**setenta y siete**
36	**treinta y seis**	80	**ochenta**
40	**cuarenta**	88	**ochenta y ocho**
49	**cuarenta y nueve**	90	**noventa**
50	**cincuenta**	91	**noventa y uno**
52	**cincuenta y dos**	100	**cien**

Note: Numbers ending in **-uno**, such as **veintiuno, setenta y uno**, become **ventiún, setenta y un** before a masculine noun. Examples: **veintiún estudiantes, setenta y un años**.

Exercise 1

Arrange these numbers in order of value and write next to the word or phrase the corresponding figure.

(a)	**cien**	(g)	**quince**
(b)	**noventa y tres**	(h)	**doce**
(c)	**uno**	(i)	**noventa y cuatro**

(d) **treinta y cuatro**	(j) **siete**
(e) **trece**	(k) **sesenta y dos**
(f) **veintisiete**	(l) **setenta y nueve**

Exercise 2

Write the Spanish word for the answer to these operations.

(a) $16 + 9 =$	(c) $91 - 15 =$	(e) $27 + 17 =$
(b) $17 \times 4 =$	(d) $39 \div 3 =$	

Exercise 3

These are the dates of birth of some people. How old were they on 1st January 2001? Write the Spanish words for the answers. (Note: **años** = years.)

Carlos	27/07/1981	_____ **años**
Luisa	19/03/1978	_____ **años**
Milagros	02/12/1946	_____ **años**
Carolina	25/05/1974	_____ **años**
Esteban	28/07/1903	_____ **años**

Language points

Saludos

These are the phrases most frequently used to greet somebody:

Hola	Hello
Buenos días	Good morning
Buenas tardes	Good afternoon
Buenas noches	Good evening; Good night

During the evening/night **Buenas noches** is used to say 'Hello' or 'Goodbye'.

Sometimes in informal spoken language to greet somebody, **Buenas** replaces the phrases **Buenos días, Buenas tardes, Buenas noches**.

Despedidas

Saying goodbye

Chao/Chau	Goodbye (informal)
Adiós	Goodbye (more formal)

| **Hasta luego** | See you later (slightly formal) |
| **Nos vemos** | See you (informal) |

In Latin America the most common way of saying goodbye is **chao** or **chau**, while in Spain it is **adiós**.

Exercise 4

Write in your notebook what you would say to greet somebody in Spanish at these times:

(a) 10.00 a.m.   (d) 10.00 p.m.
(b) 2.00 p.m.   (e) 11.30 p.m.
(c) 6.00 a.m.

Language points

The infinitive

The infinitive is the form of a verb given in a dictionary. It is also the form that you will find in the glossary at the back of this book. According to the ending of the infinitive there are three types of verbs in Spanish:

verbs ending in **-ar**   also called verbs of the first conjugation
verbs ending in **-er**   also called verbs of the second conjugation
verbs ending in **-ir**   also called verbs of the third conjugation

Examples:

-ar	**comprar**	to buy
	trabajar	to work
	estudiar	to study
-er	**comer**	to eat
	vender	to sell
	comprender	to understand
-ir	**vivir**	to live
	escribir	to write
	subir	to go up

The present tense indicative

The present tense indicative is used with actions which are habitual or timeless.

Examples:

habitual

Siempre voy en tren.	I always go by train.
Teresa no trabaja los sábados.	Teresa does not work on Saturdays.

timeless

Mi gato come mucho queso.	My cat eats a lot of cheese.
Martha es peruana.	Martha is Peruvian.

Subject pronouns

Usually, it is not necessary to use the words for 'I', 'you', 'he', etc. to indicate who performs the action. For example, **tengo** means 'I have'. You do not need to include **yo** 'I'.

Pronouns may be used to emphasize the subject of a verb or to avoid ambiguity. For example:

Yo trabajo en Lima, María no.	I work in Lima, María doesn't.

There are two ways of addressing a second person in Spanish.
Tú for friends, relations, people of the same age group as you, your classmates. **Usted** for people you do not know, somebody you have just met, somebody much older than you, your superior. **Usted** is abbreviated as **Ud**. In the plural **ustedes**, abbreviated as **Uds.**, is used for both formal and informal situations. (In Spain the abbreviated forms are written **Vd**. and **Vds.**)

yo	I	**nosotros**	we
tú	you (informal)	**ustedes**	you (formal and informal)
usted	you (formal)	**ellos**	they (masculine)
él	he	**ellas**	they (feminine)
ella	she		

Unlike Peninsular Spanish, Latin American Spanish does not use the **vosotros** form of a verb for the informal second person plural. Compare these sentences:

Vosotros trabajáis en Guatemala. (Spain)
Ustedes trabajan en Guatemala. (Latin America)

You (pl.) work in Guatemala.

¿Habéis visto a Juan? (Spain)
¿Han visto a Juan? (Latin America)

Have you seen Juan?

¿A qué hora os vais? (Spain)
¿A qué hora se van? (Latin America)

What time do you leave?

Regular verbs

Most Spanish verbs are regular. They follow a certain pattern or rule when changing their endings, depending on which person performs the action. Here are three examples of regular verbs: **trabajar, comer** and **escribir.**

trabajo	I work
trabajas	you work (informal)
trabaja	you work (formal); he/she works
trabajamos	we work
trabajan	you work (formal and informal)
trabajan	they work
como	I eat
comes	you eat (informal)
come	you eat (formal); he/she eats
comemos	we eat
comen	you eat (formal and informal)
comen	they eat
escribo	I write
escribes	you write (informal)
escribe	you write (formal); he/she writes
escribimos	we write
escriben	you write (formal and informal)
escriben	they write

Irregular verbs

Some verbs do not follow the pattern or rule of regular verbs. For that reason they are called *irregular*. Here is one example: **tener.**

tengo	I have
tienes	you have (informal)
tiene	you have (formal); he/she/it has

tenemos	we have
tienen	you have
tienen	they have

See Chapter 2 for more irregular verbs.

Forming questions

Both regular and irregular verbs form questions by adding question marks to affirmative and negative statements. When speaking you sound as if you are asking a question. Unlike English, you do not need an auxiliary word like 'do'.

| **Trabajan mucho.** | They work hard. |
| **¿Trabajan mucho?** | Do they work hard? |

| **No tienes tiempo.** | You don't have time. |
| **¿No tienes tiempo?** | Don't you have time? |

As in English, questions can begin with a question word (who, what, etc.) as shown below:

qué (what)	**¿Qué tienes ahí?**	What have you got there?
quién (who)	**¿Quién tiene uno?**	Who has one?
cuál (which)	**¿Cuál tienes?**	Which one have you got?
cómo (how)	**¿Cómo es?**	What is it like?
cuándo (when)	**¿Cuándo es?**	When is it?
dónde (where)	**¿Dónde está?**	Where is it?

Exercise 5

Give the Spanish equivalent for these expressions:

1 Arturo has a car.
2 Lupe works in Mexico.
3 The travel agency has a fax.
4 Do you work?

Exercise 6

Complete the sentences with the correct form of **tener**.

1 **Yo _____ el asiento 7D y María _____ el 7C.**
2 **(Nosotros) _____ problemas en el hotel.**
3 **¿Ustedes _____ un periódico?**
4 **La impresora no _____ papel.**
5 **Silvia y Luisa _____ clase.**

asiento	seat
impresora	printer
papel	paper
clase	lesson, class

Dialogue 2 ▨

¿Cambia dólares?

While reading the dialogue below, see if you can find answers to these questions:

> How much money does Amalia want to change?
> Does she have traveler's checks to change?

AMALIA: Buenas tardes.
JAVIER: Buenas tardes. ¿Qué desea?
AMALIA: ¿Cambia dólares?
JAVIER: Sí, señora. ¿Billetes o cheques de viajero?
AMALIA: Billetes.
JAVIER: ¿Cuántos dólares?
AMALIA: Doscientos cuarenta.
JAVIER: Un momento, por favor. Acá tiene. Doscientos cuarenta dólares en moneda nacional.
AMALIA: Gracias.
JAVIER: A usted.

AMALIA: *Good afternoon.*
JAVIER: *Good afternoon. Can I help you?*
AMALIA: *Do you change dollars?*
JAVIER: *Yes, madam. Notes or traveler's checks?*
AMALIA: *Notes.*
JAVIER: *How many dollars?*
AMALIA: *Two hundred and forty.*
JAVIER: *One moment, please. Here you are. Two hundred and forty dollars in local currency.*

AMALIA: *Thanks.*
JAVIER: *Thank you.*

Language points

¿Qué desea?

The polite expression **¿Qué desea?** 'Can I help you?' is usually used by assistants in shops to greet you as a potential customer.

¿Cuánto?/¿Cuántos?

To find out amounts you use **¿cuánto?** 'how much' and **¿cuántos?** 'how many' – masculine – or **¿cuánta?** and **¿cuántas?** – feminine.

¿Cúanta plata tienes?	How much money do you have?
¿Cuántos empleados trabajan acá?	How many employees work here?

Addressing people

Señor is the usual polite expression to address a man, **joven** if it is a young man, **señora** for a lady and **señorita** for a young lady. In the case of children, **niño** is for a boy and **niña** for a girl. In everyday language there are several ways of referring to children, for example: **chamaco/chamaca** in Mexico; **pibe/piba** in Argentina; **chiquillo/chiquilla** in Peru.

Acá tiene/Aquí tiene

Acá tiene/Aquí tiene 'Here you are' is an expression said when you hand over something to another person, e.g. money to the taxi driver, passport to the immigration officer, etc. **Acá tienes/Aquí tienes** is used when addressing somebody informally.

Reading

While reading the passage below, see if you can find answers to these questions:

Is Spanish the only language in Latin America?
Are any indigenous languages spoken?

Idiomas de Latinoamérica 〇〇

La mayoría de la población de Latinoamérica habla castellano. En Brasil hablan portugués y en algunos países del Caribe, inglés o francés. Los indígenas del Perú y Bolivia hablan quechua y aymara.

Note: In Paraguay Guarani is widely spoken.

idiomas	languages	**quechua**	indigenous
mayoría	majority		language spoken
población	population		in the Andes
habla	speaks	**aymara**	indigenous
castellano	Spanish		language spoken
portugués	Portuguese		in Peru and
inglés	English		Bolivia
francés	French	**nahuatl**	indigenous
indígenas	indigenous people		language spoken
			in Mexico and
			Guatemala

2 Salgo a las seis

I leave at six

> **By the end of this chapter you should be able to:**
>
> - Use some irregular verbs in the present tense
> - Identify and use colors
> - Use numbers over 100
> - Ask and give information about times
> - Make negative statements using **no**

Dialogue 1 ▭

¿A qué hora sales?

MARINA: ¿A qué hora sales?
GABRIEL: Salgo a las seis. A esa hora podemos discutir el plan para mañana.
MARINA: Muy bien. Yo vengo a la cafetería de abajo a las seis y cuarto.
GABRIEL: Muy bien. Hasta más tarde.

MARINA: *What time do you leave?*
GABRIEL: *I leave at six. Then we can discuss our plan for tomorrow.*
MARINA: *Fine. I'll come to the cafe downstairs at a quarter past six.*
GABRIEL: *Fine. See you later.*

Language points

The present tense indicative of irregular verbs

Apart from the verb **tener** studied in Chapter 1, there are other irregular verbs. The irregularity of these verbs is sometimes only in the first person singular (the 'I' form), sometimes in several forms. The following are the most commonly used irregular verbs in the present tense.

decir to say

digo	**decimos**
dices	**dicen**
dice	**dicen**

Example:

Rosario dice la verdad.   Rosario tells the truth.

hacer to do, to make

hago	**hacemos**
haces	**hacen**
hace	**hacen**

Examples:

¿Qué haces los sábados?   What do you do on Saturdays?
Quiero hacer una torta.   I want to make a cake.

ir to go

voy	**vamos**
vas	**van**
va	**van**

Example:

¿Vas al colegio?   Do you go to school?

salir to leave, to go out

salgo	**salimos**
sales	**salen**
sale	**salen**

Example:

Salgo de casa a las seis.   I leave home at six.

venir to come

vengo	**venimos**
vienes	**vienen**
viene	**vienen**

Example:

¿A qué hora viene Eduardo? What time is Eduardo coming?

Negative statements

The particle **no** is always used before a verb to make a negative statement:

Gabriela no trabaja.	Gabriela doesn't work.
Hugo no habla inglés.	Hugo doesn't speak English.

Exercise 1

Complete the sentences below with the correct present indicative form of the verb in brackets.

1 **Delia (venir) temprano al trabajo.**
2 **¿A qué hora sales de la reunión?**
   (Yo) (salir) a las siete.
3 **Víctor no (ir) a clases de noche.**
4 **Oscar no (hacer) sus tareas.**
5 **Nosotros (decir) lo mismo.**

Language points

¿Qué hora es? 🔲

¿Qué hora es? is the question to ask the time. Sometimes the plural version **¿Qué horas son?** is used, especially in spoken Spanish in Latin America. In Spain, only **¿Qué hora es?** is used.

las doce

la una

las cuatro y media

las tres y cuarto

las ocho y veinte

diez para las nueve

un cuarto para las doce

Note: in Latin America the expression **para** is used to indicate minutes 'to the hour'. In Spain, **menos** is used.

Examples:

> **Son veinte para las cuatro**. (Lat. Am.)   It's twenty to four.
> **Son las cuatro menos veinte**. (Spain)
>
> **La cita es a un cuarto para las once**.   The appointment is at a
>   (Lat. Am.)   quarter to eleven.
> **La cita es a las once menos cuarto**. (Spain)

¿A qué hora? ▭

¿A qué hora . . . ? is the question you ask to find out at what time something takes place.

> **¿A qué hora es el concierto?** At what time is the concert?
> **¿A qué hora terminas?**   At what time do you finish?

As in British English, Spanish speakers sometimes use the 24-hour clock for departures and arrivals of trains, flights, etc.

12.05	**las doce cero cinco**
17.52	**las diecisiete cincuenta y dos**
23.10	**las veintitres diez**
07.15	**las cero siete quince**

Exercise 2

Look at the departure and arrival chart below and then ask and answer questions as in the example.

Example:

> **¿A qué hora sale el avión a Miami?**
> **Sale a las once.**
> **¿A qué hora llega el avión de La Habana?**
> **Llega a las quince cero cinco.**

Salidas		**Llegadas**	
Miami	11.00	La Habana	15.05
Caracas	13.45	Madrid	11.45
Lima	09.20	Santiago	11.50
Quito	06.00	México D.F.	10.20

sale	it leaves	**salida**	departure
llega	it arrives	**llegada**	arrival

Dialogue 2 ▣

En la tienda

While reading the dialogue below, see if you can find answers to these questions:

Does Pablo ask for a particular color of shirt?
Does he buy the shirt?

Pablo sees a shirt he likes in a shop in Lima.

PABLO: Buenas tardes, ¿tiene esta camisa para caballero en talla 15?
EMPLEADA: Sí, tengo en blanco, azul, verde o marrón.
PABLO: ¿Cuánto cuesta?
EMPLEADA: 35 soles.
PABLO: ¡Muy cara!
EMPLEADA: Pero . . . muy fina.

PABLO: *Good afternoon, have you got this shirt in size 15?*
ASSISTANT: *Yes, I have it in white, blue, green or brown.*
PABLO: *How much is it?*
ASSISTANT: *35 soles.*
PABLO: *That's very expensive!*
ASSISTANT: *But . . . it is very good quality.*

Language points

¿Cuánto cuesta?

¿Cuánto cuesta? is used to find out the price of an item. If it is more than one item, you use **¿Cuánto cuestan?**

¿Cuánto cuestan las blusas? How much are the blouses?

¿Cuánto es? is the expression used to find out how much it all adds up to at the end.

Muy

Muy is used to intensify the meaning of the adjective which follows. Here are some examples:

muy inteligente	very intelligent
muy interesante	very interesting
muy bonita/o	very nice
muy barata/o	very cheap

Colores 🔳

blanco	white	**verde**	green
negro	black	**amarillo**	yellow
rojo	red	**marrón**	brown
azul	blue		

Examples:

blusa blanca	white blouse
auto verde	green car

Exercise 3

The following products are reduced. What is their new selling price? Give the answers in full, in Spanish.

artículo	precio normal	descuento	precio de venta
Camisas	$40.00	10%	
Blusas	$35.00	20%	
Abrigos	$99.00	5%	
Pañuelos	$6.00	10%	
Pantalones	$48.00	20%	
Camisetas	$12.00	10%	

Exercise 4 🔳

Arrange the following words in three groups under the headings **Hombres** (items usually worn by men), **Mujeres** (items usually worn by women) and **Ambos** (items usually worn by either sex).

camisa	suéter/chompa
zapatos	blusa
corbata	calzoncillo
medias	pañuelo
vestido	aretes
falda	lápiz labial

Dialogue 3 ⬛

Hay un problema

While reading the dialogue below, see if you can find answers to these questions:

Is the problem something to do with the room itself?
Can the problem be solved at once?

Mr Carter explains to the receptionist at the hotel where he is staying that something is not working

SR CARTER: Disculpe. Hay un problema. El televisor no funciona.
RECEPCIONISTA: ¿Qué número de habitación?
SR CARTER: Cuarenta y uno.
RECEPCIONISTA: Bien. Vamos.
(*They go in the room, and the receptionist tests the TV.*)
Un momento, por favor.
(*He leaves the room and comes back after a few minutes with another TV set.*)
Acá tiene. Otro televisor.
SR CARTER: A ver . . . ¡Funciona! Gracias.
RECEPCIONISTA: De nada.

MR CARTER: *Excuse me. There is a problem. The TV doesn't work.*
RECEPTIONIST: *Which room number is it?*
MR CARTER: *Forty-one.*
RECEPTIONIST: *Right. Let's go.*
One moment, please.
Here you are. Another TV set.
MR CARTER: *Let me see. It works! Thank you.*
RECEPTIONIST: *You're welcome.*

Language points

Disculpe

Disculpe 'Excuse me' is one way of catching other people's attention (formal). There is also the form **disculpa** (informal).

Disculpe, ¿habla castellano? Excuse me, do you speak Spanish?
Disculpa, ¿eres mexicano? Excuse me, are you Mexican?

Disculpe/Disculpa also mean *I am sorry* (apology)

The expression **por favor**, which literally means *please*, is also frequently used with the meaning of *Excuse me* in order to catch somebody's attention. For example:

Por favor. ¿Hay menú económico? *Excuse me. Is there a set menu?*

Hay

Hay indicates existence or presence. The same word is used in singular or plural, in question or statement.

| hay | there is | ¿hay? | is there? |
| hay | there are | ¿hay? | are there? |

Examples:

Hay un problema en el hotel. There is a problem at the hotel.
¿Hay clases de castellano? Are there Spanish lessons?

No funciona

To explain that something is not working, you use the expression **no funciona**. In the dialogue above, the television doesn't work. Here are more examples:

El teléfono no funciona. The phone is not working.
La máquina no funciona. The machine does not work.
***El computador no funciona.** The computer is not working.

* To refer to a computer some Latin American countries use the feminine noun **computadora**, e.g. Peru, and others prefer the masculine **computador**, e.g. Mexico.

Exercise 5

You cannot say **no funciona** when something goes wrong for all
things listed below. But for some, you can. Which ones?

1 **la máquina de escribir**
2 **el pasaporte**
3 **la motocicleta**
4 **el carro**
5 **el diccionario**

Language point

¡Y más números!

200	**doscientos**	2,000	**dos mil**
300	**trescientos**	10,000	**diez mil**
400	**cuatrocientos**	50,000	**cincuenta mil**
500	**quinientos**	100,000	**cien mil**
600	**seiscientos**	500,000	**quinientos mil**
700	**setecientos**	1,000,000	**un millón**
800	**ochocientos**		
900	**novecientos**		
1,000	**mil**		

BANCO COMERCIAL . Fecha. . . . .

Páguese a _____

la suma de _____

_____

. . . .

Exercise 6

You have to pay Viajes El Sol (El Sol Travel Agent) a bill for 245
dollars (dólares). You are paying by cheque. Rewrite the cheque in
your notebook including the amount in words.

páguese a	payable to	**firma**	signature
la suma	the amount, the sum	**fecha**	date

Reading

While reading the passage below, see if you can find answers to these questions:

Where does Carmen want to travel to?
Does she buy a ticket?

En la agencia de viajes ⬤⬤

Carmen tiene un carro amarillo muy bonito. Carmen visita la agencia de viajes El Sol. El viaje a Canadá cuesta mucho y ella no tiene suficiente dinero. ¡Qué pena!

carro	car	**dinero**	money
viaje	trip	**qué pena**	what a pity
suficiente	enough		

3 Reserva en el hotel

Reserving a hotel room

By the end of this chapter you should be able to:

- Reserve a room at a hotel
- Ask and give information about dates
- Write a short letter
- Use definite and indefinite articles
- Introduce yourself

Dialogue 1

Reservando una habitación

While reading the dialogue below, see if you can find answers to these questions:

When is Mr Carter starting his stay at the hotel?
How many nights will he be staying?

RECEPCIONISTA:	¡Aló! Buenas tardes. Hotel Excelsior.
SR CARTER:	Buenas tardes. ¿Tiene una habitación libre a partir de mañana?
RECEPCIONISTA:	¿Individual o doble?
SR CARTER:	Individual.
RECEPCIONISTA:	¿Para cuántas noches?
SR CARTER:	Para cinco noches.
RECEPCIONISTA:	Un momento, por favor.
	Aló. Sí, tenemos una habitación individual libre. 90 dólares por noche.
SR CARTER:	Está bien. Mi nombre es Carter.
RECEPCIONISTA:	Bueno, Sr. Carter. Hasta mañana.
SR CARTER:	Hasta mañana.

RECEPTIONIST:	*Hello. Good afternoon. Hotel Excelsior.*
MR CARTER:	*Good afternoon. Do you have a room available from tomorrow?*
RECEPTIONIST:	*Single or double?*
MR CARTER:	*Single.*
RECEPTIONIST:	*How many nights?*
MR CARTER:	*Five nights.*
RECEPTIONIST:	*Just one moment, please.*
	Hello. Yes, we have one single room free. It is 90 dollars per night.
MR CARTER:	*That's all right. My name is Carter.*
RECEPTIONIST:	*Right, Mr Carter. See you tomorrow.*
MR CARTER:	*See you tomorrow.*

Language points

Aló

When somebody answers the phone, the usual expression is **Aló**. It is also used when you want to resume a conversation after a brief pause. In Mexico, **Bueno** is used instead.

Me llamo . . .

Me llamo . . . 'I am called . . .' is one way of telling somebody else what your name is.

Me llamo Esteban.
Me llamo Juan García.

Another way to introduce yourself is to use **Mi nombre es**, followed by your name.

Mi nombre es Guillermo.
Mi nombre es Jorge Castañeda.

¿Cómo te llamas?

You say **¿Cómo te llamas?** to ask somebody else what his or her name is, addressing that person informally. **¿Cómo se llama?** or **¿Cómo se llama usted?** is the formal question.

Another way of asking a name is **¿Cuál es tu nombre?** (informal) or **¿Cuál es su nombre?** (formal).

Masculine and feminine nouns

Spanish nouns are either masculine or feminine. Usually nouns ending in **-o** are masculine and those ending in **-a** are feminine. This rule is for guidance only, since there are exceptions. It is advisable to try to learn the gender as you learn the noun. The glossary at the end of the book will help you.

Examples:

libro (m.)	book
vuelo (m.)	flight
revista (f.)	magazine
impresora (f.)	printer
estudiante (m. & f.)	student
papel (m.)	paper

The definite article

El/la

The words **el** and **la** correspond to the English 'the'. The definite article **el** is used before masculine singular nouns and the definite article **la** is used before feminine singular nouns:

el colegio	the school
la niña	the girl

The majority of nouns ending in **-nte** keep the same form for masculine and feminine.

el estudiante	the student (m.)
la estudiante	the student (f.)

Nouns ending in a consonant are usually masculine.

el actor	the actor
el campeón	the champion

Los/las

The definite article **los** is used before masculine plural nouns and the definite article **las** is used before feminine plural nouns. There has to be agreement between article and noun in both gender and number.

los colegios	the schools
los libros	the books
las mañanas	the mornings
las motocicletas	the motorcycles

Exercise 1

Which definite article should be before these nouns?

1	**documentos**	6	**profesor**
2	**casa**	7	**bailarina**
3	**carro**	8	**representante**
4	**alumnos**	9	**amigos**
5	**adolescente**	10	**papel**

The indefinite article

The words **un** and **una** correspond to the English 'a/an'. **Un** is used before a masculine noun and **una** is used before a feminine noun.

un libro	a book
una pregunta	a question
un animal	an animal

In English the indefinite article appears in a sentence before a noun indicating profession or occupation. In Spanish this is not the case.

Elena es secretaria.	Elena is a secretary.
Jorge es arquitecto.	Jorge is an architect.

Exercise 2

Match the symbol with the word or words:

1 **céntrico** (a)

2 **estacionamiento** (b)

3 **acceso para minusválidos** (c)

4 **servicio médico** (d)

5 **televisión en la habitación** (e)

6 **aire acondicionado** (f)

7 **bar/cafetería** (g)

8 **calefacción** (h)

9 **cabina Internet** (i)

10 **correo electrónico** (j)

Exercise 3

Write down the facilities mentioned in the previous exercise in order of priority when you choose a hotel.

In your opinion,

What is most important for a disabled person?
What is most important for a business person?
What is most important for a family on holiday?

Exercise 4

You want to reserve a room in a hotel. You like quiet places. At the moment it is very hot in the city you are going to. You sort out your travel money in advance and you like to have all your meals in nice little cafés and local restaurants. Which of the following facilities are advantages (**ventajas**) and which are disadvantages (**desventajas**) in your case? Write them down in two separate lists.

céntrico	desayuno incluido
piscina	cambio de moneda
calefacción central	restaurante
aire acondicionado	teléfono en la habitación
caja fuerte individual	

Language points

Días de la semana 🔊

Days of the week

domingo	Sunday		**jueves**	Thursday
lunes	Monday		**viernes**	Friday
martes	Tuesday		**sábado**	Saturday
miércoles	Wednesday			

In Spanish it is not necessary to write the days of the week beginning with a capital letter, except at the start of a sentence.

El sábado llega mi hermana. My sister arrives on Saturday.
Domingos: de 10 a 5. Sundays: from 10 to 5.

Exercise 5

Explain what you plan to do each day based on the page of a diary below. (The abbreviated form of each day in Spanish is given in brackets.)

Example:

¿Qué piensas hacer el lunes?
Mis planes para el lunes … comprar los boletos de avión y comprar una maleta nueva.

Lunes	**(Lun)**	**Comprar los boletos de avión**
		Comprar una maleta nueva
Martes	**(Mar)**	**Leer la guía turística**
		Comprar un mapa
Miércoles	**(Mié)**	**Buscar información**
		Navegar en Internet
Jueves	**(Jue)**	**Estudiar el informe**
		Escribir comentarios

Viernes	(Vie)	Preparar documentos
		Hacer las maletas
Sábado	(Sáb)	Llegar al aeropuerto a las 2.30
		Comprar una novela
Domingo	(Dom)	Descansar

comprar	to buy	informe	report
boleto de avión	flight ticket	preparar	to prepare
maleta	suitcase	llegar	to arrive
nuevo, nueva	new	novela	novel
guía turística	tourist guide	descansar	to rest
buscar	to look for	mapa	map
comentarios	comments	navegar en Internet	to surf the Net

¡Hasta mañana!

Hasta, meaning 'until', is used to form expressions of farewell like the following:

Hasta mañana	Until/See you tomorrow
Hasta el sábado	Until/See you Saturday
Hasta la próxima clase	Until/See you next lesson
Hasta luego	Until/See you later

Exercise 6

How could you say goodbye using **hasta** in the following circumstances?

1 Your next lesson is on Monday.
2 You will see this person this coming Saturday.
3 You will meet again on Sunday.
4 You will see each other on Tuesday.
5 Your next meeting is tomorrow.

Meses del año

Months of the year

enero	julio
febrero	agosto
marzo	septiembre
abril	octubre
mayo	noviembre
junio	diciembre

Exercise 7

Say and write in Spanish the date of the following events.

Example:

    New Year's Eve   **31 de diciembre**

1 Christmas
2 Your birthday
3 New Year
4 Today
5 Your mother's birthday

Exercise 8

Answer these questions about the fax below.

1 What type of room does Mrs Stewart want?
2 Which day of the week will she leave the hotel?

TELEFAX

Dirigido a: Sr. A. Sánchez   Fax No 00 52 74 298765
              HOTEL EXCELSIOR

Estimado señor:
Le ruego reservar una habitación individual con baño para 5 noches a partir del domingo próximo.

Atentamente

Helen Stewart

---

le ruego	would you please (literally: *I beg you*)	**próximo**	next
a partir de	as from	**dirigido a**	for the attention of

Language points

Starting a letter

In Spanish, a colon appears after the salutation in written corre-
spondence. In English a comma is used. Here are some examples:

Estimada señora:	Dear Madam,	(formal, no name used)
Querido Esteban:	Dear Esteban,	(informal, first name used)
Distinguido señor:	Dear Sir,	(formal, no name used)
Querido señor Milla:	Dear Mr Milla,	(formal, followed by surname)

Ending a letter

A straightforward way of finishing a formal letter in Spanish is by
using one of the following expressions:

Muy atentamente	Yours faithfully
Le saluda atentamente	Yours sincerely

If it is a more informal letter, it can be finished with:

Saludos	Regards
Con cariño	Love

Exercise 9

Write a fax to reserve a room at Hotel Embajador. You want a
double room for three nights from next Saturday, with bathroom
and telephone in the room. The person in charge is Sra Urrutia.

Reading

Ecuador

While reading the passage below, see if you can find answers to
these questions:

What type of terrain predominates in Ecuador?
Which racial groups are in the majority in Ecuador?

La mitad del territorio de Ecuador es zona de selva. Una tercera parte es zona de montañas y el resto lo forman la costa y las Islas Galápagos. Los mestizos y los indígenas forman el ochenta por ciento de la población (40% cada grupo) y los blancos y negros forman el otro veinte por ciento. La capital es Quito y otra ciudad muy importante es Guayaquil. Quito está a unos tres mil metros de altura. Guayaquil es un puerto.

mitad	half	**población**	population
selva	jungle	**otro**	other, another
el resto	the rest	**ciudad**	city
mestizos	mixed-race people	**puerto**	port

4 ¿Dónde está?

Where is it?

By the end of this chapter you should be able to:

- Enquire about location
- Describe people and objects
- Talk about nationality
- Use the verbs **ser** and **estar** (to be)

Dialogue 1 ▣

Rentar un carro

While reading the dialogue below, see if you can find answers to these questions:

Does Karen find the car she wants?
Does she want the car for that same day?

Karen Stewart wants to rent a car in Mexico City

ANA: ¿En qué puedo servirle?
KAREN: Quisiera rentar un carro.
ANA: Aquí tiene la lista de modelos.
KAREN: ¿Hay un Citroen libre para mañana?
ANA: Citroen no hay, pero tenemos un Renault.
KAREN: ¿Es económico?
ANA: Sí, es económico y cómodo.
KAREN: Muy bien. ¿A qué hora mañana?
ANA: A partir de las siete y media de la mañana.

ANA: *How can I help you?*
KAREN: *I would like to hire a car.*

ANA: *Here you are. The list of models.*
KAREN: *Is there a Citroen free for tomorrow?*
ANA: *There isn't a Citroen, but we have a Renault.*
KAREN: *Is it economical?*
ANA: *Yes, it's economical and comfortable.*
KAREN: *Fine. At what time tomorrow?*
ANA: *From half past seven in the morning.*

Exercise 1

¿Cómo es tu carro?

Describe your car (or the car you would like to have, if you do not have one at the moment) choosing features from the list below. Start your answer like this:

Mi carro es ...

potente	**cómodo**	**chico**
deportivo	**incómodo**	**antiguo**
ecológico	**grande**	**económico**
nuevo	**mediano**	

potente	powerful	**grande**	large
deportivo	sporty	**mediano**	medium
ecológico	ecological, 'green'	**chico**	small
cómodo	comfortable	**antiguo**	old
incómodo	uncomfortable	**económico**	economical

Dialogue 2

Congreso empresarial

Three people attending a business conference introduce themselves to each other at the bar during a break

HELEN: Me llamo Helen Stewart. Soy consultora de negocios. ¿Es usted consultor, también?
PETER: No, soy representante de ventas. Mi nombre es Peter Harris.
LUPE: Yo me llamo Lupe Arenas. Soy agente de viajes.

HELEN: *I'm Helen Stewart. I'm a business consultant. Are you a consultant as well?*
PETER: *No. I'm a sales representative. My name is Peter Harris.*
LUPE: *I'm Lupe Arenas. I'm a travel agent.*

Language point

Ser

One equivalent of 'to be' is **ser**. The other, **estar**, is explained later on in this chapter. The difference between the two is not easily learned by an English speaker.

Ser is used to explain the nature of people or objects and also to identify them.

Ramón es respetuoso.	Ramón is respectful.
¿Eres socialista?	Are you a socialist?
Bogotá es la capital de Colombia.	Bogotá is the capital of Colombia.
Es un libro de castellano.	It is a Spanish book.

To describe your occupation or profession you use **soy**, as in **soy consultora** 'I am a consultant', **soy representante** 'I am a representative'.

To describe somebody else's occupation or profession you say **es**, as in **Lorena es profesora** 'Lorena is a teacher'. For the second person (formal) you also use **es**, as in **¿Es usted consultor?** 'Are you a consultant?'.

In the case of the second person (informal) you use **eres**. For example: **¿Eres turista?** 'Are you a tourist?', **Eres estudiante. Yo también** 'You are a student. Me, too'.

These are all the forms:

soy	I am
eres	you are (informal)
es	You are (formal), he/she/it is
somos	we are
son	you are (formal and informal)
son	they are

Exercise 2

Match the unfinished sentence with the correct word in the column on the right.

1 **Edward Kennedy es** _____   (a) **lago**
2 **Gabriel García Márquez es** _____   (b) **capital**

3 **Managua es una** _____   (c) **río**
4 **El Amazonas es un** _____   (d) **escritor**
5 **El Titicaca es un** _____   (e) **político**

Soy mexicano

In the following short dialogue three people talk about their nationalities

PERSONA 1: Soy inglesa. ¿Usted es inglés también?
PERSONA 2: No, soy mexicano. Mi padre es inglés.
PERSONA 3: Yo soy nicaragüense.

PERSON 1: _I am English. Are you English too?_
PERSON 2: _No, I am Mexican. My father is English._
PERSON 3: _I am Nicaraguan._

Language point
Nationality

Soy, **es**, **eres** can be used to describe nationality for people. **Es** can be used for things as well. For example:

Pablo es panameño.	Pablo is Panamanian.
Todos somos latinoamericanos.	We are all Latin Americans.
El ron es cubano.	The rum is Cuban.
El producto es canadiense.	The product is Canadian.

Some more examples in the plural:

Marta y yo somos estadounidenses.	Marta and I are Americans.
Manuel y Esteban son salvadoreños.	Manuel and Esteban are Salvadorians.
Los carros son europeos.	The cars are European.
Ustedes son estudiantes.	You are students.

Exercise 3

Complete the sentences with the correct form of the verb **ser**.
Examples:

(Nosotros) ____ **estudiantes**
Somos estudiantes.

Mario _____ inteligente
Mario es inteligente.

1 **(Yo)** _____ **profesor.**
2 **Elena y Sara** _____ **amigas.**
3 **(Nosotros)** _____ **colombianos.**
4 **Caracas** _____ **la capital de Venezuela.**
5 **El Espectador y El Comercio** _____ **periódicos.**

Países y naciona/idades 🔘

Here are some useful country names and nationalities:

Argentina	argentino	Honduras	hondureño
Bolivia	boliviano	Inglaterra	inglés
Brasil	brasileño	Jamaica	jamaiquino
Canadá	canadiense	México	mexicano
Chile	chileno	Nicaragua	nicaragüense
Colombia	colombiano	Panamá	panameño
Costa Rica	costarricense	Paraguay	paraguayo
Cuba	cubano	Perú	peruano
Ecuador	ecuatoriano	Puerto Rico	puertorriqueño
El Salvador	salvadoreño	República	dominicano
Estados	estadounidense	Dominicana	
Unidos		Uruguay	uruguayo
Guatemala	guatemalteco	Venezuela	venezolano
Haití	haitiano		

¿Dónde está el carro?

Mr Carter goes to pick up the car he has hired

SR CARTER: Buenos días. Soy el Sr Carter y . . .
JULIÁN: Ah, sí. Es un Renault, ¿verdad?
SR CARTER: Sí. ¿Dónde se recoge el carro?
JULIÁN: Enfrente, en el garaje. Acá tiene las llaves.
(*Mr Carter asks Paulina, the attendant, at the garage*)
SR CARTER: Disculpe, ¿dónde está el Renault?
PAULINA: El Renault está allá a la derecha.
SR CARTER: Gracias.
PAULINA: De nada.

MR CARTER: *Good morning. I am Mr Carter and . . .*
JULIÁN: *Ah, yes. It's a Renault, isn't it?*
MR CARTER: *Yes. Where do you pick up the car?*
JULIÁN: *Opposite, at the garage. Here you are. The keys.*
MR CARTER: *Excuse me, where is the Renault?*
PAULINA: *The Renault is over there on the right.*
MR CARTER: *Thank you.*
PAULINA: *You're welcome.*

Language point

Estar

Estar also means 'to be' (see **ser**, earlier in this chapter, for the other use of 'to be'). **Estar** is used to describe location or a temporary state.

Examples of description of a state with **estar**:

Está enfermo.	He is ill.
Estoy triste.	I am sad.
Estamos seguros de eso.	We are sure about that.

Examples indicating location with **estar**:

El carro está a la derecha.	The car is on the right.
Guadalajara está en México.	Guadalajara is in Mexico.
Atlanta está en los Estados Unidos.	Atlanta is in the United States.
El hotel está en el centro.	The hotel is in the center of town.

Exercise 4

Complete the sentences with the correct form of **ser** or **estar**.

1 **El restaurante _____ en la calle principal.**
2 **_____ estudiante (yo).**
3 **María _____ molesta.**
4 **_____ en la casa de mi hermana (nosotros).**
5 **Estela y Lucrecia _____ pintoras.**
6 **Guadalajara _____ en México.**
7 **El autor del libro _____ peruano.**
8 **El banco _____ cerca.**
9 **_____ vendedores (Nosotros).**
10 **No _____ en su casa (ella).**

Prepositions of place

en

al lado de

enfrente de

sobre

abajo de/debajo de

delante de

atrás de/detrás de

entre

Exercise 5

A LA IZQUIERDA

A LA DERECHA

(a) Ask and/or answer questions based on the street plan above.

Example:

¿Dónde está el bar?
El bar está a la izquierda.

Continue: **¿Dónde está el hotel?**, etc.

(b) Look again at the street plan and ask and/or answer questions, as in the following example.

¿Dónde está el bar?
El bar está a la izquierda, enfrente del hotel.

Now continue asking and/or answering questions about the hotel, supermarket, etc.

(c) Look once again at the street plan and ask and/or answer questions, as in the following example:

¿Dónde está el bar?
El bar está a la izquierda, enfrente del hotel, al lado de la librería.

Juan está *enfrente de* Luis

Juan está *al lado de* Lucía.

Continue asking and answering questions about the hotel, super-market, etc., giving as much information as possible.

Exercise 6

Complete the sentence on the left with one (or more) expression(s) from the column on the right.

1 **Viajar es** _____ (a) **agradable(s)**
2 **La comida latinoamericana es** _____ (b) **interesante(s)**
3 **La Ciudad de México es** _____ (c) **variada(s)**
4 **Comer fruta es** _____ (d) **saludable(s)**
5 **Los animales domésticos son** _____ (e) **grande(s)**
6 **La política es** _____ (f) **complicado (/a)(s)**
7 **Las reuniones de negocios son** _____ (g) **necesario (/a)(s)**
8 **Los problemas ecológicos son** _____ (h) **urgente(s)**

Language point

Pero

As in English, **pero** ('but') is used to contrast two ideas or state-ments without contradicting the first one.

Hablo francés, pero sólo un poco.	I speak French, but only a little.
No tengo auto, pero no me importa.	I haven't got a car, but I don't mind.

Note: For more on **pero**, see Chapter 19.

Reading

Costa Rica

Costa Rica es uno de los países latinoamericanos con menos población. Cuenta con unos tres millones de habitantes. El ochenta por ciento de los habitantes de Costa Rica son de raza blanca y el diecisiete por ciento son mestizos. El resto son de raza negra e indígena. San José es su capital. En su zona metropolitana se encuentra medio millón de habitantes. Costa Rica es un país que no tiene ejército. Es un país exportador de café.

raza	race
ejército	army
indígena	indigenous

Exercise 7

Based on the passage above, say if the following statements are **verdadero** (true) or **falso** (false).

1 **Costa Rica no tiene ejército.**
2 **La mayoría de la población es de raza mestiza.**
3 **Es uno de los países más poblados.**
4 **El café es un producto importante para su economía.**
5 **San José es su capital.**

5 El clima y los viajes

Weather and travel

By the end of this chapter you should be able to:

- Comment about the weather
- Talk about transport
- Express frequency
- Refer to the parts of the day

Dialogue 1 ▨

¿Como está el clima?

While reading the dialogue below, see if you can find answers to these questions:

Is it a sunny place?
Does it rain much?

Mr Carter is talking to one of the local women in the resort where he is spending his holiday

SR CARTER:	¿Hace calor aquí?
SRA LOPEZ:	Generalmente sí, pero la temperatura es agradable.
SR CARTER:	¿Cuál es la temperatura media?
SRA LOPEZ:	En enero es de 28 grados centígrados.
SR CARTER:	¿Y hace mucho sol?
SRA LOPEZ:	Sí, normalmente ocho horas diarias.
SR CARTER:	¿Llueve también?
SRA LOPEZ:	Muy poco.

MR CARTER:	*Is it hot here?*
SRA LOPEZ:	*Usually it is, but the average temperature is pleasant.*

MR CARTER: *What is the average temperature?*
SRA LOPEZ: *In January it is 28 degrees centigrade.*
MR CARTER: *And is it very sunny?*
SRA LOPEZ: *Yes, usually the sun shines eight hours a day.*
MR CARTER: *Does it rain too?*
SRA LOPEZ: *Very little.*

Language points

Hace

The word **hace** is used to form some expressions which refer to the
weather. (For another use of **hace** see Chapter 12.)

hace calor   it's hot

hace frío
it's cold

hace viento
it's windy

hace sol
it's sunny

The four expressions above can be used to describe the usual climatic conditions, e.g. **En enero hace calor en Lima** (January is hot in Lima.), or to refer to what the weather is like at the time of speaking, e.g. **Hoy no hace sol** (It's not sunny today.).

In the following cases a different expression is needed:

está lloviendo	it's raining
llueve	it rains

está nevando	it's snowing
nieva	it snows

Poco/mucho

When you use **poco** and **mucho** as adjectives, they agree in number and gender with the noun they refer to.

Hay pocos estudiantes.	There are few students.
Llueve poco en enero.	It doesn't rain much in January.
Tengo poca información.	I have little information.
No hay muchas mujeres en este grupo.	There aren't many women in this group.
Hace mucho calor	It is very hot
Tiene mucha suerte.	He is very lucky.

Expressions of frequency/habit/routine

generalmente	generally
normalmente	normally

Examples:

Normalmente salimos a las siete.	Normally we leave at seven.
Generalmente hace calor en diciembre.	Generally it is hot in December.

siempre	always
nunca	never

Examples:

Siempre vamos al mercado los sábados.	We always go to the market on Saturdays.
Nunca viajamos al extranjero.	We never travel abroad.

a veces	sometimes

Examples:

A veces vamos al cine.	Sometimes we go to the cinema.
A veces juego fútbol.	Sometimes I play football.

Daily, weekly, etc.

These expressions have the same meaning in English, but some are used as an adjective – to indicate the characteristic of a noun – or as an adverb – to indicate the manner in which it is done.

diario (/a)	daily	**diariamente**
semanal	weekly	**semanalmente**
mensual	monthly	**mensualmente**
trimestral	quarterly	**trimestralmente**
semestral	six-monthly	**semestralmente**
anual	yearly	**anualmente**

Es una publicación diaria.	It is a daily publication.
Se publica diariamente.	It is published daily.
Es una visita semanal al club.	It is a weekly visit to the club.

Voy al club semanalmente.	I go to the club weekly.
Este es un pago mensual.	This is a monthly payment.
Escribo a esos amigos mensualmente.	I write to those friends monthly.

Exercise 1

Classify the following activities according to their frequency in your life, e.g. **diario**, **mensual**, etc.

1 **desayuno**
2 **vacaciones**
3 **cuenta del teléfono**
4 **sueldo**
5 **compras en el supermercado**

desayuno	breakfast
vacaciones	holiday
cuenta del teléfono	telephone bill
sueldo	salary
compras	shopping
supermercado	supermarket

Cada

It is also possible to form expressions of frequency using the word **cada**:

cada día	each day
cada semana	each week
cada mes	each month
cada tres meses	every three months
cada año	every year

Vez/veces

These words are used to form expressions of frequency such as 'once', 'twice', etc.

una vez	once
dos veces	twice
tres veces	three times
a veces	sometimes

Por

The word **por** can also express frequency:

Desayuno en el tren dos veces por semana.	I have breakfast on the train twice a week.
Limpian las ventanas dos veces por mes.	The windows are cleaned twice a month.

Exercise 2

Complete the phrases with a suitable expression of frequency.

1 **Limpio el carro** _____
2 **Escucho la radio** _____
3 **Compro leche** _____
4 **Voy a Latinoamérica** _____
5 **Voy de vacaciones** _____

Exercise 3

Complete the phrases with something that you do with the frequency suggested.

1 _____ **una vez por semana.**
2 _____ **anualmente.**
3 _____ **a veces.**
4 _____ **diariamente.**
5 _____ **cada domingo.**

Exercise 4

Answer the following survey:

In your own town or city, what happens to the weather in January?

1 **Hace calor**	sí	no	poco	**mucho**	**a veces**
2 **Hace frío**	sí	no	poco	**mucho**	**a veces**
3 **Hace viento**	sí	no	poco	**mucho**	**a veces**
4 **Llueve**	sí	no	poco	**mucho**	**a veces**
5 **Nieva**	sí	no	poco	**mucho**	**a veces**
6 **Hace sol**	sí	no	poco	**mucho**	**a veces**

Dialogue 2 🔳

A Cancún

Sr Ruiz wants to make a reservation to fly to Cancún in Mexico the next morning. Unfortunately that flight is full

SR RUIZ: Quisiera reservar un pasaje para Cancún.
EMPLEADA: ¿En qué vuelo?
SR RUIZ: Mañana por la mañana.
EMPLEADA: Por la mañana está completo, pero hay espacio en el vuelo de la tarde, a las 14:20.
SR RUIZ: Muy bien. Por la tarde.
EMPLEADA: ¿Fumador o no fumador?
SR RUIZ: No fumador.
EMPLEADA: ¿Pasillo o ventanilla?
SR. RUIZ: Ventanilla.

MR RUIZ: *I would like to book a seat to Cancún.*
ASSISTANT: *When is it for?*
MR RUIZ: *Tomorrow morning.*
ASSISTANT: *The one in the morning is full, but there is room on the 14:20 afternoon flight.*
MR RUIZ: *That's fine. In the afternoon then.*
ASSISTANT: *Smoking or no smoking?*
MR RUIZ: *No smoking.*
ASSISTANT: *Aisle or window?*
MR RUIZ: *Window.*

Language point

Quisiera 🔳

Quisiera is used to express what you would like. It is usually followed by a verb in the infinitive.

Quisiera hablar con el Sr Fuentes.	I would like to talk to Mr Fuentes.
¿Quisiera hablar con él en privado?	Would you like to talk to him in private?
Quisiera un boleto para el vuelo de las diez.	I would like a ticket for the ten o'clock flight.
Quisiéramos una habitación doble.	We would like a double room.

Here are all the forms:

quisiera	**quisiéramos**
quisieras	**quisieran**
quisiera	**quisieran**

Exercise 5 ⬤⬤

Give Spanish equivalents for the following:

1 I would like to buy a newspaper.
2 We would like to visit the museum.
3 We would like two single rooms.
4 I would like a new book.
5 I would like to go to Uruguay.

Language point

Parts of the day

To explain which part of the day you refer to, these expressions are used:

por la mañana/en la mañana	in the morning
por la tarde/en la tarde	in the afternoon
por la noche/en la noche	in the evening/at night
al mediodía	at noon
a la medianoche	at midnight
en la madrugada	in the early hours

Note: in Latin America **por** and **en** are used with parts of the day. In Spain usually **por** is the only form used.

Exercise 6

Write the expression indicating the part of the day for each of these times:
(a) 10.00 a.m.
(b) 2.30 a.m.
(c) 7.45 p.m.
(d) 2.30 p.m.
(e) 11.15 p.m.

Exercise 7

Write out things that are usually done in the morning, in the afternoon and in the evening/at night. Write the usual time when most people do it or when you do it. Below there are some suggestions of activities.

Example:

POR LA MAÑANA   POR LA TARDE
desayunar: 7.30 a.m.   **almorzar**: 1.30 p.m.

POR LA MAÑANA	POR LA TARDE	POR LA NOCHE
_____	_____	_____
_____	_____	_____
_____	_____	_____

tomar un café	to have a coffee	**ver televisión**	to watch television
pasear	to go for a walk	**escuchar música**	to listen to music
comprar el	to buy the	**volver a casa**	to return home
periódico	newspaper	**almorzar**	to have lunch
ir a trabajar	to go to work		

Dialogue 3 🔲

Viajar en el metro

Miguel wants to go to Emilio's house in Mexico City later the same day. Emilio suggests the Metro (subway) as the quickest way to get there

MIGUEL: ¿Dónde está tu casa, entonces?
EMILIO: Está en Panteones. Acá tienes la dirección exacta.
MIGUEL: ¿Cómo voy hasta allá?
EMILIO: Lo mejor es ir en Metro. La estación Revolución está cerca de aquí. Tomas la línea a Cuatro Caminos y te bajas en Panteones.
MIGUEL: ¿Es caro?
EMILIO: No, es barato y rápido.

MIGUEL: *Where is your house, then?*
EMILIO: *It's in Panteones. Here is the exact address.*
MIGUEL: *How do I get there?*

EMILIO: *The best way is by subway. The Revolución station is*
          nearby. You get on the Cuatro Caminos line and get off at
          Panteones.

MIGUEL: *Is it expensive?*

EMILIO: *No, it's cheap and fast.*

Language point

¿Cómo? 🔲🔲

This is the question word used to ask the way you do things.

¿Cómo voy hasta allá?   How do I get there?
¿Cómo funciona esta   How does this machine work?
  máquina?

In informal speech, **¿Cómo?** is also the expression used when you
do not hear what somebody has just said and you want that person
to repeat the message.

A: **Mario está en casa.**
B: **¿Cómo?**
A: **Digo que Mario está en casa.**
B: **Ah, sí. Está enfermo.**

A: Mario is at home.
B: Pardon?
A: I'm saying that Mario is at home.
B: Oh, yes. He's ill.

Exercise 8 🔲🔲

Match the word in the left column with its opposite on the right.

1	**cerca**	(a) **subir**
2	**acá**	(b) **barato**
3	**caro**	(c) **rápido**
4	**lento**	(d) **lejos**
5	**bajar**	(e) **allá**

Reading

México 〔OO〕

México es el país más poblado de habla castellana. Su población llega a aproximadamente 100 millones. Su capital tiene más de 20 millones. Otras dos ciudades importantes son Guadalajara y Monterrey.

México es el principal productor de plata en el mundo. Es también un importante exportador de petróleo. Entre los productos agrícolas que ofrecen beneficios para el país están el algodón, la caña de azúcar, el café, el cacao y el garbanzo. El turismo es también una importante fuente de divisas.

poblado	populated	**algodón**	cotton
de habla	Spanish-	**cacao**	cacao
castellana	speaking	**garbanzo**	chickpea
plata	silver	**fuente de divisas**	source of foreign exchange

Exercise 9

Based on the paragraph above, say if the following statements are **verdadero** (true) or **falso** (false).

1 **México es el país con más población de habla castellana.**
2 **Monterrey no es una ciudad de México.**
3 **México no exporta petróleo.**
4 **El comercio de algodón y caña de azúcar ofrece beneficios al país.**
5 **El turismo no aporta beneficios económicos.**

6 De compras

Shopping

By the end of this chapter you should be able to:

- Make comparisons using adjectives
- Express possibility or impossibility
- Express likes and dislikes
- Use radical changing verbs

Dialogue 1

Comprando regalos

Martha works in a gift shop. A customer wants to buy a present and is comparing two ornaments

CLIENTE:	¿Cuánto cuesta ese adorno?
MARTHA:	Doscientos cuarenta el grande y ciento noventa el más pequeño.
CLIENTE:	¿Puedo ver el grande un momento?
MARTHA:	Por supuesto. Puede ver los dos.
CLIENTE:	Los dos son lindos, pero prefiero el grande. ¿Acepta tarjetas de crédito?
MARTHA:	Sí, aceptamos todas las principales tarjetas de crédito.

CUSTOMER:	*How much is that ornament?*
MARTHA:	*Two hundred and forty for the big one and one hundred and ninety for the smaller one.*
CUSTOMER:	*Can I have a look at the big one for a moment?*
MARTHA:	*Of course. You can have a look at both of them.*
CUSTOMER:	*Both are pretty, but I prefer the big one. Do you take credit cards?*
MARTHA:	*Yes, we accept all major credit cards.*

Language points

El grande/el chico

The big one/the small one

To avoid the repetition of a noun or noun phrase it is possible to use only the article + the adjective. In these cases in English you would use the adjective + 'one', as in 'the small one'.

¿Le gusta el plato grande o el chico?	Do you like the big plate or the small one?
A: **Tengo una camiseta roja y una azul.** B: **La roja, por favor.**	A: I have a red T shirt and a blue one. B: The red one, please.
¿Qué modelo busca, el liviano o el pesado?	Which model are you looking for, the light one or the heavy one?

Lindo

The word **lindo/linda** is very much used in Latin American Spanish to mean 'pretty, nice, beautiful'. In Peninsular Spanish **bonito/bonita** is preferred.

Tu hija es muy linda.	Your daughter is very pretty.
¡Qué linda casa!	What a beautiful house!

Radical changing verbs

These are verbs in Spanish which undergo a change of the stem vowel (i.e. the vowel in the part of the verb that remains the same when it is conjugated) when you conjugate them. In these verbs the vowel -**e**- in the stem becomes -**ie**-, and the vowel -**o**- becomes -**ue**-. The exception is the first person plural.

-e- → -ie-

preferir (to prefer)

prefiero	**preferimos**
prefieres	**prefieren**
prefiere	**prefieren**

pensar (to think)

pienso	**pensamos**
piensas	**piensan**
piensa	**piensan**

-o- → -ue-

dormir (to sleep)

duermo	**dormimos**
duermes	**duermen**
duerme	**duermen**

volver (to return)

vuelvo	**volvemos**
vuelves	**vuelven**
vuelve	**vuelven**

Some other common radical changing verbs are:

With vowel change -e- → -ie-

cerrar (to close)

cierro	**cerramos**
cierras	**cierran**
cierra	**cierran**

perder (to lose)

pierdo	**perdemos**
pierdes	**pierden**
pierde	**pierden**

pedir (to ask for)

pido	**pedimos**
pides	**piden**
pide	**piden**

empezar (to begin)

empiezo	**empezamos**
empiezas	**empiezan**
empieza	**empiezan**

With vowel change -**o**- → -**ue**-

morir (to die)

muero	**morimos**
mueres	**mueren**
muere	**mueren**

encontrar (to find)

encuentro	**encontramos**
encuentras	**encuentran**
encuentra	**encuentran**

recordar (to remember)

recuerdo	**recordamos**
recuerdas	**recuerdan**
recuerda	**recuerdan**

soñar (**con**) (to dream (of))

sueño	**soñamos**
sueñas	**sueñan**
sueña	**sueñan**

Exercise 1

Rewrite the following phrases using the correct form of the verb in brackets.

1 **¿A qué hora (empezar) la reunión?**
2 **Yo (recordar) la visita a Costa Rica.**
3 **Nosotros siempre (cerrar) a las 7.30.**
4 **Muchas personas (morir) de cáncer.**
5 **Enrique no (recordar) el problema.**

Language points

The comparatives

One way of comparing people or objects is by using **más** followed by the adjective, as in the examples:

más alto	taller, higher
más caro	more expensive
más grande	bigger, larger

Irregular comparatives

Some adjectives do not form their comparatives with **más**. They have a special form.

Adjective		*Comparative*	
bueno	good	**mejor**	better
malo	bad	**peor**	worse
mucho	a lot of	**más**	more
poco	little	**menos**	less

Más . . . que

When expressing comparison you usually use **más** + adjective + **que**:

Miami es más grande que Tampa.	Miami is bigger than Tampa.
En mi opinión el teatro es más interesante que el cine.	In my opinion, the theater is more interesting than the cinema.
El tabaco es más dañino que el café.	Tobacco is more harmful than coffee.

Exercise 2

Say if the following statements are true (**verdadero**) or false (**falso**):

1 **Londres es más grande que Nueva York.**

2 Generalmente un televisor es más caro que un carro.
3 Una computadora es más inteligente que una persona.
4 Las 6 de la mañana es más tarde que las 10 de la mañana.
5 Un carro es más pequeño que un camión.

Language point

The superlative

The superlative is formed by adding the definite article before the comparison:

El juguete más caro.	The most expensive toy.
El más flexible de todos los materiales.	The most flexible of all materials.
La película más interesante del festival.	The most interesting film of the festival.

If the adjective is in the plural, the superlative is formed with **los** or **las**:

Los juguetes más atractivos son japoneses.	The most attractive toys are Japanese.
Las bicicletas más caras están en esta sección.	The most expensive bicycles are in this section.

Exercise 3

Write an equivalent in Spanish for the following. See the glossary at the back of the book for the new words.

1 The most intelligent girl in the group.
2 It is the worst film in the festival.
3 The most functional models are here.
4 I would like the cheapest product.
5 It is the most difficult problem.

Language points

Poder

To ask if something is possible or permissible, the verb **poder** is used.

¿Puedo ver el grande?	Can I have a look at the big one?
¿Puedo usar esta computadora?	Can I use this computer?
¿Puedo mandar un mensaje por correo electrónico?	Can I send an E-mail message?

Notice that you add "no" before the relevant form of poder in order to make a negative statement showing that something is impossible, not advisable or improper.

No puedo caminar. Me fracturé el tobillo.	I cannot walk. I've broken my ankle
No puedes entrar ahí es peligroso.	You can't go in there. It's dangerous.

The forms are as follows:

puedo	can I? *or* I can
puedes	can you? *or* you can (informal)
puede	can you? *or* you can (formal); can he/she? *or* he/she can
podemos	can we? *or* we can
pueden	can you? *or* you can (formal and informal)
pueden	can they? *or* they can

Notice that this is a radical changing verb.

¿Se puede? is used to ask if something can be done without referring to a particular subject in the sentence.

¿Se puede estacionar acá?	Can you park here?
¿Se puede fumar?	Is smoking allowed?

Exercise 4

Complete the following sentences with the correct form of **poder**.

1 (Yo) No _____ asistir a la clase mañana.
2 (Nosotros) ¿ _____ ayudar?
3 (Ella) ¿ _____ venir con nosotros?
4 Usted _____ hacerlo.

5 (Yo) No _____ empezar el trabajo hoy. No tengo los materiales.

Saber

To indicate ability, as in 'Can you play the piano?', the verb **saber** is used.

¿Sabes tocar el piano?	Can you play the piano?
¿Sabes nadar?	Can you swim?
¿Sabes manejar?	Can you drive?

The forms are as follows:

sé	**sabemos**
sabes	**saben**
sabe	**saben**

Language point

Ambos/los dos

Ambos and **los dos** are used with the meaning of 'both'. If you refer to a feminine pair, then **ambas** or **las dos** is used. **Los dos** and **las dos** are preferred in spoken language, **ambos** and **ambas**, in written language.

Los dos son lindos.	**Ambos son lindos.**
Las dos son chilenas.	**Ambas son chilenas.**
Las dos estudiantes tienen problemas.	**Ambas estudiantes tienen probemas.**

Both . . . and . . .

The structure 'both . . . and . . .' can be translated by **ambos/ambas . . . y . . .** or **los/las dos . . . y . . .**, but also by the structure **tanto . . . como . . .**. Again, **ambos . . . y . . .** is preferred in written language.

Ambos Julián y María aprobaron sus exámenes.
Los dos, Julián y María aprobaron sus exámenes.
Tanto Julián como María aprobaron sus exámenes.

Both Julián and María passed their examinations.

Dialogue 2 🔲

La nueva computadora

Lucrecia has just bought a new computer

LUCRECIA: Mira mi nueva computadora. Es más potente que la anterior. Ahora también tengo una impresora de chorro de tinta, escáner, copiadora y fax. Adenás tengo una impresora láser para trabajos de alta calidad.

PABLO: ¿Tienes impresora láser a color o blanco y negro?

LUCRECIA: Es a color. No se puede trabajar con gráficos en blanco y negro.

PABLO: ¿Tienes agenda electrónica?

LUCRECIA: Sí. Presionas este botón y se pueden ver todas las citas de esta semana.
¿Te gusta mi escritorio?

PABLO: Sí, es muy funcional.

LUCRECIA: Ahora es más fácil que antes organizar mi trabajo.

LUCRECIA: *Look at my computer. It's more powerful than the previous one. I have a bubble jet printer, a scanner, a photocopier and a fax.*

PABLO: *Is it a colour printer, or black and white?*

LUCRECIA: *It's a colour printer. You can't work with graphics using a black and white printer.*

PABLO: *Does it have an electronic diary?*

LUCRECIA: *Yes. You press this button and you can see all the appointments for this week.*
Do you like my desk?

PABLO: *Yes. It's very functional.*

LUCRECIA: *Now organizing my work is easier than before.*

Note: **presionar** and **apretar** are used in Latin America with the meaning of *press* (a button or key on a keyboard) In Spain **pulsar** is preferred.

Language point

Me gusta

In order to express likes and dislikes you can use **gustar** or **no gustar**. For example:

Me gusta la camisa azul.	I like the blue shirt.
Nos gusta caminar.	We like walking.
A Miguel no le gusta el café.	Miguel doesn't like coffee.

It is also possible to use them in questions:

¿Te gusta el hotel?	Do you like the hotel?
¿No le gusta el regalo a María?	Doesn't María like the present?

Here are all the forms:

me gusta	**nos gusta**
te gusta	**les gusta**
le gusta	**les gusta**

And here are more examples:

Nos gusta montar en bicicleta.	We like to ride a bicycle.
¿Te gusta el chocolate?	Do you like chocolate?
A Gloria le gusta la moda.	Gloria likes fashion.
A ustedes les gusta la clase?	Do you like the class?

Note: Although in these exercises *like* is used as a translation of **gustar**, it must be said that the actual meaning is *to pleas*e, so for example **Me gusta la camisa azul** must be understood as *The blue shirt pleases me.*

Me gustan

If what is liked is plural, then the forms are as follows:

me gustan	**nos gustan**
te gustan	**les gustan**
le gustan	**les gustan**

Examples:

Me gustan los domingos.	I like Sundays.
A mis padres no les gustan las vacaciones en el extranjero.	My parents don't like holidays abroad.
¡Te gustan las frutillas!	You like strawberries!
Nos gustan los documentales.	We like documentaries.
No me gustan las comidas picantes.	I don't like spicy food.

Frutillas is used in Mexico. Elsewhere **fresas** is used for *strawberries*

Exercise 5 📷

Complete the phrases stating whether you like or dislike the following:

1 _____ los animales domésticos.
2 _____ las vacaciones en el extranjero.
3 _____ las ensaladas.
4 _____ visitar museos.
5 _____ escribir cartas.
6 _____ comprar regalos.
7 _____ levantarme temprano.
8 _____ comer chocolate.
9 _____ los niños.
10 _____ leer novelas.
11 _____ 'chatear' en Internet.
12 _____ viajar en transporte público.

Note: **chatear** (or **chatlear**, in Colombia) is the expression used to contact other people on the Internet.

Exercise 6

The following are types of television programs. Which ones do you like? Which ones don't you like?

	ME GUSTAN	NO ME GUSTAN
Los noticieros		
Las películas del oeste		
Las telenovelas		
Los documentales		
Los dibujos animados		
Las entrevistas		
Los programas cómicos		
Los reportajes		
Los concursos		
Los programas musicales		
Los *talk shows*		
Los programas de actualidad		
Otros		

noticieros	news	**programas cómicos**	comedy programs
películas del	westerns	**reportajes**	reports
oeste		**concursos**	contests
telenovelas	soap operas	**programas**	music programs
documentales	documentaries	**musicales**	
dibujos animados	cartoons	**programas de**	current affairs
entrevistas	interviews	**actualidad**	

Reading

Read the information in the advertisement below and answer these questions:

How much discount are you given?
What kind of keyboard does the computer have?
Can you pay with a credit card?
Are these discontinued models?

PROMOCION ESPECIAL
30% de descuento del precio de lista

CHARACTERÍSTICAS
¡ÚLTIMA TECNOLOGÍA!

Disco duro de 2 Gigabytes
Memoria de siz MB
Windows instalado
Multimedia
Teclado en castellano
Monitor de alta resolución
y baja radiación
Procesador muy veloz
Ranuras de expansión

Los precios se pueden
pagar en moneda nacional
o su equivalente en dólares.

Precios válidos únicamente en efectivo o con tarjeta
de debito.

precio de lista	list price	**ratón**	mouse
última tecnología	latest technology	**pagar**	to pay
disco duro	hard disk	**en efectivo**	in cash

páginas	pages	**tarjeta de**	debit card
teclado	keyboard	**debito**	
alta resolución	high resolution	**baja radiación**	low radiation
ranuras de expansión	expansion slots		

Archivo Editar Ver Ir Ayuda   7:55 am

Dirección: http://

Enlaces: e-mail gratuito   Enlaces personalizados   Windows

LIBROS   VIDEOS   MUSICA   FLORES

REGALOS   JUGUETES   CHOCOLATES

COMO COMPRAR EN INTERNET SIN TARJETA DE CREDITO

Con la nueva tarjeta *Intercard* del Banco Porvenir puedes comprar por Internet en cualquier lugar del mundo. El Banco Porvenir te brinda seguridad para comprar cómodamente los productos que deseas. Se puede obtener una tarjeta *Intercard* con un depósito mínimo de 25 dólares.

- Puedes hacer compras según la cantidad de dinero que tengas depositada.
- Puedes aumentar tu saldo en la cuenta en cualquier momento.
- Puedes consultar tu saldo en la página web del banco, utilizando tu contraseña.
- Puedes retirar tu dinero en las ventanillas de una sucursal o en el cajero automático.

agregar el carrito   ir a caja

enlaces:	links	**consultar du saldo:**	check your balance
tarjeta de crédito:	credit card	**contraseña:**	password,pin number
te brinda:	it provides	**retirar:**	to withdraw
deseas:	(you) wish	**sucursal:**	branch
según:	according to	**cajero automático:**	cash dispensing machine
agregar:	add	**ventanilla:**	counter
carrito:	shopping trolley	**caja:**	cash till

Based on the text above decide if the following statements are either **verdadero** (true) or **falso** (false):

1. Es necesario una tarjeta de crédito para comprar en Internet.
2. No hay un depósito minimo.
3. Es posible retirar dinero del cajero automático.
4. La tarjeta se llama *Intercard*.
5. Se puede consultar el saldo sólo en una ventanilla del banco.

7 ¿Qué estás haciendo?

What are you doing?

By the end of this chapter you should be able to:

- Refer to actions in progress using the present continuous
  e.g. (I am working)
- Use possessive adjectives (my, your, etc.)
- Use demonstrative adjectives and pronouns (this, this one,
  etc.)
- Use exclamations with **que** + adjective/noun (e.g. **¡Qué
  bonito!**)

Dialogue 1 🔊

¡Qué lindas fotos!

Ernesto is showing Maritza photographs of his birthday party

MARITZA: ¿Qué lindas fotos! ¿Qué estás haciendo en esa
          foto?
ERNESTO: Estoy celebrando mi cumpleaños.
MARITZA: ¿Y en esta foto?
ERNESTO: Julia y yo estamos bailando. Acá todos están brindando
          por mi cumpleaños.
MARITZA: Tú estás leyendo un discurso.
ERNESTO: Sí, algo chistoso.

From here on you will find the translations of dialogues in an
appendix at the back of the book.

Language point

The present continuous tense

The present continuous tense is formed by using **estar** + the gerund form of the verb. The gerund ends in **-ando** or **-iendo** (**-ando** for **-ar** verbs; **-iendo** for **-er** and **-ir** verbs.) These forms correspond to the English ending '-ing', as in 'eating', 'running', etc.

estoy estudiando	I am studying
estás estudiando	you are studying (informal)
está estudiando	you are studying (formal); he/she is studying
estamos estudiando	we are studying
están estudiando	you are studying (formal and informal)
están estudiando	they are studying

The present continuous refers to an action which is in progress at the time of speaking.

Estoy estudiando para el examen de mañana.	I am studying for tomorrow's exam.
Estamos jugando a las cartas, ¿quieres jugar?	We are playing cards, do you want to play?

Reading 🎧

After reading the following extract from a TV report transcript, answer these questions:

Who is giving a speech?
What is the speaker trying to explain?
Are people interested in the message?

Rodolfo Arias is a current affairs reporter and is giving a live report by satellite on events in a neighboring country

Locutor de televisión:	A continuación un informe de nuestro corresponsal en el extranjero.
Rodolfo:	El presidente está hablando a la nación en estos momentos. Está dando un discurso de fin de año. La radio y la televisión están transmitiendo el mensaje.

El presidente está explicando los planes del gobierno para el próximo año. En estos momentos está tratando sobre el aumento de sueldos para los empleados públicos y privados. Sin duda, todo el país está escuchando.

a continuación	now follows	**está explicando**	is explaining
informe	report	**próximo**	next
corresponsal en el extranjero	foreign correspondent	**está tratando sobre**	is dealing with
la nación	the nation	**aumento de sueldos**	wage increase
dando un discurso	giving a speech	**sin duda**	no doubt
de fin de año	end of the year	**todo el país**	the whole country
		está escuchando	is listening

Exercise 1 ⬤⬤

Answer each question as in the example:

¿Qué está haciendo Silvia? (saltar)
Está saltando.

1 **¿Qué está haciendo Pepe? (estudiar)**
2 **¿Qué están haciendo Julia y Rosana? (escribir)**
3 **¿Qué estás haciendo? (trabajar en la oficina)**
4 **¿Qué están haciendo ustedes? (arreglar el jardín)**
5 **¿Qué están haciendo las chicas? (practicar el baile)**

saltar	to jump	**el jardín**	the garden
arreglar	to tidy up	**el baile**	the dance

Exercise 2

Read the following notice put up by the telephone company on the road. Answer these questions:

1 Is it an apology? If so, what is the expression used?
2 What is the reason for this apology?

> **Compañía de Teléfonos S.A.**
> **Disculpe la molestia.**
> **Estamos instalando nuevas líneas.**

disculpe la	I/we apologize for	**instalar**	to instal
molestia	the inconvenience	**líneas**	lines

Exercise 3

Give the equivalent in English for the following sentences:

1 **Estamos entrevistando para dos puestos de trabajo.**
2 **El grupo está incursionando en el mercado internacional.**
3 **La recuperación económica está empezando.**
4 **Estoy buscando una alternativa a este producto.**
5 **Genaro está trabajando en un nuevo proyecto.**

incursionar	to make inroads	**puestos de trabajo**	jobs
buscar	to look for		

Language point

Possessive adjectives

Possessive adjectives appear in front of the noun they refer to and correspond to the English 'my', your', etc. They agree in number with the noun possessed. The possessive adjective for the first person plural ('our') also agrees in gender.

	Singular	Plural
my	**mi**	**mis**
your (informal)	**tu**	**tus**
your (formal)	**su**	**sus**
his/her/its	**su**	**sus**
our	**nuestro(/a)**	**nuestros(/as)**
your	**su**	**sus**
their	**su**	**sus**

Examples:

Mi casa está cerca.	My house is near.
Nuestra clase es a las nueve.	Our lesson is at nine.

Tus amigos están esperando.	Your friends are waiting.
¡Apúrate!	Hurry up!
Su opinión es muy importante.	Your opinion is very important.

Exercise 4

Rewrite the second sentence in each pair, adding at the beginning the correct possessive adjective for the person mentioned or implied in the first sentence.

Example:

Sandra tiene problemas.
Su madre está enferma.

1 **Marina y Lupe están adentro.**
   _____ **amigas también.**

2 **Felipe sabe manejar.**
   _____ **carro es nuevo.**

3 **El producto es bueno.**
   _____ **precio es competitivo.**

4 **Estoy contento.**
   _____ **padre ahora está bien.**

5 **Juan tiene una motocicleta.**
   _____ **hermano menor tiene una bicicleta.**

Language point

Demonstrative adjectives

The demonstrative adjectives 'this' and 'that' are translated by the Spanish **este** and **ese** and other forms associated with them (see below). They agree in number and gender with the noun they refer to. **Aquel**, which also means 'that', is preferred to indicate something that is far away.

Singular		Plural	
masc.	*fem.*	*masc.*	*fem.*
este	esta	estos	estas
ese	esa	esos	esas
aquel	aquella	aquellos	aquellas

Examples:

Este periódico es el más popular.	This newspaper is the most popular one.
Esa camisa es cara.	That shirt is expensive.
Estos amigos viven en Guadalajara.	These friends live in Guadalajara.
Estas mesas son para el colegio.	These tables are for the school.
Esas chicas estudian medicina.	Those girls study medicine.
Aquel señor es el presidente del club.	That gentleman (over there) is the president of the club.
Aquellos animales son especies en peligro.	Those animals are endangered species.

Exercise 5

Teléfono celular ◖◖

A salesperson is showing a mobile phone to a potential customer.

Vendedor: Este celular* es digital, tiene un diseño moderno y es de prepago para mayor control de su cuenta telefónica. Puede hablar a todo el país y también hacia y desde el extranjero. En ese folleto se encuentra más información.

This digital mobile phone has a modern design and it is prepaid so that you have better control over your telephone bill. It covers the whole country and also abroad. This leaflet gives you more information.

- Memoria para 90 números
- Identificación de llamadas
- Peso de 200 gramos
- Hasta 180 minutos de conversación ininterrumpida
- De 4 a 8 días en *stand by*
- 120 minutos libres por 60 dias
- Casilla de mensajes
- Mensajes por Internet
- Discado por voz
- Roaming Internacional

prepago	prepaid	**peso**	weight
cuenta telefónica	telephone bill	**ininterrumpida**	uninterrupted
		libre	free
hacia	towards, to	**casilla de**	voice
folleto	leaflet	**mensajes**	mail
llamada	telephone call	**discado por voz**	voice activated dialing

*In some Latin American countries a mobile phone is called **teléfono móvil**.

1 If you have a mobile phone, explain or write down in Spanish which features of the phone above are similar to yours.

2 Rearrange the features above in order of importance.

Language points

Demonstrative pronouns

In spoken Spanish, demonstrative pronouns are identical in form to demonstrative adjectives. In writing, the difference is that the pronouns have an accent. 'This one' and 'that one' correspond to **éste** and **ése** and their associated forms. Again, **aquél** and related forms are used for something remote.

Singular		Plural	
masc.	*fem.*	*masc.*	*fem.*
éste	ésta	éstos	éstas
ése	ésa	ésos	ésas
aquél	aquélla	aquéllos	aquéllas

Examples:

No quiero este periódico, quiero aquél.	I don't want this newspaper, I want that one.
Quisiera comprar éstas.	I would like to buy these ones.
¿Cuánto cuestan éstos?	How much are these?
Ese video no me gusta. Prefiero éste.	I don't like that video. I prefer this one.

There are also the neuter pronouns **esto** and **eso** and **aquello**, as in **¿Qué es esto?** 'What's this?', **Eso es todo** 'That's all'.

¡Qué!

The structure **qué** + adjective translates the English 'how + adjective'.

¡Qué lindo!	How lovely!
¡Qué interesante!	How interesting!
¡Qué caro!	How expensive!
¡Qué tonta!	How stupid!

The structure **qué** + noun corresponds to the English 'what (a) + noun'.

¡Qué día!	What a day!
¡Qué tiempo!	What weather!
¡Qué película!	What a film!
¡Qué desastre!	What a disaster!

Acá/aquí; allá/allí

The English 'here' is translated by **acá** or **aquí**; 'there' is translated by **ahí**, **allá** or **allí**. In Latin America, **acá** and **allá** are preferred. In

Spain, **aquí** and **allí** are preferred. In both varieties of Spanish **ahí** is used regularly. **Acá/aquí** refers to a place near the speaker. **Ahí** refers to a place not far from the speaker, perhaps near the hearer. **Allá/allí** refers to a place far from the speaker.

Acá en la tienda tenemos una amplia variedad de productos.	Here in the shop we have a wide variety of products.
Allá en el norte se vive mejor.	People live better in the north.
Ahí está. Cerca de la puerta.	It's there. By the door.

Dialogue 2 🔲

Más fotos

Ernesto and Maritza are looking at more photographs of his birthday party

ERNESTO: En esta foto estoy leyendo las tarjetas de saludos.
MARITZA: Mira, acá estás con un plato repleto.
ERNESTO: Y en ésta, Rosana está posando para el fotógrafo. Está mirando las flores.
MARITZA: Está muy bien.
ERNESTO: Sí, está bien.

Language points

Leer → leyendo

When the verb has -**ee**- in the infinitive, there is a spelling change in the gerund ('-ing') form.

leer (to read)
Está leyendo en la biblioteca. He's reading in the library.

creer (to believe)
Creyendo que era fácil de hacer, empezó a pintar el retrato. Believing that it was easy to do, she started to paint the portrait.

Construir → construyendo

When the infinitive ends in **-uir**, there is also a spelling change.

construir (to build)
Están construyendo un   They are building a new school.
colegio nuevo.

disminuir (to go down)
El nivel del agua está   The water level is going down.
disminuyendo.

Exercise 6 💿

Complete this dialogue, changing the verb in brackets to the continuous form.

Ana arrives home from work and finds her son in the kitchen.

ANA:	**¿Qué estás (hacer)?**
MARIO:	**Estoy (preparar) un informe.**
ANA:	**Y Tomás, ¿qué está (hacer)?**
MARIO:	**Está (escribir) una carta a una amiga.**
ANA:	**¿Dónde está?**
MARIO:	**En su cuarto.**

hacer	to do, to make
informe	report
carta	letter
cuarto	room, bedroom (note that other words used for bedroom are **pieza, alcoba, recámara, dormitorio**)

In Spain usually **dormitorio** and **habitación** are used for *bedroom*.

Exercise 7

Complete the following sentences with the correct form of **estar**.

1 **(Yo) _____ hablando por teléfono a Bogotá.**
2 **María _____ explicando el problema.**
3 **Dolores y Fernando _____ platicando.**
4 **El abuelo _____ tomando fotos a los niños.**
5 **Mi madre _____ exprimiendo las naranjas para el jugo.**

explicar	to explain	**exprimir**	to extract
platicar	to talk	**jugo**	juice
tomar fotos	to take photographs		

Exercise 8

Choose the correct answer from the words in brackets.

1 **(Maribel/Nosotros) está viendo televisión.**
2 **(Asunción y Genaro/Yo) están hablando por teléfono.**
3 **(Tú/Usted) está preparando el informe y (tú/usted) estás preparando los gráficos, ¿verdad?**
4 **(Maritza/Yo) estoy cantando en esta foto.**
5 **(La radio/Los periódicos) está transmitiendo el partido de fútbol.**

el informe	the report	**cantando**	singing
los gráficos	graphics	**transmitiendo**	broadcasting
¿verdad?	right?	**partido**	match

Language point

Conjunctions

The conjunctions **y** and **o** correspond to 'and' and 'or' in English and are used in a similar way.

When **y** precedes another word beginning with the sound **i**, it changes to **e**, as in **Felipe e Ignacio**.

When **o** precedes a word beginning with the sound **o**, it changes to **u**, as in **Aconsejar u orientar es difícil**. 'To advise or give guidance is difficult'.

Reading 🔲

While reading the passage below, see if you can find answers to these questions:

What happens on the Day of the Dead according to popular belief?
What do children usually buy?

El Día de Muertos

El dos de noviembre en todo México se celebra el Día de Muertos, una de las fiestas más importantes del país. Se cree que los muertos vuelven a visitar a su familia y se les ofrece alimentos, frutas y flores. Además, se encienden velas y se quema incienso. Por todas partes hay calaveras de 'papier-maché' y los niños compran calaveras de dulce para comer.

muertos	the dead	**se encienden**	are lit
fiesta	festival	**velas**	candles
se cree	it is believed	**incienso**	incense
alimentos	food	**por todas partes**	everywhere
frutas	fruit	**calaveras**	skulls
flores	flowers	**dulce**	sweet

8 ¿Qué tengo que hacer?

What do I have to do?

By the end of this chapter you will be able to:

- Express necessity or obligation using **tener que** and **hay que**
- Talk about your routines at work and at home
- Describe a house
- Describe a room
- Use **con** + pronoun/**conmigo**, **contigo** (with me, with you, etc.)

Dialogue 1 ▚

Tengo que ir al banco

Mark wants to change some traveler's checks

MARK: Tengo que cambiar cheques de viajero. Necesito más plata. Vamos a la casa de cambio.

CARMEN: No. El banco es mejor.

MARK: ¿Por qué?

CARMEN: El banco cobra menos comisión y paga más por dólar.

MARK: Entonces, vamos al banco.

CARMEN: Tenemos que ir rápido. El banco cierra a las tres. ¡Apúrate! Quedan diez minutos.

Language point

Tener que

To explain that something has to be done the expression **tener que** is used. This is the equivalent of the English 'to have to'. Here are all the forms:

tengo que	I have to
tienes que	you have to (informal)
tiene que	you have to (formal); he/she has to
tenemos que	we have to
tienen que	you have to (formal and informal)
tienen que	they have to

The expression **tener que** is always followed by a verb in the infinitive.

Tengo que cambiar cheques de viaje.	I have to change traveler's checks.
Tenemos que terminar pronto.	We have to finish soon.

Exercise 1

Which of these things do you do at work and at home? Use the expression **tener que** to say what you have to do both at home and at work. Then write the phrases down in your notebook.

Example:

En el trabajo tengo que presentar informes.

En el trabajo (At work)

1 **abrir la correspondencia**
2 **enviar faxes**
3 **escribir cartas**
4 **supervisar la producción**
5 **trabajar hasta tarde**
6 **presentar informes**
7 **llamar por teléfono**
8 **tratar con el público**

9 **utilizar la computadora**
10 **leer y contestar el correo electrónico**

En casa (At home)

1 **preparar la comida**
2 **limpiar**
3 **pasar la aspiradora**
4 **planchar**
5 **ayudar a los niños con sus tareas**
6 **contestar el teléfono**
7 **atender el jardín**
8 **hacer reparaciones**
9 **pagar las cuentas**
10 **ordenar las recámaras**

enviar	to send	**ayudar**	to help
hasta tarde	until late	**tareas**	homework
pasar la	to vacuum	**atender**	to attend to
aspiradora		**hacer reparaciones**	to do repairs
planchar	to iron	**ordenar**	to tidy up
las cuentas	the bills		

Now practise the same sentences again, adding some expressions of frequency/habit/routine.

generalmente	generally
normalmente	normally
a veces	sometimes
siempre	always
nunca	never

Examples:

> **En casa, generalmente tengo que contestar el teléfono.**
> **En el trabajo siempre escribo cartas.**

Reading

A professor of Economics is talking about the problems of the nation

'En mi opinión, el gobierno tiene que rebajar las tasas de interés, el sector privado tiene que invertir más, los sindicatos tienen que moderar sus expectativas, y todos tenemos que trabajar juntos para estimular la economía del país.'

gobierno	government	**sindicatos**	trade unions
rebajar	to reduce	**moderar**	to tone down,
tasas de interés	interest rates		to moderate
sector privado	private sector	**expectativas**	expectations
invertir	to invest	**juntos**	together

Exercise 2

People from various sources mentioned in the speech above have commented on the contents of it. Are they in favor (**en favor**) or against (**en contra**) what was said in the speech?

1 **Vocero del gobierno: '. . . las tasas de interés están bien . . .'**
2 **Sociedad de Empresarios: 'Tenemos que invertir más capital . . .'**
3 **Líder sindical: 'Tenemos que luchar por un salario justo.'**

vocero	spokesperson	**luchar**	to fight
sociedad de	industrialists'	**salario**	salary
empresarios	confederation	**justo**	fair, just
líder sindical	union leader		

Exercise 3

Mr Miller has a few things to do during his one-day business visit to a Latin American client. In what order does he have to do things, do you think? Write it down in your notebook. The following expressions may help you to link your sentences:

primero	first
después	afterwards
luego	next, then
entonces	then
más tarde	later
por último	lastly

Example:

Primero, tiene que preparar el informe.

tiene que visitar la fábrica

tiene que discutir precios
tiene que ver muestras
tiene que probar el producto
tiene que estudiar el contrato

la fábrica	the factory	**probar**	to try, to test
discutir	to discuss	**muestras**	samples
precios	prices		

Dialogue 2 🔲

Tareas de la casa

While reading the dialogue below, see if you can find answers to this question:

Does Sra Huertas do housework or does she do a paid job from home?

Sra Huertas explains some of the things she has to do at home

ENTREVISTADOR: ¿Qué tareas domésticas tiene que hacer en la casa Sra Huertas?

SRA HUERTAS: Tengo que lavar la ropa, tengo que lavar los platos, tengo que limpiar la casa, tengo que preparar el desayuno, tengo que llevar a los niños al colegio . . .

Language point

Personal a

After certain verbs, such as **conocer** (to know), **llevar** (to carry), **acompañar** (to accompany), **ver** (to see), **visitar** (to visit), it is necessary to use the 'personal' **a** when the direct object (i.e. the person, animal or thing directly affected by the verb) that follows is a person or the name of a person. You do not need the 'personal' **a** if the direct object is not a person.

Me gusta visitar a mi tía.	I like to visit my aunt.
Me gusta visitar Chile.	I like to visit Chile.
Llevo a los niños al colegio.	I take the children to school.
Llevo muchas cosas al colegio.	I take many things to school.

Exercise 4

Study the following examples:

Tengo que llevar mi carro al trabajo.	I have to take my car to work.
Tenemos que llevar a Julia al centro.	We have to take Julia to town.

Now make similar sentences including other things or people you have to take somewhere, e.g. **al colegio** (to school), **al trabajo** (to work), **al parque** (to the park), etc., either regularly or occasionally.

Language point

Hay que

Another way of expressing that something needs to be done is by using **hay que** followed by the infinitive.

Hay que parar la guerra.	The war must be stopped.
Hay que comprar por docenas.	You have to buy by the dozen.

In this case the expression is more impersonal than **tener que** since you do not refer to any person in particular. The emphasis is on the need to perform the action.

Exercise 5

Match the possible solutions to the problems in the following troubleshooting chart for a television set.

PROBLEMA	SOLUCIÓN POSIBLE
1 **Imagen imperfecta.**	(a) **Hay que regular el contraste.**
2 **Buen sonido, pero la pantalla no está iluminada.**	(b) **Hay que ajustar la antena.**
3 **Imagen lluviosa y ruido.**	(c) **Hay que chequear la conexión de la antena.**
4 **Aparecen líneas horizontales.**	(d) **Hay que regular el brillo.**

imagen	TV picture	**lluviosa (imagen)**	snowy (TV picture) (literally, 'rainy')
ajustar	adjust		
sonido	sound	**regular**	adjust
pantalla	screen	**ruido**	noise
antena	aerial	**líneas**	lines
chequear	check	**brillo**	brightness
contraste	contrast		

Exercise 6

Here are the names of well-known daily newspapers from Latin America. Use the map below to match each paper with the country where it is published.

1	**Excelsior**	(a)	Cuba
2	**El Mercurio**	(b)	Argentina
3	**La Nación**	(c)	Colombia
4	**El Comercio**	(d)	Uruguay
5	**El Espectador**	(e)	México
6	**ABC**	(f)	Paraguay
7	**El Universal**	(g)	Perú
8	**Gramma**	(h)	Venezuela
9	**La Prensa**	(i)	Bolivia
10	**El País**	(j)	Chile

MAR CARIBE

OCEANO PACIFICO

OCEANO ATLANTICO

Once you have finished Exercise 6, explain where each newspaper is published.
Example:

Excelsior se publica en Mexico   *Excelsior is published in Mexico.*

You may use se **publica** *it is published*, or **se lee** *it is read*. You will learn more about similar expressions in Chapter 11.

Los cuartos de la casa

1 entrada
2 sala
3 comedor
4 cocina

5 garaje
6 dormitorio
7 baño

Al entrar a la casa, en la planta baja a la izquierda está la sala. A la derecha está el patio. Más adentro, a la izquierda está el comedor y a la derecha está la cocina. En la planta alta hay dos dormitorios y un baño. También hay un estudio.

Note: in Latin America **entrar a** is usually the preferred form, while in Spain **entrar en** predominates.

al entrar	as you go in	**planta alta**	upstairs
planta baja	downstairs	**más adentro**	further inside

Exercise 7

Based on the description above, now try to describe your own house. You can start by saying: **Vivo en una casa** 'I live in a house' or **Vivo en un departamento** 'I live in a flat/apartment' and then describe the layout, i.e. **Al entrar a la casa/al departamento . . .** 'As you go into the house/flat . . .'.

Note: In Spain people use the word **piso** for a flat/apartment. **Apartamento** is also used when it is for short holiday stays.

Reading

Mi cuarto

Mi cuarto es chico, pero cómodo. A la izquierda está mi cama. Al lado de la cama está el ropero. A la derecha está mi estéreo. También a la derecha hay estantes para libros. En los estantes tengo mi cámara fotográfica y fotos. Cerca de la puerta están mis zapatos y zapatillas. La ventana es grande y da al jardín.

chico	small	**estantes**	shelves
cómodo	comfortable	**ventana**	window
cama	bed		

Note: Spanish speakers in Latin America prefer the word **chico/chica** to mean 'small'. In Spain **pequeño/pequeña** is preferred.

Now try to describe in Spanish your own room and some of the things there are in it:

¿Cómo es tu cuarto?	What's your room like?
¿Qué tienes en tu cuarto?	What do you have in your room?

Dialogue 3 🔲

Hablando por teléfono

Ana María and Adela are talking on the phone

ANA MARÍA: ¿Adela? ¿qué estás haciendo?
ADELA: Estoy escuchando mis 'compact discs'. ¿Quieres escuchar música conmigo?
ANA MARÍA: Bueno.
ADELA: Ven a mi casa, entonces.
ANA MARÍA: Sí, voy ahorita.

As well as 'compact discs' people also use the letters CD. Example:

Estoy escuchando mis CDs.   *I am listening to my CDs.*
(pronounced 'mis ce des')

Language points

Ahorita

This word is used to indicate that something will be done straight away, without delay. In Spain the equivalent expression is **enseguida**.

Conmigo/contigo

The special forms **conmigo** and **contigo** are used for 'with me' and 'with you'. For other persons **con** + pronoun is used.

conmigo	with me
contigo	with you (singular)
con él	with him
con ella	with her
con nosotros	with us
con ustedes	with you (plural)
con ellos	with them
con ellas	with them (if all are female)

Examples:

Ven conmigo.	Come with me.
¿Quieres ir a comer con ellos?	Do you want to go out for a meal with them?

Note: if you want to refer to a mixed group of people, the masculine plural form is used.

Exercise 8

Give the Spanish equivalent for the following phrases.

1 I want to go with you.
2 Sra Rosas lives in a small house with them (two daughters).
3 Come with me.
4 They want a meeting with you.
5 He always arrives with them (all male).

Reading 🔲

Here is a message from a charity collecting donations for Christmas. While reading the text, see if you can find answers to these questions:

What are they collecting for?
How can you make a donation?

CONTAMOS CONTIGO

Esta Navidad con la ayuda de todos vamos a lograr sonrisas. Como siempre, esperamos contar contigo. Toda ayuda será bienvenida: ropa, medicinas, juguetes. Llama al teléfono 49 – 4949 de 8 de la mañana a 6 de la tarde para ofrecer tu donativo.

Navidad	Christmas	**contar**	to count on
vamos a lograr	we are going to get	**bienvenida**	welcome
sonrisa	smile	**juguetes**	toys
como siempre	as always	**ofrecer**	offer
esperamos	we hope	**donativo**	donation

9 He perdido . . .

I have lost . . .

> **By the end of this chapter you will be able to:**
>
> - Refer to recent events using the present perfect tense (e.g. I have finished, we have eaten, etc.)
> - Use the present perfect continuous tense (e.g. I have been working)
> - Give a basic physical description of objects and materials
> - Use **por** and **para**

Dialogue 1

He perdido mi pasaporte

JAIME: ¿Qué pasa?
CATHERINE: He perdido mi pasaporte.
JAIME: ¿Dónde? ¿Cómo?
CATHERINE: No sé. No estoy segura. Quizás en el mercado.
JAIME: Hay que ir a la comisaría y luego al consulado.
CATHERINE: Sí. Necesito un duplicado.

Language points

¿Qué pasa?

This question is used to find out what the matter is with somebody. It is similar to 'What's happening?/What's the matter?'

The present perfect tense

The present perfect tense is formed by the auxiliary verb **haber** and the past participle of the main verb of the sentence.

Example:

He perdido mi maletín.   I have lost my briefcase.

The forms of **haber** are:

he	I have
has	you have (informal)
ha	you have (formal); he/she has
hemos	we have
han	you have (plural)
han	they have

Note: when the meaning of 'to have' is 'to possess', then you must use **tener** and not **haber**, i.e. **tengo** (I have), **tienes** (you have), etc., as in

Tengo una cámara   I have a digital camera.
digital.

You form the past participle of a verb by replacing the infinitive ending **-ar** by the ending **-ado**, and the endings **-er** and **-ir** by **-ido**.

trabajar	**trabajado**
comer	**comido**
vivir	**vivido**

The most common irregular past participles are:

abrir (to open)	**abierto**
decir (to say)	**dicho**
escribir (to write)	**escrito**

hacer (to do, to make)	**hecho**
morir (to die)	**muerto**
poner (to put)	**puesto**
romper (to break)	**roto**
ver (to see)	**visto**
volver (to return)	**vuelto**

The present perfect is used to indicate that an event has happened in a period of time in the past but which includes the present or whose effects still bear on the present.

He perdido mi pasaporte.	I have lost my passport.
Hemos terminado.	We have finished.
¿No ha llegado?	Hasn't he/she arrived?

The present perfect continuous

This tense is used to indicate that an action has been in progress over a period of time and continues to be in progress at the time of speaking. It is formed by using **haber** plus the past participle plus the gerund (e.g. **escribiendo** 'writing', **viajando** 'traveling').

Examples:

Hemos estado trabajando todo el día en este asunto.	We have been working on this matter all day.
¿Has estado estudiando todo el tiempo?	Have you been studying all the time?

Desde

The word **desde** is the equivalent of 'since'.

He estado trabajando desde las siete y media.	I have been working since half past seven.
Hemos estado preparando el congreso desde enero.	We have been preparing the conference since January.

The following structure in Spanish:

desde + hace + period of time

is similar to the English structure 'for' + period of time.

Examples:

Trabajo acá desde hace dos años.	I have been working here for two years.
¿Desde hace cuánto tiempo que estás en Santiago?	How long have you been in Santiago?
Estudio en la universidad desde hace dos meses.	I have been studying at the university for two months.

Exercise 1

Translate the following into Spanish:

1 I have finished my work.
2 I have been writing this letter for two hours.
3 Elena and I have written a letter to the newspaper.
4 Roger has been in Cali for a week.
5 Carlos Fuentes has published a new book.
6 You have lived in Paraguay for a long time.
7 The bank has opened a new branch.
8 We haven't seen Lorena since this morning.
9 They have arrived.
10 Haven't you finished?

Exercise 2

Here are two things you may have done today. Continue the list with other things you have completed during the day – on your own or with somebody else.

He escrito una carta.
Mi madre y yo hemos preparado el desayuno.

Dialogue 2 🔲

En la comisaría

While reading the dialogue below, see if you can find answers to these questions:

Why is Mark at the police station?
Would you carry the same things in your briefcase if you visited a Latin American country?

Mark has lost his briefcase and is reporting the loss at a police station

Policía:	Buenas tardes.
Mark:	He perdido mi maletín con documentos personales.
Policía:	Su nombre, por favor.
Mark:	Mark Williams.
Policía:	¿Qué hay en su maletín?
Mark:	Un momento, por favor. He escrito una lista. Acá está: mi pasaporte, boleto de avión, cheques de viajero, una guía de Latinoamérica, una lista de hoteles y una agenda.
Policía:	Voy a apuntar los detalles.
Mark:	Quisiera una copia del informe policial. Es para el seguro.
Policía:	Sí, por supuesto.

Language point

Por/para

Por usually indicates the source of the action ('because of, by, through'). **Para** usually expresses destination or purpose ('to, in order to'). These two prepositions can often be confusing to English speakers because both may also translate the English preposition 'for'.

Fue elegida por su experiencia.	She was elected for her experience.
Contestar por fax.	Answer by fax.
Por María aceptó la invitación.	Because of María he accepted the invitation.
Este regalo es para ti.	This present is for you.
¿Qué estás haciendo? Estoy mirando por la ventana.	What are you doing? I'm looking through the window.
Empuje la palanca para abrir la puerta.	Push the lever to open the door.
¿Para qué quieres esto? Para arreglarlo.	What do you want this for? To fix it.

Por is also used in the following idiomatic expressions:

por ahora	for the time being
por el momento	for the moment
por otra parte	on the other hand
por si acaso	just in case
por ejemplo	for example
por fin	at last

Exercise 3

Complete these sentences choosing **por** or **para**.

1 **Este libro es un regalo _____ Susana.**
2 **¿_____ qué no has terminado tu comida?**
3 **Estoy preparando la agenda _____ la reunión.**
4 **¿Vas _____ la tienda?** (on your way to)
5 **Hay que salir _____ esta puerta.**

Exercise 4

These are features you might find in a Latin American publication. Write down those which also belong to the journal/magazine that you usually read. Are there any others you can name?

- **Edición actualizada**
- **Direcciones útiles de Internet**
- **Informes**
- **Análisis de encuestas**
- **Cartas de lectores**
- **Entrevistas**
- **Disposiciones legales**
- **Reportajes**
- **Reseñas de publicaciones**
- **450 páginas**
- **53 cuadros estadísticos**
- **90 gráficos**
- **Glosario técnico**
- **Terminología en castellano, francés e inglés**
- **Mapas y fotos**
- **Temas: sociedad, nutrición, pobreza, mujer, sector informal, pequeña y mediana empresa.**

actualizada	up to date	**nutrición**	nutrition
cuadro		**pobreza**	poverty
estadístico	chart	**sector informal**	the 'informal'
gráfico	graphics		sector (of the
temas	topics, themes,		economy)
	subjects	**empresa**	firm, company
sociedad	society	**direcciones**	addresses
útil, útiles	useful	**entrevistas**	interviews
informes	reports	**reportajes**	report (special feature)
encuestas	surveys	**reseñas**	reviews
lectores	readers	**publicaciones**	publications

Reading 📼

While reading the passage below, see if you can find answers to these questions:

Why are there so many street vendors in Latin America?
How do they announce the goods they sell?

Vendedores ambulantes

Los vendedores ambulantes, hombres, mujeres y niños, llenan las calles de las principales ciudades latinoamericanas. Ofrecen todo tipo de productos, alimentos, artículos de tocador importados, verduras, bebidas gaseosas, etc. El desempleo y la pobreza obligan a muchos a trabajar horas y horas voceando sus productos. Son parte del sector informal de la economía.

vendedores	street sellers	**verduras**	vegetables
ambulantes		**bebidas gaseosas**	soft drinks
llenan	fill	**voceando**	shouting
artículos de		**desempleo**	unemployment
tocador	toiletries	**pobreza**	poverty

Are there any street sellers in your city/town/village? What do they sell? Can you think of the names of some of their products in Spanish?

Dialogue 3 🔘

¿Por qué estás triste?

Mark has not yet recovered his briefcase

DELIA: ¿Por qué estás triste?
MARK: Porque he perdido mi maletín con mi agenda.
DELIA: ¿Cuándo?
MARK: El otro día. He ido a la comisaría, pero no han encontrado el maletín.
DELIA: ¿Por qué no te compras otra agenda?
MARK: Ya tengo una nueva. Pero he perdido nombres y direcciones con contactos importantes.

Language point

¿Por qué?/porque

¿Por qué?, the equivalent of 'why?', is written as two words. **Porqué**, the equivalent of 'because', is one word.

¿Por qué no ha venido Sofía?	Why hasn't Sofía come?
Porque está enferma.	Because she is ill.

Exercise 5

Below is a list of possible presents. Which one would you choose for . . .

un enamorado/una enamorada	a boyfriend/girlfriend
tu niño o niña	your child
tu abuela	your grandmother
un amigo	a friend
tu oficina	your office
¿y para ti?	and for you?

Juegos de construcción
en plástico sólido
transparente y cálido.

Carpeta para guardar
facturas o apuntes.
Hecha de plástico.
Muy útil.

Silla plegable. El asiento es de lona y cuero. Para
conciertos al aire libre. Es cómoda.

Sortija de plata. Elegante.

Llavero de oro. Atractivo.

Caja fuerte de acero. Con sistema electrónico. Muy segura.

Poleras/Polos de algodón. De moda.

Abrigos de lana. Gruesos.

Algunos otros materiales:

madera	wood
metal	metal
cartón	cardboard
fibra de vidrio	glass fiber
vidrio	glass
plástico	plastic
tela	fabric

Reading 🔘🔘

While reading the passage below, see if you can find answers to these questions:

When did Europeans arrive in Latin America?
What does Latin America buy from industrialized countries?
Does your own country produce or import one or more of these products?

Latinoamérica exporta

Desde la llegada de los europeos en el siglo XVI, América Latina ha exportado materias primas y ha importado productos manufacturados de los países industrializados. Algunas de las principales materias primas que exporta Latinoamérica son petróleo, café, azúcar de caña, algodón, cobre.

desde la llegada	since the arrival	**petróleo**	oil
siglo	century	**café**	coffee
materias primas	raw materials	**azúcar de caña**	cane sugar
países	countries	**algodón**	cotton
algunas	some	**cobre**	copper

10 ¿Qué vamos a hacer hoy?

What are we going to do today?

> By the end of this chapter you should be able to:
>
> - Explain what you intend to do using **ir a**
> - Order a meal and/or a drink
> - Use subject relative clauses (e.g. the music that I like)
> - Use expressions of agreement (e.g. according to)

Dialogue 1

En Lima

While reading the dialogue below, see if you can find answers to these questions:

What are the tourists going to visit?
Are they going to do anything in the afternoon?

A group of tourists are visiting Lima. The travel agent is talking to them about their itinerary for the day

TURISTA: ¿Qué vamos a hacer hoy?
GUÍA: Primero, vamos a visitar el Museo Arqueológico. Aparte de la exposición van a ver un video de diez minutos y luego vamos a almorzar en un restaurante criollo. En la tarde vamos a recorrer las iglesias antiguas de la capital y a comprar recuerdos. El guía va a explicar . . .

Language point

ir a *+ infinitive*

One way of expressing the future is by using the present tense of the verb **ir** (to go) followed by **a** plus the infinitive expressing the intended action. This is similar to the English structure 'to be going to + infinitive'

Vamos a visitar el museo.	We are going to visit the museum.
Elena va a viajar a México.	Elena is going to travel to Mexico.

Here are all the forms of the verb **ir + a**:

voy a	I am going to
vas a	you are going to (informal)
va a	you are going to (formal); he/she/it is going to
vamos a	we are going to
van a	you are going to
van a	they are going to

Exercise 1

This is what a tourist intends to do one day while visiting Lima:

1 **Voy a visitar el Museo de la Inquisición.**
2 **Voy a pasear por el malecón.**
3 **Voy a nadar en el mar.**
4 **Voy a mirar tiendas.**
5 **Voy a tomar helados.**
6 **Voy a cambiar plata.**

And this is what a local person has to say about each activity. Can you match the comment with the corresponding sentence above?

(a) **En el mercado paralelo pagan más.**
(b) **Es muy romántico.**
(c) **Está cerca de la catedral.**
(d) **El de frambuesa es muy rico.**
(e) **Yo prefiero la piscina.**
(f) **Hay un centro comercial muy cerca.**

pasear	to walk about, to go for a stroll	**tomar helados**	to have ice cream
malecón	promenade	**mercado paralelo**	free rate currency market
nadar	to swim	**frambuesa**	raspberry
mar	sea	**piscina**	swimming pool
mirar tiendas	window shopping	**cambiar plata**	change money

Exercise 2 ▣▣

¿Qué vas a hacer?

This is a list of possible activities for the week ahead. Look at the example and practise similar questions and answers for each day. Use **y también** 'and also' to link both sentences.

Example:

¿Qué vas a hacer el lunes?
El lunes voy a telefonear a casa y también voy a preparar la reunión.

LUNES	**telefonear a casa**
	preparar la reunión
MARTES	**asistir a la reunión**
	comer en un restaurante céntrico
MIÉRCOLES	**estudiar el reglamento**
	escribir cartas
JUEVES	**probar el equipo nuevo**
	entrevistar a posible jefe de ventas
VIERNES	**recoger la nueva impresora láser**
	comprar 'compact discs'
SÁBADO	**descansar**
DOMINGO	**descansar**

asistir	to attend	**jefe de ventas**	head of sales
reglamento	regulations	**recoger**	to pick up
equipo	equipment	**impresora**	printer
entrevistar	to interview	**descansar**	to rest

Some more useful connectors:

en primer lugar	first, in the first place
luego	then
más adelante	later
finalmente	finally, lastly

Exercise 3

Say what you are going to do at the weekend. Use events from the list below. Here is an example:

A: **¿Adónde vas a ir el viernes?**
B: **Voy a ir a la Exposición de Juguetes.**
A: **¿Dónde es?**
B: **En el Museo Antropológico.**
A: **¿A qué hora?**
B: **A las cinco de la tarde.**

Guía de Fin de Semana

VIERNES
P.M.
5.00   Exposición. Ganadores del Concurso de Pintores Jóvenes. Auditorio Municipal.
5.00   Exposición. Juguetes de otra época. Museo Antropológico. Sala Especial 1.
8.00   El grupo Arena interpreta los temas de su nuevo compact. Restaurante Bartolo. Playa Las Piedritas.
9.00   La cantante Tania ofrece una noche de rock en el teatro La Primavera. Cerca de la Catedral.

SÁBADO
P.M.
4.00   Exposición fotográfica. 'Paisajes y personas'. En blanco y negro y en color. Entrada gratis. Instituto de Cultura.
7.00   Ballet Nacional. Danzas folklóricas y modernas. Palacio de la Música.
8.00   Teatro Marsano. Obra cómica. 'Las Brujas'. Décima semana en cartelera.
9.30   Bar El Auténtico. Jazz hasta las 2 de la madrugada.

DOMINGO
A.M.
9.00   Competencia automovilística. En la Vía Expresa.
10.00   Exposición de monedas antiguas. Banco Central.
2.00   Final del Campeonato de Vóley. Estadio Nacional.

fin de semana	weekend	**entrada**	admission, ticket
ganadores	winners	**obra cómica**	comedy
concurso	competition	**en cartelera**	on at the theater or
juguetes	toys		cinema
otra época	bygone era	**madrugada**	early hours of the
sala	hall		morning
interpreta	sings	**monedas**	old coins
ofrece	gives	**antiguas**	
cantante	singer	**campeonato**	championship
paisajes	landscapes	**estadio**	stadium

Exercise 4

RESTAURANTE 'TERRENAL'

Dirección:	Lisina 844
Teléfono:	343–9983
Tarjetas:	Visa y Diners
Horario:	Lunes a Sábado a partir del mediodía
Reservas:	Recomendables
Nivel de Precios:	De S/.10 (menús especiales) a S/.25

tarjeta	card	**nivel de precios**	price range
horario	opening hours	**a partir de**	from, as from

Based on the information above, say which of the following statements are possible and which are not. Use the words **Sí es posible** 'It is possible' or **No es posible** 'It is not possible' for your answers.

1 **Voy a pagar con tarjeta Visa.**
2 **Vamos a almorzar el domingo.**
3 **Vamos a almorzar a las 11.30 de la mañana.**
4 **Voy a pedir el menú más barato de diez pesos.**
5 **Vas a reservar una mesa por teléfono.**

Language point

The relative pronoun que

Que is the relative pronoun normally used to link two phrases in one sentence. In English it can be 'that', 'which' or 'who':

Los jóvenes *que* **prefieren un** Young people *who* prefer a quiet
ambiente tranquilo. atmosphere.
El restaurante *que* **está en la** The restaurant *which* is on the
esquina. corner.
El plato *que* **me gusta.** The dish *that* I like.

Dialogue 2

En el restaurante

After reading the dialogue below and looking at the menu, answer the following questions:

Do the customers both choose the same?
What would you choose?

A couple are choosing something to eat from the menu below at a restaurant in Buenos Aires

CLIENTE: (*To the waiter*) ¿Qué es lenguado? ¿Carne? ¿Pescado? ¿Verdura?
MOZO: Es pescado. Es muy agradable.
CLIENTE: Para mí un lomo. Para mi esposo, lenguado con jenjibre.
MOZO: ¿Para beber?
CLIENTE: Vino blanco, por favor.

```
┌──────────────────────────────────────────────────┐
│  ╭────────────────────────────────────────────╮  │
│  │      ❧ 𝒜𝑒𝓃𝓊 𝒯𝓇𝒶𝒹𝒾𝒸𝒾𝑜𝓃𝒶𝓁 ❧      │  │
│  │                  10 pesos                      │  │
│                                                      │
```

<table>
<tr><td>Ensaladas</td><td>A escoger del bar de las ensaladas</td></tr>
<tr><td>(Salads)</td><td>(To choose from the salad bar)</td></tr>
<tr><td></td><td></td></tr>
<tr><td>Broqueta de pollo</td><td>(Chicken brochettes)</td></tr>
<tr><td>Broqueta de carne</td><td>(Meat brochette)</td></tr>
<tr><td>Panqueques de espinaca</td><td>(Spinach pancakes)</td></tr>
<tr><td>Milanesas</td><td>(Escalope)</td></tr>
<tr><td></td><td></td></tr>
<tr><td>Ensalada de fruta con helado</td><td>(Fruit salad and ice cream)</td></tr>
</table>

❧ Platos Especiales ❧

Lomo con salsa de berenjenas	(Beefsteak in aubergine sauce)
Lenguado con jenjibre	(Sole with ginger)
'Hojas' de pollo con champiñones	(Chicken with mushrooms)
Parrillada	(Grilled meats)

❧ Postres ❧

Ensalada de frutas	(Fruit salad)
Torta de chocolate	(Chocolate cake)

Language point

Para mí

To indicate for whom something is intended, such as a meal at a restaurant or a drink at a bar, the usual expression is **para** followed by the object of the order. Here are all the forms:

para mí	for me
para ti	for you (informal)
para usted	for you (formal)
para él	for him
para ella	for her

para nosotros	for us
para ustedes	for you (formal and informal)
para ellos	for them (all masculine or mixed group)
para ellas	for them (all feminine)

Examples:

| **La chica es para Mariana.** | The small one is for Mariana. |
| **Estos regalos son para ustedes.** | These presents are for you. |

Reading

In each issue a weekly magazine recommends some restaurants following the International Classification System, giving points for cooking, service, decoration, etc. Read this week's results and then answer the questions in Exercise 5:

CLASIFICACIÓN

0–10 puntos	Malo/Regular
11–15 puntos	Promedio
16–20 puntos	Bueno
21–25 puntos	Muy bueno
26–30 puntos	Excelente

Según el sistema de clasificación internacional, se otorgan puntos por cada aspecto del restaurante: cocina, servicio, decorado, etc.

Esta semana recomendamos

24 puntos   *El Jardín*, Calle Ugarteche 315. Reservas al 802–1555. Cocina argentina moderna y de rápida preparación 'fast-food'. Broquetas de langostinos y champiñones. Todos los días desde las 12 del mediodía hasta las 4 de la madrugada. De $10 a $30 por persona.

18 puntos   *The Grill*, Calle Reconquista 1875. Reservas al 312–2477. Cocina inglesa y porteña. Lunes a viernes mediodía y noche. $20 a $40 por persona.

| 17 puntos | *Marítimo*, Costanera Norte. Reservas al 788–0409. Pescados y mariscos. Broqueta de pez espada con tagliatelle. Todos los días al mediodía y por la noche. $30 a $40 por persona. |
| 14 puntos | *Sabor*, Pelliza 319. Reservas al 726–5341. Cocina europea. Martes a domingo por la noche. $30 a $50 por persona. |

Exercise 5

Decide if the following statements are true (**verdadero**) or false (**falso**).

1 **El Jardín está en la calle Ugarteche.**
2 **El Jardín abre sólo por las tardes.**
3 **El Grill es un restaurante promedio.**
4 **El Marítimo se especializa en pescados.**
5 **El Sabor es un restaurante malo.**

Language point

Según

This word means 'according to', as in **Según el gobierno, la inflación está bajo control.** 'According to the government, inflation is under control.'

Other expressions with similar meaning are:

> **de acuerdo con**
> **conforme a**
> **de conformidad con**

Conforme a and **de conformidad con** are used in a more formal or legal context.

De acuerdo con las normas.	According to the rules.
De conformidad con la ley actual.	According to current legislation.

Readings

While reading the advertisement below, see if you can find answers to these questions:

Is the advertisement offering travel abroad?
What does the Gran Hotel offer, and what is required from you?

★ **EL GRAN HOTEL** ★
P R E S E N T A

NOCHE CUBANA
NOCHE BRASILEÑA
NOCHE PERUANA
NOCHE PARAGUAYA
NOCHE MEJICANA*

Cada fin de semana viaje
con su imaginación a otros países.

Nosotros ofrecemos el ambiente,
la música, el baile, la comida
adecuada.

Usted aporta su grata presencia.

---

viaje	travel	**comida**	food
imaginación	imagination	**aporta**	contribute
ambiente	atmosphere	**grata**	pleasant
baile	dance	**presencia**	presence

While reading the list of food and drinks from a health food shop, see if you can find answers to these questions:

Can you ask them to deliver or do you have to collect?
How many dishes a day are recommended?

tarta de verduras	vegetable pie		
tarta dulce dietética	low-fat sweet pie		
		bizcochuelo de zanahoria	carrot cake
bocaditos dietéticos	'healthy' snacks	**pan de salvado**	bran bread
empanadas dietéticas	low-fat pasties	**pan de queso**	cheese bread
		elaboramos	we make
jugos y licuados energéticos	isotonic drinks	**bajar de peso**	to loose weight
		mantener el peso	to maintain a certain weight
budín dietético	low-fat bread pudding	**deseado**	that you want
		reparto a domicilio	home delivery

*Note : The usual spelling is *Mexico* and *Mexicana/o;* but occasionally you find the alternative spelling using a ' j ' instead of an ' x '.

> ### COMIDA DIETETICA Y NATURAL
>
> Dos platos diarios: uno de carbohidrato y otro de proteínas.
>
> **Tarta de verduras**
> **Tarta dulce dietética**
> **Bocaditos dietéticos**
> **Empanadas dietéticas**
> **Jugos y licuados energéticos**
> **Budín dietético**
> **Bizcochuelo de zanahoria**
> **Pan de salvado**
> **Pan de queso**
>
> Elaboramos menús dietéticos para bajar y/o
> mantenerse en el peso deseado.
>
> Reparto a domicilio.

Note: health food shops usually announce their products as **dietéticos** .

Exercise 6

Match the food/drink on the left with the country on the right where it is a typical dish/drink. The glossary at the back of the book might help.

1	**chipa**	(a) Perú
2	**guacamole**	(b) Colombia
3	**carapulcra**	(c) Paraguay
4	**tinto**	(d) México
5	**mate**	(e) Argentina

Exercise 7

You have just ordered sole as the main course. Which of these two wines goes well with it?

VINOS

Naturaleza Blanca	Clásico
buen color	aroma tradicional
aroma débil	neutro
algo dulce	frutal
ligero	cuerpo medio
agradable	
Buena combinación con jamón, melón o con frutas en general.	Adecuado para acompañar a mariscos o pescados asados.

Reading 🔊

While reading the passage below, see if you can find answers to these questions:

What's the atmosphere like in this restaurant?
What are the restaurant's special attractions?

El restaurante 'La Plata'

El restaurante 'La Plata' está situado en la zona del sur de la Plaza de Mayo en Buenos Aires, donde hay un ambiente romántico y melancólico. Los restaurantes tienen un aire de antiguos, aunque muchos son edificios nuevos. La zona es concurrida por adultos y también por jóvenes que prefieren un ambiente tranquilo. Esta parte de Buenos Aires es diferente del norte o del oeste. El restaurante 'La Plata' está en un inmenso local decorado con pinturas modernas. Se utiliza un proyector de video láser para mostrar video clips sobre una amplia pared.

está situado	is located	**concurrido**	well attended, busy (of a place but not a person)
zona	area		
ambiente	atmosphere		
tiene un aire de	has an air of	**jóvenes**	young people
antiguo	old	**tranquilo**	quiet
edificio	building	**norte**	north
sur	south	**pinturas**	paintings
este	east	**se utiliza**	it is used
oeste	west	**mostrar**	to show
inmenso local	huge premises	**amplia pared**	large wall

11 Se dice que . . .

It is said that . . .

By the end of this chapter you should be able to:

- Make impersonal statements using **se**
- Understand basic travel and leisure information
- Use some expressions of comparison with **tan . . . como** (as . . . as)
- Make comparisons using **más de** (more than) and **menos de** (less than) followed by numbers or quantities

Dialogue 1 💿

Turismo en Mar Del Plata

While reading the dialogue below, see if you can find answers to these questions:

Is tourism on the increase?
What has been done to attract more tourists?

The mayor of Mar del Plata is being interviewed about tourism in his town

ENTREVISTADOR: Este año el turismo muestra un incremento del 30 por ciento. ¿Cómo se logró esto?

ALCALDE: Se trabaja para el crecimiento. Anualmente se destina 25 por ciento de los recursos a obras públicas. Se ha reducido el personal (en 35 por ciento). Se mejora continuamente la limpieza de plazas, paseos y calles. Hay que atraer al turista.

ENTREVISTADOR: ¿Qué otros planes hay?

ALCALDE: Se van a construir atracciones deportivas y culturales. El turismo está relacionado con el deporte y la cultura.

Language point

Impersonal se

Se with a third person verb usually has an impersonal meaning. In English, the usual equivalent is a sentence in the passive voice. (See also Chapter 19.)

Examples:

Se dice que tiene cáncer.	It is said that he/she has cancer.
Se iniciará en 1999.	It will be started in 1999.
Se van a construir veinte casas.	Twenty houses are going to be built.
Se ha aumentado el precio.	The price has been increased.
Se habla español.	Spanish spoken.
El grupo musical 'Los Gitanos' se presenta en distintos estadios en las próximas semanas.	The band 'Los Gitanos' will perform in various stadia in the next few weeks.
Las canciones de Daniela se inspiran en su trabajo de maestra.	Daniela's songs are inspired by her work as a teacher.
Con una computadora:	With a computer,
se puede procesar textos	you can do word processing
se puede hacer una base de datos	you can create a database
se puede emplear una hoja de cálculo	you can use a spreadsheet
se puede hacer gráficos	you can create graphics

Exercise 1

Give the equivalent in Spanish using the impersonal **se**.

1 It opens early.
2 Cars are made here.
3 Computers repaired.
4 A report is prepared daily.
5 It is said that he is very ill.

Exercise 2

Read the following information about holidays and then complete the chart given below.

DE LUJO

Hotel Amsterdam

7 noches en Hotel de Primera Categoría con desayuno, piscina. Precio incluye pasaje aéreo y asistencia médica durante la estadía.

$495.00

ESPECIAL

Hotel Central

5 noches, con desayuno. Incluye pasaje aéreo. Entrada al casino. Asistencia médica durante la estadía.

$435.00

ALOJAMIENTO INDEPENDIENTE

7 noches en apartamentos de dos ambientes con kitchenette.
Auto compacto con kilometraje ilimitado.
El precio incluye el pasaje aéreo y laasistencia médica durante toda la
estadía.

$680.00

Based on the information about holidays above, complete the following:

Hotel	Nº de noches	desayuno	piscina	pasaje incluido	asistencia médica incluida
Amsterdam					
Central					
Apartamento					

Reading

Read the following information about a weekly publication called *Pasatiempo*, devoted to outdoor activities, then answer the following questions:

What are the main features of the magazine?
What are the activities covered?
Which of the activities mentioned do you like?

Pasatiempo

Una publicación semanal completa y actualizada para planificar su fin de semana.

Información indispensable:

lugares   hojas de ruta
paseos   tarifas

atracciones	medios de transporte
campings	itinerarios
hoteles	pronóstico del tiempo

La revista para los que gustan del descanso. Para disfrutar del tiempo libre en contacto con la naturaleza y el aire puro.

Actividades que incluimos:

turismo	montañismo
salidas cortas	fauna
campamentismo	bicicleta de montaña
pesca	todo terreno
buceo	aventuras

Exercise 3

Match each present to the most suitable recipient:

1 **billetera para hombre**
2 **cartera en negro y marrón**
3 **garrafa de vidrio para vino**
4 **reloj despertador**
5 **mochila colegial**
6 **malla entera de baño**
7 **lapicero**
8 **adorno de porcelana**
9 **un ramo de flores**
10 **un CD/stereo personal**

(a) **esposo**
(b) **esposa**
(c) **enamorado**
(d) **enamorada**
(e) **una joven de 15 años**
(f) **una abuela**
(g) **tu mejor amigo**
(h) **tu pareja**
(i) **tu mejor amiga**

billetera	wallet	**malla entera de**	one-piece
cartera	purse	**baño**	swimsuit
garrafa	carafe	**lapicero**	ball-point pen

reloj	watch/clock	**adorno**	ornament
despertador	alarm clock	**esposo**	husband
mochila	rucksack	**esposa**	wife
colegial	school (adjective)	**enamorado**	boyfriend
enamorada	girlfriend	**una joven**	a young lady
abuela	grandmother	**pareja**	partner
mejor amigo	best friend		

Suggest other suitable presents for the people mentioned above.

Dialogue 2

Una bici

While reading the dialogue below, see if you can find answers to these questions:

When does the child want the bike?
Why is it a good time to buy one now?

HIJO: Papi, quiero una bici. Una bicicleta de montaña.
PADRE: Tienes que esperar hasta la Navidad. Además, las bicicletas de montaña son más caras que las bicicletas tradicionales.
HIJO: Pero ahora están de oferta hasta el sábado.
PADRE: Montar bicicleta puede ser peligroso.
HIJO: Sí, pero voy a usar un casco protector. He visto uno amarillo que me gusta. No es tan grande como un casco para ir en moto.

Although the correct phase is 'montar bicicleta', many people say 'montar en bicicleta' in casual speech.

Language point

Tan . . . como

When you compare in terms of equality you use the expression **tan . . . como**. It translates as 'as . . . as', often with an adjective in the middle. The adjective describes the nature of the equality. Here are some examples:

La bicicleta es tan necesaria como el aire puro.	A bicycle is as necessary as fresh air.
Yo tengo 49 años. Tú tienes 20. Yo no soy tan joven como tú.	I am 49 years old. You are 20. I am not as young as you are.
El otro libro no es tan interesante como éste.	The other book is not as interesting as this one.

Exercise 4

Express the following comparisons as in the example, using the clue in brackets.

Example:

El mapa cuesta 20 pesos. El libro cuesta 250 pesos. (caro)
El mapa no es tan caro como el libro.

1 **Carlos vive a dos horas de aquí. Graciela vive a cinco horas de aquí. (cerca)**
2 **Carolina mide 1.78m y su hermano José también mide 1.78m (alto/a)**
3 **La rosa es una flor muy linda. El clavel también es una flor muy linda. (linda/o)**
4 **Mi televisor es de 14". El televisor de mi novia es de 17". (grande)**
5 **Esta impresora produce 4 páginas por minuto. La otra impresora produce 8 páginas por minuto. (rápida)**

Exercise 5

Read the following advertisement offering prizes, then match the prizes 1 to 5 with their use (a) to (e).

(a) para escuchar música en diversas formas
(b) para ver programas
(c) para pasear
(d) para preparar la comida
(e) para grabar música

BICI REINA

Con la compra de una Bici Reina recibes un termo de regalo.
En el termo hay un cupón para un sorteo de grandes premios.

PREMIOS PARA LOS COMPRADORES:

1 Un ciclomotor 50 cc.
2 Un televisor a color de 14".
3 Un equipo de sonido.
4 Una cocina de 4 hornallas.
5 Una radiograbadora stereo.

Fecha del sorteo: 22 de diciembre

Reading

While reading the advertisement below, see if you can find answers to these questions:

Can you win a prize if you buy this product?
How do you enter the draw?

ADELGAZAR CON 'GELA SLIM'

Más sabor y más color

Gela Slim es un 'postre' que adelgaza. Es una gelatina deliciosa con todo su color y sabor.

Sólo 1.8 calorías en cada porción de 100 gramos.
Consumir media hora antes de las comidas.

Gela Slim absorbe grasas y azúcares.

Menos de 2 calorías. Más de 10 sabores para escoger.

Es posible ganar un automóvil 0 km.

En cada envase de Gela Slim hay un formulario. Rellenar los espacios con sus datos y a participar en el sorteo.

(Concurso sin obligación de compra.)

adelgazar	to slim	**formulario**	form
sabor	flavor, taste	**rellenar**	to fill in
todo	all	**datos**	information, data
porción	portion, serving	**sorteo**	draw, raffle
antes de	before	**concurso**	contest,
comidas	meals		competition
grasas	fats	**sin**	without
azúcares	sugars	**obligación**	obligation
ganar	to win	**compra**	purchase
envase	packet, container		

Note: the phrase **Concurso sin obligación de compra** is the equivalent of the English 'No purchase necessary'.

Language point

Más de/menos de

The expressions **más de** and **menos de** ('more than' and 'less than') are used to establish comparison before numbers or quantities.

Hay más de 10 sabores.	There are more than 10 flavors.
Tiene menos de 2 calorías.	It has less than 2 calories.
Hay más de 100 personas.	There are more than 100 people.
Hay menos de 50 dólares en la cuenta.	There is less than 50 dollars in the account.

Exercise 6

Complete with **más de** or **menos de**:

1 **Tienen 23 empleados. Tienen _____ de veinte empleados.**
2 **Hay 1,050 asistentes. Hay _____ mil asistentes.**
3 **Cuesta $64.99 por semana. Cuesta _____ sesenta y cinco dolares.**
4 **Ha viajado 32,045 km. en ese carro. Ha viajado _____ treinta y cinco mil km.**
5 **Normalmente asisten 107 diputados. Normalmente asisten _____ de cien diputados.**

Exercise 7

Read the following advertisements:

INSTITUTO INTERNACIONAL
Turno diurno y nocturno
Inglés
Procesamiento de textos
Computación
Mecánica de automóviles
Jr Córdoba 911

FUNDACIÓN LEXIS
Cursos por correspondencia
Manualidades en 10 lecciones
Pintura sobre madera en 12 lecciones
Contabilidad básica en 15 lecciones
Precio de cada lección $20
Pagar al cartero
Solicite información al 825 3257

INSTITUTO DE DEPORTES
Natatorio climatizado
Clases individuales y grupales de natación
Bebés – Niños – Adultos
Jr Zepita 765

Say if the following statements are **verdadero** (true) or **falso** (false) based on the three advertisements above.

1 **Para estudiar inglés se puede ir al Instituto de Deportes.**
2 **Es posible estudiar inglés por correspondencia en la Fundación Lexis.**
3 **Manualidades por correspondencia se estudia en diez lecciones.**
4 **El curso de contabilidad básica cuesta $300.**
5 **Cuando se estudia por correspondencia en Fundación Lexis se paga directamente en la oficina principal.**
6 **Procesamiento de textos es un curso que ofrece el Instituto Internacional.**
7 **Sólo se puede estudiar de día en el Instituto Internacional.**
8 **Pintura sobre madera lleva más tiempo que manualidades.**
9 **Un niño de seis meses puede empezar a nadar en el Instituto de Deportes.**
10 **Se puede aprender mecánica de automóviles por correspondencia.**

Exercise 8 🔲

Read the following invitation:

CLUB DE TENIS

Se invita a los socios a una reunión el miércoles 3 de diciembre a partir de las 19.30 horas, a fin de conformar la subcomisión de tenis del club.

Based on the information above, say if the following statements are **verdadero** (true) or **falso** (false).

1 Members and non-members are invited.
2 The meeting is on a Friday.
3 The meeting starts at 7.30 p.m.
4 The purpose of the meeting is to form a subcommittee.
5 The meeeting is at the beginning of the year.

a partir de	as from, beginning from	**reunión**	meeting
a fin de	in order to	**subcomisión**	sub-committee

Reading 🔲

While reading the passage below see if you can answer this question. Is there African and Spanish influence in Cuban music?

Cuba

Cuba es la mayor de las islas antillanas. Está situada en el Mar Caribe. Tiene una problación aproximada de doce millones de habitantes, de los cuales más de dos millones viven en La Habana, la capital. Dos productos cubanos conocidos por todo el mundo son el ron y los puros. El azúcar y el turismo son las dos actividades económicas principales de su economía. El *son* es el origen de la música actual conocida como *salsa*. El *son* es una manifestación de la fusión entre la herencia musical africana y la hispánica.

la mayor	the largest
ron	rum
puros	cigars
fusión	fusion, merge
africana	African
hispánica	Hispanic

12 ¿Qué hiciste?

What did you do?

By the end of this chapter you should be able to:

- Use the past tense with regular verbs
- Use the past tense with irregular verbs
- Use a range of expressions for past time reference

Reading

Below are some news headlines from a newspaper.

LOS TITULARES

- Ayer llegó a Lima el nuevo embajador de la República de Chile.
- El dólar subió diez céntimos en el mercado de cambios.
- Empatamos en fútbol, ganamos en vóley.
- Anoche terminó la Primera Jornada de Educadores Latino-americanos.
- Volvió la cantante Tania Libertad.

THE HEADLINES

- The new ambassador from Chile arrived in Lima yesterday.
- The dollar rose ten cents in the currency market.
- We drew in football and won in volleyball.
- The first conference of Latin American teachers came to an end last night.
- The singer Tania Libertad is back.

Note: it is not unusual to find headlines written in the past tense in Latin American newspapers.

Language points

The past tense or preterite

The past tense, or preterite, is used to express an action in the past already complete at the time of speaking.

Ayer comimos en un restaurante.	Yesterday we went to a restaurant for a meal.
Al fin terminamos el proyecto.	At last we finished the project.
Vivimos en Quito durante dos años.	We lived in Quito for two years.

Regular verbs

The past tense of regular verbs, i.e. those which follow a certain pattern or rule, is formed using endings which vary according to the person.

-ar verbs: **terminar** (to finish)

terminé	I finished
termin*aste*	you finished (informal)
termin*ó*	you finished (formal); he/she/it finished
termin*amos*	we finished
termin*aron*	you finished
termin*aron*	they finished

Note that the form for the first person plural is the same as the present tense. The context of the sentence, or the addition of a reference to the time when the action took place, usually avoids any confusion.

-er verbs: **comer**

com*í*	**com*imos***
com*iste*	**com*ieron***
com*ió*	**com*ieron***

-ir verbs: **vivir**

viv*í*	**viv*imos***
viv*iste*	**viv*ieron***
viv*ió*	**viv*ieron***

Dialogue 1 📼

El fin de semana

Carola tells Elsa about her weekend in Lima

CAROLA: Hola, cuéntame de tu fin de semana.

ELSA: El viernes por la noche comimos en un restaurante típico. Bailamos 'landó' y luego regresamos al departamento. El sábado por la mañana compramos varias cosas en el centro, luego compramos comida para llevar y almorzamos en el departamento. Por la tarde vimos una película en un cine de estreno y luego vimos la obra *No me toquen ese vals* en un teatrito de la Avenida Brasil. Muy linda la obra.

CAROLA: ¿Y el domingo?

ELSA: El domingo, descansamos.

Exercise 1

Give an account in Spanish of your (or somebody else's) weekend in Lima, based on the information below. Say the sentences in the preterite, and in the order that you find most suitable. Omit some and/or add others if you wish.

Useful connectors:

después	afterwards
luego	then
más tarde	later

Comprar la revista *Quehacer*.
Ver una obra de teatro en Barranco.
Visitar una exposición de pintura en la galería Forum.
Asistir a la clase de quena.
Llamar por teléfono a un amigo/una amiga.
Bailar en la discoteca.
Practicar aeróbicos en el gimnasio.
Comer un cebiche.
Preparar unos cocteles.

Quehacer	current affairs publication in Perú
Barranco	district of Lima where many cultural events take place and where many restaurants which offer live shows are located
pintura	painting
Forum	well-known art gallery in Lima
asistir	to attend (a lesson, a meeting, etc.)
quena	traditional Andean musical instrument
llamar	to call
cebiche	popular dish made with raw fish marinated in lemon
coctel	cocktail

Language points

Expressions of time in the past

Here are some useful expressions for specific reference to time in the past.

ayer	yesterday
anteayer	the day before yesterday
anoche	last night
la semana pasada	last week
el lunes pasado	last Monday
el viernes pasado	last Friday
el mes pasado	last month

As you can see, **pasado/a** can be used to form a number of expressions in the past. It is not the literal translation of 'last' (**último**). **Último** is used to indicate that something or somebody is the last of a series; that there are no more, as in: **Esta es la última función.** 'This is the last show'.

Hace

Hace is used to indicate how long ago something happened.

Examples:

¿Cuándo llegó? Hace dos días.   When did she arrive? Two days ago.

Terminó la universidad hace un año.   He finished college a year ago.

Exercise 2

Match the phrases 1 to 5 with the phrases (a) to (e).

1 **Leí un cuento . . .**
2 **Vimos una linda pintura modernista . . .**
3 **Visitamos tres iglesias . . .**
4 **Anoche . . .**
5 **Rellenamos el formulario . . .**

(a) **. . . en la galería Forum.**
(b) **. . . para renovar el pasaporte.**
(c) **. . . en el centro de la capital.**
(d) **. . . soñé contigo.**
(e) **. . . en la biblioteca.**

cuento	short story	**soñar**	to dream (of)
renovar	to renew		

Dialogue 2 📼

¿Dónde nació?

Here is an interview with a young painter from Paraguay

PERIODISTA: ¿Dónde nació?
COLLAR: Nací en Itauguá Guazú en 1964.
PERIODISTA: ¿Dónde pasó sus primeros años?
COLLAR: Pasé mis primeros años con mi abuela materna. Aprendí guaraní como primera lengua. Luego me adapté al castellano.
PERIODISTA: ¿Tuvo una infancia feliz?

COLLAR:	Desde los diez años tuve que trabajar. Primero en una farmacia y luego como ayudante de imprenta. Luego tuve mi propia oficina de diseño gráfico.
PERIODISTA:	¿Cómo nace su trabajo de pintor?
COLLAR:	Estudié en la Escuela de Bellas Artes. Poco a poco participé en muestras individuales y colectivas.
PERIODISTA:	¿Qué premio importante ha obtenido?
COLLAR:	Recientemente gané el Premio Martel de Artes Plásticas.

Reading

De visita en ciudad de México

Ayer empezamos nuestra visita de la ciudad de México. Primero partimos del Zócalo y fuimos al Palacio de Bellas Artes que está construido de mármol. Luego estuvimos en el Museo Antropológico y más tarde en el Museo de Arte Moderno. De ahí, fuimos al Bosque de Chapultepec, que está muy cerca del Museo de Arte Moderno. Yo compré artesanía de Oaxaca en un mercado local. Los tapetes son lindos. La señora Chávez va muy seguido a ese mercado. Dice que allí venden más barato.

empezamos	we started	**tapetes**	tapestries
partimos	we set off	**lindos**	pretty
mármol	marble	**muy seguido**	very often
artesanía	handicraft	**barato**	cheap

Language points

Irregular verbs in the past

Irregular verbs do not follow the rules which apply to the majority of verbs. Their stems or their endings differ from those of regular verbs.

Compare these verbs in the past:

escribir (regular)		ir (irregular)	
escribí	escribimos	fui	fuimos
escribiste	escribieron	fuiste	fueron
escribió	escribieron	fue	fueron

As you see, the stem in the past forms of **ir** has changed.

comer (regular)		hacer (irregular)	
comí	comimos	hice	hicimos
comiste	comieron	hiciste	hicieron
comió	comieron	hizo	hicieron

Other frequently used irregular verbs in the past are:

ser		venir	
fui	fuimos	vine	vinimos
fuiste	fuisteis	viniste	vinisteis
fue	fueron	vino	vinieron

tener		estar	
tuve	tuvimos	estuve	estuvimos
tuviste	tuvieron	estuviste	estuvieron
tuvo	tuvieron	estuvo	estuvieron

saber		dar	
supe	supimos	di	dimos
supiste	supieron	diste	dieron
supo	supieron	dio	dieron

Exercise 3

Replace the infinitives with the correct past form.

1 **La semana pasada (ir)(yo) al Museo de Arte Moderno.**
2 **(Nosotros)(ver) obras de Frida Kahlo.**
3 **Ayer Julián y Carmela (visitar) Guadalajara por primera vez.**
4 **(Yo)(comprar) dos libros en la librería del Sótano.**
5 **¿(Tú)(visitar) el Salón de la Informática en el Hotel María Isabel – Sheraton?**
6 **¿Cuándo (Ud.)(llegar) a Ciudad de México?**
7 **(Yo)(aprender) el castellano en la escuela secundaria.**
8 **Anoche (nosotros)(estar) en el restaurante Santa Anita.**

9 (Nosotros)(ver) mariachis y otros conjuntos musicales.
10 María (escribir) dos cartas muy largas a sus hermanos.

Exercise 4

Somebody attended a short training course for two weeks. Say in Spanish what this person did during that time based on the information below. Consult the glossary at the end of the book if necessary.

You can start your sentences like this:

En la primera semana ...   The first week ...
En la segunda semana ...   The second week ...

Semana 1
Estudiar el sistema operativo.
Escribir texto y fórmulas.
Imprimir la hoja de cálculo.
Diseñar pantallas.
Alimentar datos.

Semana 2
Analizar economía empresarial.
Preparar estrategias financieras.
Aplicar estadísticas y probabilidades.
Desarrollar métodos de valuación de proyectos.

Exercise 5

Change these sentences to the preterite using the information in brackets.

Example:

Compro una revista de deportes. (ayer)
Ayer compré una revista de deportes.

1 **Escucho un programa de radio. (anoche)**
2 **Marcelo y Estela diseñan ropa para una firma extranjera. (el año pasado)**
3 **Carlos imita a Elvis Presley en la tele. (el sábado pasado)**
4 **La revista *Decoración* sale los viernes. (ayer)**

5 **El servicio médico es criticado siempre.** (ayer)
6 **Siempre gana las carreras.** (el sábado pasado)
7 **Pochita entrena todos los domingos.** (ayer y anteayer)
8 **Leonardo come en casa.** (anoche)
9 **El jefe organiza una reunión de ejecutivos cada semana.** (el viernes pasado)
10 **Steven vuelve los lunes.** (hace dos horas)

Reading 🔊

While reading the passage below about working hours in Paraguay, see if you can find answers to these questions:

Are working hours in Uruguay the same as in your own country?
Do banks open on Saturdays in Uruguay?

Horarios de trabajo

Los horarios promedio para la actividad comercial son de 9.00 de la mañana a 7.00 de la noche, de lunes a viernes y de 8.30 de la mañana a 12.30 de la tarde los sábados. Los servicios esenciales públicos y privados se mantienen sin interrupción todo el día. Las oficinas públicas, los bancos e industrias no trabajan sábado ni domingo. La mayor parte abre de 12.00 a 5.00 de la tarde y algunos sólo cierran a las siete de la noche. Las oficinas privadas y la industria abren desde las 9.00 de la mañana hasta las 5.00 de la tarde.

horarios	opening hours	**la mayor parte**	most
promedio	average	**algunos**	some

13 Irán al mercado

They will go to the market

By the end of this chapter you should be able to:

- Express ideas using the future tense (I will)
- Use specific time reference in the future
- Use irregular verbs in the future tense

Reading 🔲

While reading the following newspaper article, see if you can find answers to these questions:

Have the price increases taken effect already?
What is the highest increase expected in domestic bills?

Tarifas de electricidad aumentarán entre el 5% y 10%

El incremento se efectivizará en julio. La próxima semana se publicarán las tarifas que cobrarán a los usuarios.

Las tarifas eléctricas se incrementarán entre 5% y 10% a partir del primero de julio. Así lo manifestó el Presidente de la Comisión de Tarifas Eléctricas.

Las tarifas de los consumos industriales y comerciales experimentarán un incremento promedio de 10%. El incremento máximo de las tarifas de consumo doméstico será de 5%. Con estos aumentos las tarifas comerciales e industriales estarán muy cerca de las tarifas objetivo.

Electricity prices to go up between 5% and 10%

The increase will be implemented in July. The new prices to be charged to the users will be published next week.

Electricity prices will be increased between 5% and 10% from 1 July, said the Chairman of the Electricity Price Regulation Committee.

Prices for industrial and commercial consumption will go up by an average of 10%. The maximum increase in domestic electricity prices will be 5%. After this adjustment, prices for commercial and industrial consumption will be very near the target price.

Language points

The future tense

To form the future of regular verbs you add the same endings to the infinitive of all -**ar**, -**er** or -**ir** verbs.

trabajar	comer	vivir
trabajaré	comeré	viviré
trabajarás	comerás	vivirás
trabajará	comerá	vivirá
trabajaremos	comeremos	viviremos
trabajarán	comerán	vivirán
trabajarán	comerán	vivirán

Examples:

La empresa ampliará sus actividades.	The firm will expand its activities.
El gobierno aplicará las medidas necesarias.	The government will take the necessary action.

The future tense is used mainly in written language. In conversation the future tense is less common than its equivalent in English. Spanish speakers tend to prefer the '**ir** + **a** + verb' structure (see Chapter 10) to express ideas in the future.

El Presidente viajará a Europa.	The President will travel to Europe.
El nuevo entrenador del equipo llegará esta noche.	The new team manager will arrive tonight.
Mañana vamos a ir a la playa.	We are going to go to the beach tomorrow.

Voy a empezar un curso de castellano.	I am going to start a Spanish course.

Exercise 1

Change these sentences to the future tense. See page 238 for a list of irregular verbs in the future.

Example:

> **Voy a ir al centro en la mañana.**
> **Iré al centro en la mañana.**

1 **Vamos a comer juntos.**
2 **Marcelo va a preparar la comida mañana.**
3 **Esteban y yo vamos a escribir el informe.**
4 **Vamos a esperar hasta que llegue la nueva computadora.**
5 **Van a abrir a las 9.30, en vez de las 10.00.**
6 **Tú vas a venir mañana temprano, ¿no?**
7 **Se van a llevar todo.**
8 **Elena va a empezar a trabajar el lunes.**
9 **La reunión va a ser en mi despacho.**
10 **Voy a dejar a mi hija en la escuela.**

El próximo/la próxima

When expressing ideas in the future, such phrases as **la próxima semana**, **el próximo domingo**, etc., may be useful. Generally speaking, **próximo/próxima** means 'next', as in 'next week'.

el próximo lunes
la próxima semana
el próximo mes
el próximo verano
las próximas vacaciones
el próximo año

El lunes que viene

Another way to express a specific moment in the future is by using the phrase **que viene** (literally 'the one which is coming').

> **el lunes que viene**
> **la semana que viene**
> **el mes que viene**
> **el verano que viene**
> **las vacaciones que vienen**
> **el año que viene**

Expressions with **que viene** have the same meaning as and are interchangeable with those using **el próximo/la próxima**, especially in spoken Spanish.

There is a tendency in Spanish to prefer expressions of time at the beginning of a sentence rather than at the end, although both are correct.

Example:

> **Mañana iremos al centro.**   We will go to town tomorrow.

Exercise 2

Translate these sentences into Spanish:

1 Ann and I will go to the travel agent's next Tuesday.
2 I will travel to Guatemala and Nicaragua next year.
3 We will discuss prices at our next meeting.
4 The company will grow in the next few years.
5 New prices for gas will be announced next week.

Exercise 3

Rewrite these sentences using the alternative way of expressing time.

Example:

> **El próximo año visitaremos Cuba.**
> **El año que viene visitaremos Cuba.**

1 **La próxima semana saldremos de paseo al campo.**
2 **El próximo lunes firmaremos el contrato.**
3 **El próximo semestre será decisivo para la empresa.**
4 **El próximo mes terminamos el proyecto.**
5 **La próxima entrevista será con el Director.**

Language point

Dentro de

To explain when something will be completed, Spanish uses the expression **dentro de** followed by the period of time.

Dentro de dos días se clausurará la Feria.	The Fair will close in two days' time.
El grupo rockero llegará dentro de tres semanas.	The rock band will arrive in three weeks' time.

Exercise 4

This is somebody's plan of activities for next week. Say what he or she will do each day and explain each action using the future tense. Then do it again using the 'ir + a + verb' pattern. The glossary at the back of the book will help you with new vocabulary.

Example:

El lunes estará en una reunión de diez a once.

La próxima semana en el trabajo

LUNES	Estar en la reunión (10 –11) Ir a la feria de informática Comprar nuevo equipo
MARTES	Visitar la tienda de repuestos
MIÉRCOLES	Enviar fax a las sucursales Informar sobre cambios en el horario
JUEVES	Terminar el informe anual
VIERNES	Empezar las negociaciones con nuevo socio

Say what your main activities at work or at home will be next week. Again, use the future tense. Write them down in your notebook. You might start like this:

El lunes iré a la oficina a las ocho.

Exercise 5

Read the following paragraph and then answer the questions below.

Al mercado

Ana y María irán al mercado a las ocho de la mañana el sábado. Comprarán frutas y verduras. A eso de las nueve, se reunirán con Javier en la cafetería El Sol para tomar un refresco o un café. Luego a las diez y media estarán en casa de Cecilia, una amiga de los tres. Los cuatro amigos saldrán para el centro de la ciudad a las doce. Almorzarán en un restaurante céntrico y luego asistirán a una exposición de pintura en un parque situado en el Norte de la ciudad. Quizás comprarán uno o dos cuadros y más tarde tomarán helados con un grupo de tres amigos de la universidad.

Are the following **verdadero** (true) or **falso** (false)?

1 **Ana y María irán al mercado el sábado a las ocho.**
2 **Más tarde tomarán un café o refresco.**
3 **No irán al centro de la ciudad.**
4 **A sus amigos no les gustan los helados.**
5 **Quizás comprarán cuadros en una exposición de pinturas.**

Dialogue 1 🔲

¿Qué harás?

Carmen and Santiago are making plans for the afternoon

CARMEN: ¿Qué vas a hacer esta tarde? ¿Irás al centro o vendrás a la universidad?

SANTIAGO: Iré a la universidad y pondremos el toque final al trabajo que estamos preparando. Los otros estudiantes de nuestro grupo querrán saber cómo va el proyecto. Tendremos una reunión a las siete en la cafetería. ¿Qué te parece?

CARMEN: Está bien. ¿Qué harás después de la reunión?

SANTIAGO: Raúl, Silvia y yo saldremos al cine. ¿Quieres ir también?

CARMEN: Sí, claro.

Language point

Irregular verbs in the future

These are verbs which do not follow the standard rule or pattern of formation of verbs in the future.

vivir		**salir**	
viviré	**viviremos**	**saldré**	**saldremos**
vivirás	**vivirán**	**saldrás**	**saldrán**
vivirá	**vivirán**	**saldrá**	**saldrán**

Notice how the irregular verb **salir** undergoes changes in the stem as it is conjugated.

Here are the most common irregular verbs in the future:

decir		**hacer**	
diré	**diremos**	**haré**	**haremos**
dirás	**dirán**	**harás**	**harán**
dirá	**dirán**	**hará**	**harán**

poder		poner	
podré	podremos	pondré	pondremos
podrás	podrán	pondrás	pondrán
podrá	podrán	pondrá	pondrán
querer		saber	
querré	querremos	sabré	sabremos
querrás	querrán	sabrás	sabrán
querrá	querrán	sabrá	sabrán
tener		venir	
tendré	tendremos	vendré	vendremos
tendrás	tendrán	vendrás	vendrán
tendrá	tendrán	vendrá	vendrán

Exercise 6

Complete the sentences with the future tense of the verb in brackets.
Use the glossary at the back of the book to check the meaning of any
new words.

1 **Los visitantes (venir) a la reunión el próximo sábado.**
2 **La charla (empezar) a las diez de la mañana.**
3 **Nosotros (regresar) al local del sindicato a la una.**
4 **Leonor (poner) el anuncio en el periódico.**
5 **Ellos (establecer) nuevas normas de calidad para el producto.**
6 **El 23 de abril se (celebrar) el Día del Idioma.**
7 **Pronto (aparecer) un nuevo libro del mismo autor.**
8 **La Galería de Arte (presentar) una exposición de arte colonial.**
9 **Un especialista en el tema (hablar) a los asistentes.**
10 **Dentro de cinco minutos nosotros (ver) un video sobre el histori-
al de la empresa.**

Exercise 7

Match the phrases in 1 to 5 with (a) to (e).

1 **Voy a llegar tarde a la reunión.**
2 **Estaremos en el centro mañana.**
3 **Ayer compramos un nuevo juego de muebles.**
4 **Se ha dislocado el brazo.**
5 **Hace frío.**

(a) **Hay que llevarla al hospital.**
(b) **Ponte una chaqueta.**
(c) **No hay problema. Se ha postergado para mañana.**
(d) **¿Es de roble o caoba?**
(e) **Yo también. Tengo que hacer compras.**

Reading 📷

El Día de la Tierra

El 22 de abril se celebrará el Día de la Tierra. La municipalidad entregará distinciones a los pioneros de la conservación local. El acto tendrá lugar el viernes 22 a las 8.00 de la noche en el auditorio municipal. El sábado 23 habrá un gran concierto en el auditorio del Parque Central en el cual tomarán parte varios grupos musicales que interpretarán temas ecologistas. El concierto se llevará a cabo a partir de las 6.00 de la tarde. Este evento durará aproximadamente tres horas.

entregar	to give, to deliver	**tomar parte**	to take part
pioneros	pioneers	**llevar a cabo**	to take place,
conservación	conservation		to carry out
el acto	the event	**temas**	themes
tener lugar	to take place	**durar**	to last

Exercise 8

Answer the following questions stating whether each statement is **verdadero** (true) or **falso** (false) based on the reading passage above.

1 **El Día de la Tierra no se celebra.**
2 **Los pioneros de la conservación recibirán distinciones.**
3 **Habrá un concierto en el Parque Central.**
4 **El concierto terminará a las seis de la tarde.**
5 **El concierto incluye temas ecologistas.**

14 Yo estudiaba . . .

I used to study . . .

By the end of this chapter you should be able to:

- Use the imperfect tense (e.g. I used to study)
- Use the imperfect continuous tense (e.g. I was studying)
- Use negative words

Dialogue 1 🔲

Yo estudiaba por la noche

Ramón is telling Julia about his time at college

RAMÓN: En esa época, yo estudiaba en la universidad. Era una casona antigua donde había patios y balcones. Las clases se daban desde las cuatro de la tarde hasta las diez de la noche. Muchos de los estudiantes trabajaban y por eso el horario era conveniente.

JULIA: ¿Era difícil estudiar y trabajar?

RAMÓN: Sí. Llegábamos a clases medio dormidos. Estábamos cansados por el trabajo durante el día. A veces perdíamos la primera hora de clase y sólo asistíamos a partir de la segunda hora.

JULIA: ¿Cómo hacían para estar al día?

RAMÓN: Los fines de semana nos reuníamos en grupos y tratábamos de ponernos al día en todos los cursos.

Language points

The imperfect indicative tense

The imperfect tense is used to indicate a habitual or repeated action in the past. It is the equivalent of verbs with 'used to' or 'was' in English.

Los fines de semana nos reuníamos en grupos.	We used to gather in groups at the weekends.
Íbamos a la playa todos los domingos durante el verano.	We used to go to the beach every Sunday during the summer.

It is also used to describe characteristics in the past when such characteristics continued to exist for a period of time. In the preterite actions are finite.

La gata se llamaba Magdalena. (imperfect)	The cat used to be called/was called Magdalena.
Tomás llamó a su gata. (preterite)	Tomás called for his cat.

More examples with the imperfect:

La casa estaba muy cerca del centro.	The house was very near the center of town.
Todo costaba menos en aquellos días.	Everything cost less in those days.

Regular verbs have their forms in the imperfect indicative as follows:

comprar	**vender**	**vivir**
compraba	vendía	vivía
comprabas	vendías	vivías
compraba	vendía	vivía
comprábamos	vendíamos	vivíamos
compraban	vendían	vivían
compraban	vendían	vivían

There are only three verbs which are irregular in the imperfect indicative:

ir	ser	ver
iba	era	veía
ibas	eras	veías
iba	era	veía
íbamos	éramos	veíamos
iban	eran	veían
iban	eran	veían

Examples:

Entonces iba al colegio a pie. Then I used to go to school on foot.

Eramos veintitres en la clase. We used to be twenty-three in our class.

Antes veía mucha televisión. She used to watch television a lot.

The imperfect continuous tense

Example:

Estaba estudiando. I was studying.

This tense in Spanish is very similar in use to its English equivalent. In Latin America it is very common. In Spain however, there is a tendency to use the imperfect indicative instead (**estudiaba**).

The imperfect continuous is used to refer to an action already in progress in the past when something else happened, interrupting the first action.

Estaba escuchando música cuando sonó el timbre. I was listening to music when the bell rang.

El cartero llegó cuando estaba tomando desayuno. The postman arrived when I was having breakfast.

Estábamos preparando el almuerzo cuando se apagó la luz. We were making lunch when there was a power cut.

In the imperfect continuous you use the verb **estar** in the imperfect indicative together with the continuous form of the main verb.

estaba trabajando	estábamos trabajando
estabas trabajando	estaban trabajando
estaba trabajando	estaban trabajando

Exercise 1

Complete the sentences with either the preterite or the imperfect of the verb in brackets.

1 Estela antes (trabajar) los sábados. Ahora ya no.
2 Cuando era niña (ir) al cine con su mamá.
3 Ayer (llegar) el nuevo director de la empresa.
4 Este periódico (costar) un dólar hasta el año pasado.
5 El sábado pasado (llamar) a mi hermana que vive en Panamá.
6 Ana y Julio (ir) al mercado a comprar y (volver) hace una hora.
7 Fue a la tienda y (comprar) frutas exóticas.
8 Antes no (tener) aire acondicionado. Ahora lo han instalado.
9 La casa (tener) cuatro habitaciones. Luego la ampliaron.
10 Anoche (volver) Estela.

Exercise 2

Give the English equivalent for these sentences.

1 Iris trabajaba en una agencia de viajes.
2 Nosotros estudiábamos por la noche.
3 Estábamos mirando la televisión cuando llegó Rosana.
4 Todos los domingos venía a visitar a sus abuelos.
5 Las computadoras estaban a disposición de los estudiantes.

Exercise 3

Give the Spanish equivalent for these sentences.

1 What were you doing when the telephone rang?
2 The airplane was landing when we heard the explosion.
3 He used to travel a lot.
4 Food was cheap in those days.
5 The office used to be on the second floor.

Exercise 4

Below is information from an old leaflet used to promote a private school ten years ago. Read it and then answer the questions that follow.

Colegio San Antonio
Avenida de la Montaña 2759
Tel. 782–9981

Primaria
Secundaria
Bachillerato Internacional
Laboratorio de Idiomas
Educación personalizada
Estudio dirigido
Orientación personal
Olimpiadas estudiantiles
Viajes estudiantiles a Brasil, EE. UU, Canadá, Inglaterra y
**   España y Japón.**

Campo de deportes propio	**Gimnasio cubierto**
** (50 hectáreas)**	**4 canchas de tenis**
Estadio	**2 piletas de natación**
Pista de Atletismo	

idiomas	languages	**campo de**	sports field
dirigido	planned, directed	** deportes**	
orientación	guidance,	**estadio**	stadium
	counselling	**pista**	track
olimpiadas	school sports	**atletismo**	athletics
** estudiantiles**	festival including	**gimnasio**	indoor
	many or all of the	** cubierto**	gymnasium
	games which are	**cancha**	court
	part of the	**pileta**	swimming pool
	Olympics	**natación**	swimming
viajes	school trips		
** estudiantiles**			

1 ¿Cómo se llamaba el Colegio?
2 ¿Dónde estaba el Colegio?
3 ¿Qué facilidades tenía para aprender idiomas?
4 ¿Qué viajes hacían?
5 ¿Aconsejaban a los alumnos?
6 ¿Qué deportes practicaban?

7 ¿El campo de deportes era grande?
8 ¿Ofrecía sólo primaria y secundaria?
9 ¿Cuántas canchas de tenis había?
10 ¿Había pista de atletismo?

Language point

Había

The imperfect of **hay** (there is/there are) is **había** and only the singular form exists.

Había dos canchas de tenis.	There were two tennis courts.
Había una pista de atletismo.	There was an athletics track.

Dialogue 2

Nadie tenía carro

Ramón continues to talk about his university days

JULIA: ¿Cómo iban a la universidad?
RAMÓN: Era difícil llegar al campus. En mi grupo nadie tenía carro. Ninguno de nosotros tenía suficiente dinero para comprar ni siquiera un auto chico usado. Todos teníamos que ir en ómnibus que se demoraba casi una hora para recorrer diez kilómetros. Nada me molestaba más que viajar parado una hora. Aunque tenía veinte años, ya tenía artritis reumatoide.

Language points

Negative words

As in English, negative words, e.g. **nada** (nothing), **nadie** (nobody), **ni** (nor), may precede a verb.

Nadie tenía dinero.	Nobody had money.
Ninguno quería viajar en omnibús.	No one wanted to travel by bus.

Nada parecía apropiado.	Nothing seemed suitable.

When the negative word appears after the verb, there must be another negative word before the verb.

Nunca venía nadie a la tienda.	Nobody would ever come to the shop.
No habla ni inglés ni francés.	She speaks neither English nor French.

The most frequently used negative words are:

nada	nothing
nadie	nobody
ninguno/ninguna	no one
ni	nor
nunca	never

No más

In Latin American Spanish this expression is more frequently used than in Spain, with the meaning of 'just', 'only' or 'no more'. In Spain **nada más** is preferred.

Cincuenta gramos no más. (Latin America)	Just fifty grams.
Cincuenta gramos nada más. (Spain)	

Una no más. (Latin America)	Only one.
Una nada más. (Spain)	

The expression **no más** also has other meanings peculiar to Latin American Spanish:

to encourage others to do something

Sírvete no más.	Do help yourself.
Escríbeme no más. Yo te contesto enseguida.	Do write to me. I'll answer straight away.

to convey the idea of 'very recently' or 'very near'

Llegó ayer no más.	He only arrived yesterday.
Aquí no más voy.	I am not going very far.
Voy a la tienda no más.	I'm just going to the shop.

Exercise 5

Give the English equivalent for the following:

1 **Nadie tiene nada.**
2 **Nunca compra ningún regalo.**
3 **Estela no come ni carne ni huevos.**
4 **Nadie aprende un idioma en un día.**
5 **Aquí no más está el museo.**

Exercise 6

Compare the two results of a survey on the use of the Internet and report as in the example below. Three phases will be particularly useful: **Sigue igual** *It remains the same*, **Ha subido** *It's gone up* and **Ha bajado** *It's gone down*.

Ejemplo: **En al año 2000 el 9% de los usuarios utilizaba Internet para leer noticias. Ahora, el 9% de los usuarios utiliza Internet para leer noticias. Sigue igual.**

Uso del Internet	Año 2000	Ahora
LEER NOTICIAS	9%	9%
HACER COMPRAS EN GENERAL	7%	6%
BAJAR MUSICA	4%	7%
ENTRETENIMIENTO	21%	17.5%
BUSCAR INFORMACION	30%	27%
COMPRAR / VENDER EN SUBASTAS	3%	6%
MANDAR / RECIBIR e-mail	19%	23%
ORGANIZAR VIAJES	4%	2%

$	HACER NEGOCIOS	2.5%	4%
?	OTROS USOS	0.5%	0.5%

hacer compras   do shopping
bajar música   download music
entretenimiento   entertainment
subasta   auction

Reading 📼

While reading the following passage, see if you can find answers to these questions:

In which present day countries did the Maya civilization flourish?
What were their main interests?

Los Mayas

Los antiguos Mayas ocupaban la península de Yucatán al sur de México y la mayor parte de lo que hoy es Guatemala. Los Mayas empezaron a construir su civilización en el siglo V antes de Cristo. Los mayas se dedicaban a la arquitectura, escultura, pintura, escritura jeroglífica, matemáticas y astronomía.

antiguos   old
se dedicaban a   were devoted to
escritura jeroglífica   hieroglyphic writing
astronomía   astronomy

El Castillo, Chichen Itzá, Yucatan, Mexico © James Folan.

15 Espero que puedas

I hope you can

By the end of this chapter you should be able to:

- Use the present subjunctive with regular verbs
- Use the present subjunctive with irregular verbs
- Use expressions related to health (e.g. I've got a headache)

Dialogue 1

Estoy buscando a alguien que me oriente

Tania hopes to find somebody to help her with her project

TANIA: Estoy buscando a alguien que me oriente sobre el proyecto de consultoría.

LAURA: No creo que tengas que buscar más. Yo conozco a una persona con mucha experiencia en el asunto. Es Iris Vidal, Directora de una firma de Consultoría y Asesoramiento de Empresas.

TANIA: ¿Me puedes dar su número de teléfono?

LAURA: Claro. Acá lo tengo en mi agenda.

Language points

The present subjunctive

The subjunctive is a mood which denotes attitude and is mainly used in sentences expressing wish, hope or doubt. It is used to indicate actions which are only hypothetical or a possibility in the future, at the moment of speaking.

Espero que puedas venir a la fiesta.	I hope you can make it to the party.
Quisiera que ayudes a Isabel.	I would like you to help Isabel.
Rosa me ha pedido que vaya a la oficina.	Rose has asked me to go to the office.
Su papá lo ha convencido para que vaya a Quito.	His dad has persuaded him to go to Quito.

The present subjunctive of regular verbs is formed as follows:

trabajar	**comer**	**vivir**
trabaje	**coma**	**viva**
trabajes	**comas**	**vivas**
trabaje	**coma**	**viva**
trabajemos	**comamos**	**vivamos**
trabajen	**coman**	**vivan**
trabajen	**coman**	**vivan**

Examples:

No quiero que trabaje.	I don't want her to work.
Quizás trabajemos el sábado.	We may go to work on Saturday.
Es importante que comamos frutas y verduras.	It is important for us to eat fruit and vegetables.
No creo que coman en casa esta noche.	I don't think they will eat at home tonight.
Le han recomendado que viva en el campo.	They have recommended that he should live in the countryside.
No creo que tengan una casa tan grande.	I don't believe that they own such a big house.

The most commonly used irregular verbs in the present subjunctive are:

dar	dé, des, dé, demos, den, den
decir	diga, digas, diga, digamos, digan, digan
estar	esté, estés, esté, estemos, estén, estén
haber	haya, hayas, haya, hayamos, hayan, hayan
hacer	haga, hagas, haga, hagamos, hagan, hagan
ir	vaya, vayas, vaya, vayamos, vayan, vayan
oir	oiga, oigas, oiga, oigamos, oigan, oigan
poder	pueda, puedas, pueda, podamos, puedan, puedan
poner	ponga, pongas, ponga, pongamos, pongan, pongan
querer	quiera, quieras, quiera, querramos, quieran, quieran
saber	sepa, sepas, sepa, sepamos, sepan, sepan
salir	salga, salgas, salga, salgamos, salgan, salgan
ser	sea, seas, sea, seamos, sean, sean
tener	tenga, tengas, tenga, tengamos, tengan, tengan
traer	traiga, traigas, traiga, traigamos, traigan, traigan
valer	valga, valgas, valga, valgamos, valgan, valgan

Use of the subjunctive

A first use of the subjunctive is after verbs indicating the exercise of some kind of influence (persuasion, recommendation, etc.). Commonly used verbs in this context are **querer** (to want) **aconsejar** (to advise), **recomendar** (to recommend), **sugerir** (to suggest).

Quiero que termines pronto.	I want you to finish soon.
Recomiendo que salgan por la puerta lateral.	I recommend that you leave through the side door.
La señora dice que vuelva mañana.	The lady says that you should come back tomorrow.
Sugerimos que viajen durante la noche.	We suggest that you travel overnight.

Dialogue 2 ▣

Quizá tenga el número

Lola and Mirtha are talking about a mutual friend

LOLA: Es una pena que José no esté en su casa.

MIRTHA:	Sí. Yo creo que es necesario que le llamemos.
LOLA:	Quizá tenga el número en mi cartera. A ver . . . Sí acá está. No creo que se sorprenda cuando escuche mi voz. Pero nunca se sabe.
MIRTHA:	¿Cuándo hablaste con él por última vez?
LOLA:	Hace tres o cuatro días. Sara y yo estábamos en el centro y él se acercó.
MIRTHA:	¿Cuándo volverá por acá?
LOLA:	No creo que sea esta semana.

Language point

More uses of the subjunctive

After expressions which indicate judgement or emotion:

Es necesario que vengas a la oficina.	It is necessary that you come to the office.
¡Qué pena que Carlos no esté!	What a shame Carlos is not in!
¿No te fastidia que te hable de ese modo?	Are you not bothered that he talks to you like that?
Es mejor que no salgas. Está lloviendo mucho.	It's better if you don't go out. It's raining heavily.

After expressions which indicate probability, possibility or doubt:

Es posible que traiga la maqueta esta noche.	It is possible that he will bring the scale model tonight.
Dudo que compre más de una docena.	I doubt whether she will buy more than a dozen.
No creemos que salga bien.	We don't think it will work out well.

When the person or object is not specified, and you use words like **alguien** (somebody), **algo** (something), etc.

Estoy buscando a alguien que me oriente en este asunto.	I am looking for somebody to give me some guidance in this matter.
Quiero algo que me alivie el dolor.	I want something to relieve the pain.

After ¡qué! or ¡ojalá! (expressions of hope or wish):

¡Qué te vaya bien!	Have a good time!
¡Qué te diviertas!	Enjoy it!
¡Ojalá no necesite una operación!	Let's hope he doesn't need an operation.
¡Ojalá esté en casa!	Let's hope she is at home.

Exercise 1

Give English equivalents for these sentences.

1 **No creo que termine todo.**
2 **Qué interesante que incluya esto en su libro.**
3 **Es probable que salga esta noche.**
4 **Quiero que vayas al médico.**
5 **Te pido que continúes en tu puesto.**
6 **No les parece que ofrezca posibilidades.**
7 **Nos molesta que no llegue temprano.**
8 **Es importante que comamos verduras y frutas.**
9 **Dudamos que escriba desde Ecuador.**
10 **Lamento que usted no pueda venir a la reunión.**

Exercise 2

Give Spanish equivalents for these sentences. Use the subjunctive in your answers.

1 It is necessary that you eat less.
2 It's interesting that she answers in Spanish.
3 I am looking for something that will help everybody.
4 We advise you to do it.
5 They ask you to answer promptly.

Language point

Another use of the subjunctive

The subjunctive is always used after these expressions:

antes que	before
para que	in order that
con tal que	provided that
(or con tal de que)	
a menos que	unless

Examples:

Terminaremos antes que venga tu amiga.	We will finish before your friend arrives.
Aquí está el dinero para que compres los regalos.	Here is the money so that you buy the presents.
Puedes llevarte el libro, con tal que lo devuelvas mañana.	You can take the book, provided you return it tomorrow.
A menos que diga dónde está, no lo encontraremos.	Unless she says where it is, we will not find it.

Exercise 3

Complete the sentences with the correct form, choosing from the ones given in brackets.

1 **Carlos (vendrá/venga) el viernes a la casa.**
2 **Espero que Linda (vendrá/venga) mañana.**
3 **Quiero que (prepare/prepara) este informe para el lunes.**
4 **Esteban (trajo/traiga) la nueva computadora ayer.**
5 **Le recomiendo que no (comprará/compre) el tamaño grande.**
6 **¡Qué pena que Marcelo (estuvo/esté) ocupado mañana!**
7 **Dudamos que (encontrará/encuentre) al encargado.**
8 **Puedes comer dulces con tal de que no (es/sea) en exceso.**
9 **Creo que me (escuchará/escuche) cuando (habla/hable) con él.**
10 **El próximo domingo (empezarán/empiecen) las clases.**

Exercise 4

Explain that you would like to see the following features in your new car. Make use of the subjunctive in your sentences.

Example:

Tener levantacristales eléctricos.
Quiero que tenga levantacristales eléctricos.

1 **Tener capacidad para cinco pasajeros.**
2 **Ser económico con el combustible.**
3 **Ser de tamaño mediano.**
4 **Incluir cierre electrónico de puertas.**
5 **Contar con motor de 1,300 o 1,400 centímetros cúbicos.**
6 **Venir con caja de cambios de cinco velocidades.**
7 **Ser de un precio razonable.**
8 **Funcionar con gasolina sin plomo.**
9 **Ofrecer fiabilidad.**
10 **Estar entre los líderes del mercado.**

Exercise 5

Match each of the expressions 1 to 10 with one of the responses (a) to (j).

1 **Tiene hambre la niña.**
2 **No arranca el coche.**
3 **Necesitamos una secretaria más para mañana.**
4 **Casi se ha terminado el dinero en efectivo.**
5 **Tenemos que pagar la cuenta del teléfono.**
6 **No saben adónde ir a comer.**
7 **¿Vendrá Carlos hoy?**
8 **Le duele la muela.**
9 **¿Qué dice del informe?**
10 **¿Puede llevarse la guía telefónica?**

(a) **No creo que venga.**
(b) **Que coma algo en el comedor.**
(c) **Dile al encargado que saque dinero de la cuenta corriente.**
(d) **Siempre que la devuelva pronto.**
(e) **Que llamen al mecánico.**
(f) **Dile que haga una cita con el dentista.**
(g) **Recomiéndales el restaurante típico de la esquina.**

(h) **Espera que no tengas que volver a escribirlo.**
(i) **Pide a la secretaria que pague mañana.**
(j) **Es posible que contraten a otra esta tarde.**

Exercise 6

Choose the correct alternative for each sentence.

1 **Espero que (tienes/tengas) plata. Yo no tengo.**
2 **No creo que (sea/es) auténtico.**
3 **Este carro (tiene/tenga) cuatro puertas.**
4 **Milagros (dice/diga) que quiere hablar contigo.**
5 **Dudo que (preparará/prepare) un informe.**
6 **Puedes llevarte el libro con tal que lo (devolverás/ devuelvas).**
7 **Juan Carlos (llegue/llegará) mañana.**
8 **¡Ojalá (traen/traigan) una muestra!**
9 **No esperamos que nos (ayudan/ayuden).**
10 **Mañana (sea/será) la reunión.**

Dialogue 3

¡Qué te diviertas!

While reading the dialogue below, see if you can find the answer to this question:

Has Genaro actually forgotten something?

Genaro is about to leave for the airport. Luisa is seeing him off, trying to make sure he hasn't forgotten anything.

GENARO: Bueno. Me voy. Tengo que llegar al aeropuerto en veinte minutos.
LUISA: Sí apúrate. No te olvides de nada.
GENARO: Todo está en la maleta.
LUISA: ¡Qué te vaya bien! ¡Qué te diviertas!
GENARO: Gracias. Vuelvo el domingo.

Language point

Apurarse

This verb in Latin America has the meaning of 'to hurry up', while in Spain it is mainly used to mean 'to worry'.

¡Apúrate! ¡Van a cerrar la tienda!	Hurry up! The shop is going to close!
No te apures. Hay tiempo.	Don't rush. There's time.

Dialogue 4 ▭▭

Me duele la cabeza

While reading the dialogue below, see if you can find the answer to this question:

What will Olga do if she can't get rid of her headache?

Elisa realizes that Olga is not feeling well

ELISA: ¿Qué te pasa?
OLGA: No me siento bien. Me duele mucho la cabeza.
ELISA: Toma una pastilla para calmar el dolor.
OLGA: Ya tomé una y no me pasa. Creo que voy a acostarme.
ELISA: Sí. Te hará bien.
OLGA: Si no me pasa, consultaré al médico mañana.
ELISA: Avísame, y te acompaño.
OLGA: Gracias. Te llamaré mañana a las diez.
ELISA: Chau.
OLGA: Chau.

Language point

Me duele

To explain that you have some kind of pain you use the expression **Me duele** followed by the part of the body that hurts.

la cabeza (head)
el oído (ear)
la muela (tooth)
la garganta (throat)
la mano (hand)
el brazo (arm)
el estómago (stomach)
la espalda (back)
la pierna (leg)
el pie (foot)

Me duele la cabeza
       la muela
       el oído
       la pierna
       el brazo
       el pie
       la mano
       la espalda
       el estómago
       la garganta

It is possible to use **Tengo dolor de** instead of **Me duele**. In this case you do not use the article **el** or **la**.

Tengo dolor de cabeza.
Tengo dolor de muela.

Reading 📖

While reading the passage below, see if you can find answers to these questions:

Is the airport near the center of town?
What are the main destinations of the national airline?

El transporte aéreo en Uruguay

El aeropuerto internacional de Carrasco se encuentra ubicado a 17 km de Montevideo. En este aeropuerto operan las líneas aéreas internacionales y hay un servicio diario de puente aéreo con Argentina. Un taxi del aeropuerto al centro de Montevideo cuesta aproximadamente veinte dólares. La línea aérea nacional controlada por el estado se llama PLUNA. Vuela a Europa y a países cercanos al Uruguay, especialmente a Argentina, Brasil, Chile y Paraguay.

ubicado	located
puente aéreo	shuttle service
cercano	nearby

16 Me gustaría . . .

I would like . . .

By the end of this chapter you should be able to:

- Use the conditional tense (e.g. I would go, etc.)
- Use ordinal numbers (first, second, etc.)
- Use the imperative (i.e. the command form)

Dialogue 1 ▣

¿Qué le gustaría?

While reading the dialogue below, see if you can find answers to these questions:

Do all the people interviewed agree?
Are there any advantages in having a tram service?

Some people are being asked about their views on a local issue

ENTREVISTADOR: ¿Le gustaría tener un servicio de tranvías por aquí?

TRANSEÚNTE 1: No. Sería una pérdida de dinero público y destruiría el ambiente de la calle principal que data de tiempos coloniales.

ENTREVISTADOR: ¿Estaría de acuerdo con un servicio de tranvías por aquí?

TRANSEÚNTE 2: Sí. Primero, porque sería más rápido que los ómnibus y segundo porque es más limpio. Menos contaminante. Pero supongo que costaría más, ¿no?

ENTREVISTADOR: ¿Le parecería bien tener un servicio de tranvías por aquí, por la calle principal?

Transeúnte 3:   Sí, claro. Necesitamos transporte rápido. Hace
                  años había tranvías. Eran una gran cosa.

Reading 🔲

While reading the passage below see if you can answer the question:
Why do people access the Internet?

Internet
Internet es una red mundial de computadoras para intercambiar
información. Cuando una persona se conecta a la red, puede entrar
en contacto con cualquier otra computadora conectada a la red en
cualquier parte del planeta. A través de Internet es posible enviar
correo electrónico, hacer compras, consultar información, leer periódicos, escuchar estaciones de radio, organizar viajes, preparar
trabajos académicos, realizar operaciones bancarias, entrar en grupos de *chat* y otras actividades más.

red	network
se conecta	is linked
enviar	to send
cualquier	any
a través	by means of
operaciones bancarias	bank transactions

Language points

The conditional tense

The conditional tense (in English 'I would go', etc.) is formed by
adding the following endings to the infinitive: **-ía**, **-ías**, **-ía**, **-íamos**, **-ían**. The same endings are used with the three conjugations.

trabajar	**comer**	**vivir**
trabajaría	**comería**	**viviría**
trabajarías	**comerías**	**vivirías**
trabajaría	**comería**	**viviría**
trabajaríamos	**comeríamos**	**viviríamos**
trabajarían	**comerían**	**vivirían**
trabajarían	**comerían**	**vivirían**

Examples:

Caroline dijo que estaría en su casa.	Caroline said that she would be at home.
¿Dónde te gustaría vivir?	Where would you like to live?
¿Irías al cine con Julián?	Would you go to the cinema with Julián?

Irregular verbs in the conditional tense

Some verbs are irregular. Although the endings present no irregularities in the conditional, the stem of the verb shows variations. Here are the main irregular verbs:

decir	haber	hacer
diría	habría	haría
dirías	habrías	harías
diría	habría	haría
diríamos	habríamos	haríamos
dirían	habrían	harían
dirían	habrían	harían

poder	poner	querer
podría	pondría	querría
podrías	pondrías	querrías
podría	pondría	querría
podríamos	pondríamos	querríamos
podrían	pondrían	querrían
podrían	pondrían	querrían

salir	tener	venir
saldría	tendría	vendría
saldrías	tendrías	vendrías
saldría	tendría	vendría
saldríamos	tendríamos	vendríamos
saldrían	tendrían	vendrían
saldrían	tendrían	vendrían

Ordinal numbers

primero	first	**sexto**	sixth
segundo	second	**séptimo**	seventh
tercero	third	**octavo**	eighth

cuarto	fourth	**noveno**	ninth
quinto	fifth	**décimo**	tenth

Primero to **décimo** are used in everyday speech. When preceding nouns there must be agreement in gender and number. After **décimo**, there is a tendency to use the cardinal numbers (**once** 'eleven', **doce** 'twelve', etc.)

Es la primera vez que lo hace.	It is the first time she has done that.
El cuarto concursante de hoy.	The fourth contestant today.
Los europeos llegaron en el siglo XVI (dieciseis).	The Europeans arrived in the sixteenth century.

Note that **primero** and **tercero** become **primer** and **tercer** when they precede a noun.

Vive en un departamento del primer piso.	She lives in an apartment on the first floor.
Gané el tercer premio.	I won the third prize.

Exercise 1

¿Qué programas te gustaría ver?

Say what kind of programs you might like to watch on TV. Use the expression **Me gustaría ver . . . .** Choose from the list below. Write the sentences down in your notebook.

Programas de televisión

informativos	cómicos
noticiarios	infantiles
culturales	musicales
telenovelas	femeninos
películas	deportivos
concursos	reportajes
policiales	talk shows
documentales	No veo televisión

Exercise 2

Match the situations in the column on the left with the possible course of action you would take from the list on the right.

1 **Un incendio**	(a)	**Llamaría a un médico**
2 **El teléfono no funciona**	(b)	**Encendería la calefacción**
3 **No comprendo una palabra**	(c)	**Cambiaría el cartucho**
4 **El carro no arranca**	(d)	**Tomaría una bebida refrescante**
5 **Tienes hambre**	(e)	**La limpiaría**
6 **Tienes sed**	(f)	**Llamaría a los bomberos**
7 **Alguien está enfermo**	(g)	**Me comunicaría con la compañía telefónica**
8 **La impresora no imprime bien**	(h)	**Comprobaría la batería**
9 **La mesa está sucia**	(i)	**La buscaría en el diccionario**
10 **Hace frío en la casa**	(j)	**Comería algo**

Dialogue 2 ▣

Ponga la cebolla a macerar

Adela is explaining how to prepare a typical dish

ADELA: Exprima los 4 limones y ponga la cebolla a macerar en este jugo luego de picarla. Sancoche y luego pele las papas.

MARIANA: ¿Se forma una masa?

ADELA: Sí. Machuque las papas y forme una masa con la papa machucada, la cebolla y el jugo de limón. Añada aceite si es necesario. Coloque la masa en un molde y decore con mitades de huevo duro, aceitunas y queso.

Language point

The imperative

The imperative form is used to give commands, orders or instructions.

Prepare un informe para mañana. (usted)	Prepare a report for tomorrow.
Toma estas pastillas. (tú)	Take these tablets.

The imperative for the second person singular informal (**tú**) is the same as the form for the third person singular in the present indicative, in the case of regular verbs.

preparar	**prepar***a*
comer	**com***e*
subir	**sub***e*

Examples:

Prepara la camioneta. Vamos a salir.	Have the van ready. We are going out.
Come toda tu comida.	Eat your meal up.
Sube al carro.	Get in the car.

There are some irregular verbs. The most frequently used irregular verbs in the imperative for the second person informal (**tú**) are:

decir	**di**	**salir**	**sal**
estar	**está**	**ser**	**sé**
hacer	**haz**	**tener**	**ten**
ir	**ve**	**venir**	**ven**
oír	**oye**		

The imperative for the second person singular formal (**usted**) is the same as the present subjunctive for **usted**, **él** or **ella**.

preparar	**prepar***e*
comer	**com***a*
subir	**sub***a*

Examples:

Prepare el informe para mañana.	Have the report ready for tomorrow.
Coma antes de ir al examen médico.	Eat before going to the medical examination.
Suba al cuarto piso.	Go up to the fourth floor.

The imperative for the second person plural (**ustedes**) is the same as the present subjunctive for **ustedes**, **ellos** or **ellas**.

preparar	**prepar***en*
comer	**com***an*
subir	**sub***an*

Examples:

Preparen todo enseguida.	Have everything ready straight away.
Coman despacio.	Eat slowly.
Suban por la escalera, no por el ascensor.	Go up the stairs, not the lift.

Negative commands

These are formed using the negative particle **no** before the imperative. The negative imperative in the informal singular uses the present subjunctive.

Affirmative	*Negative*
prepara	*no* **prepar***es*
come	*no* **com***as*
sube	*no* **sub***as*

Examples:

No prepares nada.	Don't prepare anything.
No comas antes de acostarte.	Don't eat before going to bed.
No subas al despacho hasta las diez.	Don't go to the office until ten.

The negative imperative in the formal singular also uses the subjunctive.

Affirmative	*Negative*
prepare	**no prepare**
coma	**no coma**
suba	**no suba**

Examples:

No prepare una presentación larga.	Don't prepare a long presentation.
No coma dulces.	Don't eat sweet things.
No suba por el ascensor.	Don't go up in the elevator.

The negative imperative in the plural is the same as the affirmative, but preceded by **no**.

no **preparen**
no **coman**
no **suban**

Examples:

No preparen las cuentas hasta mañana.	Do not prepare the accounts until tomorrow.
No coman muy tarde.	Do not eat too late.
No suban al tren cuando esté en movimiento.	Do not board the train while it is moving.

Exercise 3

Change these commands to the negative.

Example:

Compren revistas.
No compren revistas.

1 **Vengan a la fiesta.**
2 **Llama a tu novia.**
3 **Compra cigarrillos.**
4 **Abra la ventana.**
5 **Copien el documento en diskette.**
6 **Pide diez cuadernos.**
7 **Ven con tu novio.**
8 **Tome fotos.**
9 **Prepare el plato que le recomendé.**
10 **Instala la antena.**

Exercise 4

Change the following sentences to the imperative form.

Examples:

Ustedes deben venir mañana.
Vengan mañana.

Tienes que decir cuál es el problema.
Di cuál es el problema.

1 **Tienes que bajar al primer piso.**
2 **Usted debe ser más eficiente.**
3 **Tienes que tomar esto.**
4 **Ustedes deben revisar este contrato.**
5 **Debes regresar pronto.**
6 **Tienes que comer más proteinas.**
7 **Usted debe enviar el paquete por vía aérea.**
8 **Tiene que ir el próximo domingo.**
9 **Tienes que hacer lo que dice esta señorita.**
10 **Ustedes deben vender la máquina.**

Reading

While reading the passage below, see if you can find answers to these questions:

Does Colombia have a strategic location?
Which racial group is in the majority in Colombia?

Colombia

Colombia tiene costas en el Océano Pacífico y en el Océano Atlántico. Su situación geográfica es muy estratégica. Además está cerca del Canal de Panamá. Como el resto de América Latina, su población crece aceleradamente. La mitad de la población es mestiza, alrededor del 20 ciento es blanca, otro 20 por ciento está formado por mulatos y zambos y el resto por gente de raza negra e india.

estratégica	strategic
como el resto	like the rest, like the others
crece	grows
aceleradamente	fast
mitad	half
mestiza	Spanish and indigenous mixed-blood race
mulatos	people who have one white and one black parent
zambos	people who have one black and one Indian parent

17 Si yo tuviera . . .

If I had . . .

By the end of this chapter you should be able to:

- Use the imperfect subjunctive
- Use open conditional sentences (e.g. If I arrive early)
- Use remote/hypothetical conditional sentences (e.g. If I had a car)

Dialogue 1

Si yo tuviera un ingreso extra

After reading the dialogue below, see if you can find answers to these questions:

Would both people do the same things with the extra money?
What would you do?

Two people are talking about hypothetical plans

GENARO: Si tuviera un ingreso extra, compraría algo para la casa.

ALAN: ¿Qué comprarías?

GENARO: Compraría una nueva aspiradora, porque la que tenemos ya es muy antigua, y también un escritorio para los chicos.

ALAN: ¿Pagarías a crédito?

GENARO: Sí. Hay buenas ofertas para pagar en 24 meses sin intereses.

Language point

The imperfect subjunctive

Similar to the present subjunctive, the imperfect subjunctive indicates actions which are hypothetical, but also remote possibilities at the time of speaking. Compared to the present subjunctive, the action is less likely to take place. The imperfect subjunctive is used for sentences expressing hopes or wishes which are unlikely to happen. (Another use, in hypothetical conditional sentences, is explained later in this chapter.)

Ojalá llame.	I hope he rings. (And he probably will.)
Ojalá llamase.	I wish he would ring. (But he probably won't.)

The imperfect subjunctive has two alternative conjugations, which are interchangeable.

Examples of regular verbs:

trabajar

trabajara	**trabajase**
trabajaras	**trabajases**
trabajara	**trabajase**
trabajáramos	**trabajásemos**
trabajaran	**trabajasen**
trabajaran	**trabajasen**

comer

comiera	**comiese**
comieras	**comieses**
comiera	**comiese**
comiéramos	**comiésemos**
comieran	**comiesen**
comieran	**comiesen**

vivir

viviera	**viviese**
vivieras	**vivieses**
viviera	**viviese**
viviéramos	**viviésemos**

vivieran	viviesen
vivieran	viviesen

The most common irregular verbs used in the imperfect subjunctive are:

dar	diera, dieras, diera, diéramos, dieran, dieran
decir	dijera, dijeras, dijera, dijéramos, dijeran, dijeran
estar	estuviera, estuvieras, estuviera, estuviéramos, estuvieran, estuvieran
haber	hubiera, hubieras, hubiera, hubiéramos, hubieran, hubieran
hacer	hiciera, hicieras, hiciera, hiciéramos, hicieran, hicieran
ir	fuera, fueras, fuera, fuéramos, fueran, fueran
oir	oyera, oyeras, oyera, oyéramos, oyeran, oyeran
poder	pudiera, pudieras, pudiera, pudiéramos, pudieran, pudieran
poner	pusiera, pusieras, pusiera, pusiéramos, pusieran, pusieran
querer	quisiera, quisieras, quisiera, quisiéramos, quisieran, quisieran
saber	supiera, supieras, supiera, supiéramos, supieran, supieran
salir	saliera, salieras, saliera, saliéramos, salieran, salieran
ser	fuera, fueras, fuera, fuéramos, fueran, fueran
tener	tuviera, tuvieras, tuviera, tuviéramos, tuvieran, tuvieran
traer	trajera, trajeras, trajera, trajéramos, trajeran, trajeran
valer	valiera, valieras, valiera, valiéramos, valieran, valieran
venir	viniera, vinieras, viniera, viniéramos, vinieran, vinieran
ver	viera, vieras, viera, viéramos, vieran, vieran

Note: **yo/usted/él/ella** share the same verb form, e.g. **viera**, and **ustedes/ellos/ellas** share the same verb form, e.g. **vieran**.

Dialogue 2 🔲

Si quieres . . .

Two friends are making arrangements to meet

ALBERTO: Si vienes esta tarde, salimos al cine juntos.
EMILIA: Bueno, ya que insistes.

ALBERTO: ¿A qué hora vienes?

EMILIA: No sé. Depende. Quizás vaya en el auto o quizás vaya a pie. Como vives tan cerca.

ALBERTO: Si vienes en el auto llegas rápido y podemos ir a la primera función. Si quieres, luego podemos ir a tomar algo.

EMILIA: Me parece bien. Voy en el auto.

Language points

Open conditional sentences

In an open conditional sentence (e.g. If I go . . .) you use the present indicative.

Condition	*Conclusion*
si + present indicative	present indicative

Examples:

Si vienes temprano, vamos al cine.	If you come early, we can go to the cinema.
Si mandas el formulario, recibes un cupón a vuelta de correo.	If you send the form, you get a voucher by return of post.

Como

In the appropriate context the word **como** means 'since'/'because', as in these examples:

Como vives cerca, voy a pie.	Since you live nearby I'll walk.
Como no tienes los boletos, no podemos entrar.	Since you don't have the tickets, we can't go in.
Como pasaste los exámenes, te compramos una bici.	Since you passed your exams, we'll buy you a bike.

Dialogue 3 📼

Si tuviera la plata

José Luis: Si tuviera la plata, compraría la computadora que que-remos.

Marcelo: No importa. Mi papá dijo que es posible que la com-premos a plazos.

José Luis: Pero mi mamá dudaba que mi papá pudiera pagar las cuotas mensuales ya que está pagando también el carro.

Marcelo: Si tuvieramos la oportunidad de trabajar este verano durante las vacaciones, podríamos ayudar a pagar cada mes.

José Luis: Vamos a hablar con Antonio.

Marcelo: Sí, vamos.

Language point

Remote/Hypothetical conditional sentences

In a remote/hypothetical conditional sentence (e.g. If I had the money I would buy it.) you use the imperfect subjunctive for the condition and a conditional tense in the conclusion. When you use this type of conditional sentence the conclusion is hypothetical, since the condition expressed by the imperfect subjunctive is contrary to fact or unlikely to be fulfilled. (The imperfect subjunctive is discussed earlier in this chapter and the conditional tense appears in Chapter 16.)

Condition	*Conclusion*
si + imperfect subjunctive	conditional tense

Examples:

Si tuviera un diccionario, buscaría la palabra.	If I had a dictionary, I would look the word up.
Si fueran puntuales, no causarían problemas.	If they turned up on time, they would not cause problems.
Si la tienda estuviera en el	If the shop was in the town center,

centro, iría ahorita.	I would go right now.
Si vendiésemos más, podríamos ampliar la gama.	If we sold more, we could extend the range.

Compare the following examples of two types of conditional sentences:

Si tengo tiempo, te escribo.	If I have time, I'll write to you. (I think it is likely that I will have the time.)
Si tuviera tiempo, te escribiría.	If I had time, I would write to you. (But I don't have the time.)
Si eres socio te dejan entrar.	If you are a member, they let you in. (There is a possibility that you will become one.)
Si fueras socio, te dejarían entrar.	If you were a member, they would let you in. (But you are not and probably will never become one.)

Exercise 1

Si usted tuviera un ingreso extra a partir de este mes, ¿a qué lo destinaría?
If you had extra income as from this month, what would you use it for?

Answer the survey question above, putting yourself in the position of (a), (b) and (c) below:

(a) If you were unemployed.
(b) If you and your partner had a secure job.
(c) If you were leaving secondary school.

Start your answers using:

Si tuviera un ingreso extra lo destinaría a . . .
If I had extra income I would use it for . . .

ahorros	savings
alimentación	food
artículos para el hogar	household goods
ropa/calzado	clothes/footwear
inversión	investment
estudios	studies

diversión	entertainment
otra	other
no precisa/no responde	don't know
viajes	travel

Exercise 2

Write an English equivalent for the following sentences.

1 **Si pudiera, viajaría más.**
2 **Si Marcelo fuese mejor organizado, tendría óptimos resultados.**
3 **Como vienes en auto llegarás antes que Alberto.**
4 **Si escribes un cheque deletrea bien el nombre.**
5 **Si me dieran la oportunidad, trabajaría en Uruguay.**
6 **Visitaría la capital si tuviera más tiempo, pero sólo estaré dos días por aquí.**
7 **Lo traería en diskette, si fuera compatible.**
8 **Si las cifras indicasen lo contrario, tendríamos que hacer una investigación.**
9 **Si la novela fuera más corta, tendría más éxito.**
10 **Si sabes la respuesta, ¿por qué no la dices?**

Exercise 3

Write a Spanish equivalent for the following sentences:

1 If there is a problem, I will send you a fax.
2 I do not think Helen will go to work tomorrow.
3 Would you go back if you had the chance to do so?
4 Since you only have one, take these other two.
5 If he rings, we will give him the details.

Exercise 4

Match the phrases in the first group (1 to 5) with those in the second group ((a) to (e)).

1 **¿Quisieras ir al teatro mañana?**
2 **¿Irías a la inauguración de la nueva tienda?**
3 **¿Volverías a este lugar?**
4 **En ese caso, Estela repetiría el mismo error.**
5 **Norma esperaría hasta que lleguen los pedidos.**

(a) **Sólo de vacaciones.**
(b) **Si me invitan, si iría.**
(c) **No puedo, voy a ir a hacer unas compras urgentes.**
(d) **Sí, para ver los detalles de la factura.**
(e) **Sí. Es difícil corregirla.**

Dialogue 4 📼

Si pudiera

Enrique wishes he could buy something

ENRIQUE: Si pudiera, yo lo comprara inmediatamente.
ROSARIO: Sería una decisión apresurada.
ENRIQUE: Si fueras tú, posiblemente hicieras lo mismo.
ROSARIO: Tienes razón.

Language points

The subjunctive used instead of the conditional

Frequently in spoken Spanish the **-ra** form of the subjunctive is used instead of the conditional. This makes the sentence sound more informal and therefore is used by native speakers in colloquial, familiar language. While the following example is not grammatically correct, this type of language is often heard in everyday usage.

Si pudiera, lo comprara inmediatamente.   If I could, I would buy it immediately.

Tener razón

This expression is used to indicate that somebody is right or to accept somebody's argument.

tengo razón	**tenemos razón**
tienes razón	**tienen razón**
tiene razón	**tienen razón**

Examples:

Creo que son nueve, como   I think there are nine, Yes, you're
dices tú. Sí, tienes razón.   right.
Miguel, tú siempre tienes   Miguel, you're always right.
razón.

Dialogue 5 🔘

Si tuviera más tiempo

Elena and Jorge are discussing business plans

ELENA: Si yo tuviera más tiempo prepararía la base de datos que necesitamos. Creo que tendremos que pedir ayuda a alguna firma de consultoría.

JORGE: Estoy de acuerdo. No podemos seguir adelante sin tener toda nuestra información bien organizada antes de discutir nuestros planes de expansión.

ELENA: El año pasado cuando tuvimos problemas de producción vinieron dos consultores de una firma internacional a orientarnos y lo hicieron muy bien. Creo que podríamos ponernos en contacto con ellos nuevamente.

JORGE: Sí. Tenían un enfoque muy profesional y abordaron el problema con gran eficiencia. Vamos a ponernos en contacto con ellos otra vez.

ELENA: Aquí tengo el teléfono. Voy a llamarlos.

Exercise 5

Translate the following sentences into Spanish:

1 If we had more personnel we could achieve better results.
2 We need to ask a consultancy for help.
3 Our company would expand into foreign markets if we had a better export policy.
4 Their approach is not very professional.
5 I think it is not a very good idea.

Exercise 6

Read the following advertisements:

Based on the information above, indicate if the following statements are **verdadero** (true) or **falso** (false)

1 **Si quisiera comprar lentes de contacto los encontraría en Óptica Universitaria.**
2 **En la tienda Universo se podrían comprar muebles de caoba.**
3 **Si comprara los lentes de contacto descartables, éstos serían europeos.**
4 **Los domingos a las seis de la tarde sería posible comprar módulos para estantería en la tienda universo.**
5 **La tienda Todatalla no vende ropa de cuero.**
6 **Si quisiera pagar con tarjeta de crédito, la aceptarían en la tienda Todatalla.**
7 **La tienda Universo es un distribuidor.**
8 **Solamente se puede pagar al contado en Todatalla.**
9 **Si quisiera visitar la Óptica Universitaria y la tienda Universo iría a la misma calle.**
10 **Los módulos de Universo son en blanco y negro.**

Reading 📼

Read the following passage and answer these questions:

Where is Honduras?
Are there four well defined seasons during the year?

Honduras

Honduras está situada en América Central. Tiene 112,000 kilómetros cuadrados y limita con tres países: Guatemala, Nicaragua y
El Salvador. Prácticamente sólo hay dos estaciones durante el año:
la época de lluvias y la estación seca. La época de lluvias es de junio
a octubre. Durante esta época del año las temperaturas van de 15°C
en las zonas altas a 30°C en las zonas bajas. Las temperaturas son
más altas en la época seca, que va de noviembre a mayo.

cuadrados	square	**época del año**	time of the year
limita con	has borders with	**época de lluvias**	rainy season
estaciones	seasons		

18 Si hubieras enviado . . .

If you had sent . . .

By the end of this chapter you should be able to:

- Use the pluperfect subjunctive. (e.g. If I had known)
- Use the conditional perfect (e.g. I would have come)
- Use expressions of concession (although, despite, etc.)
- Use **demasiado** + noun (e.g too many problems)
- Use **demasiado** + adjective (e.g. too long, too expensive)

Dialogue 1 ▣

Si hubieras enviado la carta

Juan and Mariela talk about things that should have been done

JUAN: Si hubieras enviado la carta, habrías obtenido la información necesaria. Así no habrías tenido que volver otra vez esta mañana con todos los documentos.

MARIELA: Lo que pasó fue que no tenía la dirección exacta. Si tú me hubieras dado los datos completos, entonces habría podido enviar la carta. ¡Pero faltaba el nombre de la calle! En fin, ya no importa.

JUAN: Discúlpame. Si hubiera notado que faltaba algo, te habría enviado un fax o te habría llamado por teléfono.

MARIELA: Está bien. Todo está resuelto ahora.

Language points

The conditional perfect tense

The verb haber in the conditional tense (habría, habrías, etc.) together with the past participle of the main verb are used to form the conditional perfect tense which is mainly used together with the pluperfect subjunctive in conditional sentences of the third type. Here are the forms of trabajar in the conditional perfect.

habría trabajado	I would have worked
habrías trabajado	you would have worked (informal)
habría trabajado	you would have worked (formal); he/she would have worked
habríamos trabajado	we would have worked
habría trabajado	you would have worked
habrían trabajado	they would have worked

The pluperfect subjunctive

To form the pluperfect subjunctive, you use the imperfect subjunctive of **haber** together with the past participle of the main verb. Here are the forms of **comprar** in the pluperfect subjunctive:

hubiera comprado	I would have bought
hubieras comprado	you would have bought (informal)
hubiera comprado	you would have bought (formal); he/she would have bought
hubiéramos comprado	we would have bought
hubieran comprado	you would have bought
hubieran comprado	they would have bought

As in the case of the imperfect subjunctive, it is possible to use the alternative form -**se**. They are interchangeable.

hubiese comprado	**hubiésemos comprado**
hubieses comprado	**hubiesen comprado**
hubiese comprado	**hubiesen comprado**

Conditional sentences of the third type

The pluperfect subjunctive is used together with the conditional perfect tense to form conditional sentences which refer to conditions that cannot be fulfilled at the time of speaking or conditions which are contrary to fact.

Condition	*Conclusion*
si + pluperfect subjunctive	conditional perfect

Examples:

Si hubiera traído el mapa, habríamos encontrado la ruta.	If I had brought the map, we would have found the route.
Muchas personas habrían muerto en la explosión si no hubiese ocurrido un domingo.	Many people would have died in the explosion if it had not happened on a Sunday.
Si hubiéramos tenido una cámara de video, habríamos grabado durante la fiesta.	If we had had a video camera, we would have recorded the party.

Exercise 1

Change the sentences below as in the example.

Example:

No visité Colombia. (tiempo)
Si hubiera tenido tiempo habría visitado Colombia.

1 **No terminé la pintura. (tiempo)**
2 **No fuimos al teatro. (entradas)**
3 **No compraste el regalo. (suficiente dinero)**
4 **Ustedes no vinieron a la fiesta. (invitación)**
5 **No preparé el informe. (datos necesarios)**

Dialogue 2 ▣

Yo que tú

SIMÓN: Yo que tú no aceptaría esas condiciones.
TERESA: No tengo alternativa. Necesito el préstamo. Si yo fuera
          una persona con un trabajo estable, entonces podría ir al
          banco a solicitar un préstamo.
SIMÓN: Tienes razón. Cuando consigas un trabajo a tiempo com-
          pleto tendrás mayor seguridad económica.
TERESA: Ojalá que sea pronto.

Language point

Yo que tú/usted

Although 'If I were you' can be translated as **Si yo fuera tú/usted**, a
more colloquial form is preferred in everyday speech, **Yo que
tú/usted**. The same applies to a third person, e.g. **Yo que Esteban** 'If
I was Esteban'.

Yo que usted no vendría más a este lugar.	If I were you I would not come back to this place.
Yo que tú lo mandaría por vía aérea.	If I were you I would send it by air mail.

Exercise 2

Match each statement in the group 1 to 10 with a suitable one from
the group (a) to (j).

1 **Me duele el estómago.**
2 **No funciona la linterna.**
3 **He traído un libro para leer durante el viaje.**
4 **La chaqueta le queda chica.**
5 **El modelo es anticuado.**
6 **No había nada de comer.**
7 **¡Cuánta gente!**
8 **Ojalá estuviera Rosana con nosotros.**
9 **Este periódico no tiene mucha información.**
10 **No encuentro la dirección de mi tía María.**

(a) **Deberíamos haber comido en casa.**
(b) **No deberías haber comido tanto.**
(c) **Deberías haber comprado uno más moderno.**
(d) **Una talla más grande habría sido mejor.**
(e) **Ojalá tuviéramos más sillas.**
(f) **Ojalá hubiera traído mi agenda. Por lo menos te podría haber dado su teléfono.**
(g) **Debería haber comprado una revista especializada.**
(h) **Sí. Nos habría ayudado mucho.**
(i) **Deberíamos haber traído más pilas.**
(j) **Si hubieras traído dos me podrías prestar uno.**

Dialogue 3 🔲

Aunque los gráficos son buenos . . .

Sr Sosa and Sr Méndez are discussing the graphics to appear in an advertisement

SR MÉNDEZ: ¿Qué le parece la publicidad que se ha preparado para el producto?

SR SOSA: Aunque los gráficos en el anuncio publicitario son muy buenos, creo que el texto es demasiado largo. Hay que recortarlo.

SR MÉNDEZ: Quizá es largo, pero así recortáramos el texto, habría que incluir suficiente información sobre las especificaciones técnicas del producto. Es un punto muy importante para atraer a los posibles compradores. Es ahí donde tenemos ventajas sobre nuestros competidores.

SR SOSA: Pienso que es cuestión de opinión. Para mí, la imagen dice más que las palabras. Quisiera que estudiases la posibilidad de recortar el texto, digamos en un quince a veinte por ciento.

SR MÉNDEZ: Bueno, a pesar de que ya pasó el plazo para entregar el texto al Departamento de Publicidad de la revista, voy a averiguar si podemos hacer algunos cambios.

Language points

Aunque

This expression of concession is used in a similar way to its English equivalent 'although'. In Spanish it can be followed by a verb in the indicative or in the subjunctive. Generally speaking they are interchangeable.

Aunque los gráficos son buenos, hay demasiado texto.	Although the graphics are good, there is too much text.
Aunque los gráficos sean buenos, hay demasiado texto.	
Aunque el producto es bueno, su presentación es deficiente.	Although the product is good, its presentation is poor.
Aunque el producto sea bueno, su presentación es deficiente.	

A pesar de que

This is another expression of concession which is also similar in use to its English equivalent 'despite the fact that'.

A pesar de que no hay subsidios o incentivos del estado, se ha logrado superar la falta de inversión en el sector de la construcción.	In spite of the fact that there aren't state subsidies or incentives, it has been possible to overcome the lack of investment in the construction sector.
A pesar de que no puede utilizar su brazo derecho, logró rescatar a la niña.	In spite of the fact that she can't use her right arm, she managed to rescue the girl.

Demasiado

When **demasiado** is used as an adjective, meaning 'too much/many', it agrees in number and gender.

Hay demasiadas fallas en esta máquina.	There are too many faults in this machine.
Tenemos demasiados problemas que resolver.	We have too many problems to solve.

When **demasiado** is used as an adverb meaning 'too/too much', it remains the same in all cases.

El texto es demasiado largo.	The text is too long.
Los vehículos todo-terreno son demasiado caros.	All-terrain vehicles are too expensive.
La cotización del dólar es demasiado baja.	The dollar exchange is too low.
Las excavaciones son demasiado profundas.	The excavations are too deep.

Exercise 3

Join the two phrases using **aunque** as in the example.

Example:

Iremos esta tarde. El museo está lejos.
Aunque el museo está lejos, iremos esta tarde.

or

Aunque el museo esté lejos, iremos esta tarde.

No compramos las camisas. Estaban rebajadas.

Aunque estaban rebajadas, no compramos las camisas.

or

Aunque estuvieran rebajadas, no compramos las camisas.

1 Manejó el auto. No tenía licencia de conducir.
2 Pagó al contado. Tenía tarjetas de crédito.
3 Compro en una tiendecita. El supermercado está cerca.
4 Le regaló una loción para después de afeitarse. No se afeita.
5 No contestó. Recibió su carta.
6 Organizó una reunión para la mañana siguiente. Llegaba de madrugada.
7 No es compatible con las demás de la oficina. La computadora es nueva.
8 No le gusta la comida picante. Es latinoamericano.
9 No tiene sistema computarizado. Es el archivo más grande del país.
10 No bajó de peso. Estuvo a dieta todo el año pasado.

Exercise 4

Give Spanish equivalents for the following:

1 There are too many students in this room.
2 Everything is too hot.
3 The temperature is too cold for this time of year.
4 It is too high. She cannot reach.
5 I put too many coins in the machine. It doesn't work.

Exercise 5

Give English equivalents for the following:

1 A pesar de que no tenía dinero, pidió comida cara.
2 Terminamos a pesar de que las condiciones eran negativas.
3 A pesar de sus quejas no recibe ayuda.
4 Visita a sus nietos muy seguido a pesar de tener muchos años.
5 A pesar de las oportunidades que tuvo, nunca triunfó.
6 A pesar de tener un gran reparto, la película no es buena.
7 A pesar de sus problemas de salud, sigue jugando fútbol.
8 No sale a pesar de que el médico se lo aconsejó.
9 A pesar de la lluvia, caminaron toda la tarde.
10 A pesar de tener un sueldo muy alto, siempre pide préstamos.

Dialogue 4 🔲

Suponiendo que . . .

JUAN: Suponiendo que no lleguen, ¿qué hacemos?
MARÍA: Nada. Hay que esperar y luego ya veremos.
JUAN: Yo creía que tú querías resolver las cosas rápido. Me
        parecía que no ibas a esperar.
MARÍA: Cambié de opinión.
JUAN: Así lleguen tarde, sería mejor a que no lleguen.

Language points

Suponiendo que . . .

Supposing . . .

This expression of concession is always followed by the subjunctive.

Suponiendo que esté armado, Supposing he is armed, what
¿qué medidas tomará la action will the police take?
policía?
Eso es suponiendo que That is supposing he was able to
pudiera asistir a la reunión. attend the meeting.

Así

Even if

Apart from its usual use (the equivalent of 'so', 'thus' in English), in
Latin American Spanish **así** can be used as an alternative to **aunque**.

Así lo castiguen, seguirá Even if he is punished, he will con-
creyendo en sus ideales. tinue to believe in his ideals.
No irá, así lo amenacen. He will not go, even if he is threat-
                             ened.

Exercise 6

Give the English equivalent for these phrases.

1 **No responderá a las preguntas, así lo torturen.**
2 **Esperará a su hijo, así llegue muy tarde.**
3 **Iremos, así llueva toda la noche.**
4 **Te avisaríamos, así fuera muy tarde.**
5 **En mi caso te habría telefoneado, así hubiera sido domingo.**

Reading 📼

While reading the passage below, see if you can find answers to these questions:

Is the lack of water going to affect Latin America in the same way as the industrialized countries?
Which sector of the economy is going to suffer most?

Falta de agua

En un futuro cercano será mayor la falta de agua en Latinoamérica. Aunque en Europa y en el resto de los países industrializados el agua disponible por habitante se reducirá en los próximos años, en Latinoamérica esta reducción será más pronunciada. Las sociedades actuales deben detener el derroche existente y la mala utilización de este elemento vital, de lo contrario habrá repercusiones para los distintos sectores económicos, especialmente para la agricultura.

la falta	lack	**sociedades**	societies
disponible	available	**derroche**	waste
se reducirá	will be reduced	**de lo contrario**	otherwise
pronunciada	marked		

19 Ha sido . . .

It has been . . .

By the end of this chapter you should be able to:

- Use the passive voice (e.g. It has been returned)
- Use the impersonal **se** in place of the passive voice
- Distinguish between **pero** and **sino**

Dialogue 1

Han sido entrevistados

While reading the dialogue below, see if you can find the answer to this question:

Do Laura and Eduardo know exactly what happened?

Laura and Eduardo are in their office talking about something in the news

LAURA: ¿Qué sabes del asunto?

EDUARDO: Sólo lo que dice el periódico. Escucha. Han sido entregados dos de los tres expedientes que se perdieron de la oficina. Los directores han sido entrevistados por la policía. Los documentos han sido devueltos esta mañana. No se sabe quién los devolvió.

LAURA: Es un misterio. Vamos a preguntar a tu hermano. Quizás él tenga más noticias.

EDUARDO: Sí, vamos.

Language point

The passive voice

The verb **ser** is used with the past participle to form the passive voice. There is agreement in number and gender with the subject of the verb **ser**. The passive voice is used to put the emphasis on the action taking place rather than on the subject performing the action (as in the active voice).

Los expedientes han sido devueltos.	The dossiers have been returned.
Los trabajadores son llevados en vehículos de la empresa.	The workers are transported in company vehicles.

The following are examples of the passive voice in various tenses.

Present	*Imperfect*
soy llevado	**era llevado**
eres llevado	**eras llevado**
es llevado	**era llevado**
somos llevados	**éramos llevados**
son llevados	**eran llevados**
son llevados	**eran llevados**

El dinero es llevado al banco en cantidades pequeñas.	The money is taken to the bank in small amounts.
Ese día los tres eran llevados a la comisaría.	That day the three of them were being taken to the police station.

Preterite	*Future*
fui llevado	**seré llevado**
fuiste llevado	**serás llevado**
fue llevado	**será llevado**
fuimos llevados	**seremos llevados**
fueron llevados	**serán llevados**
fueron llevados	**serán llevados**

El ataúd fue llevado por sus amigos más íntimos.	The coffin was carried by his closest friends.
Todos seremos llevados a la sala dos.	We will all be taken to room two.

Conditional
sería llevado
serías llevado
sería llevado
seríamos llevados
serían llevados
serían llevados

Present perfect
he sido llevado
has sido llevado
ha sido llevado
hemos sido llevados
han sido llevados
han sido llevados

El cuadro sería llevado al museo si se garantizara la seguridad del transporte.

The painting would be taken to the museum if safe transport could be guaranteed.

Los acusados han sido llevados al tribunal.

The accused have been taken to the court.

Pluperfect
había sido llevado
habías sido llevado
había sido llevado
habíamos sido llevados
habían sido llevados
habían sido llevados

Future perfect
habré sido llevado
habrás sido llevado
habrá sido llevado
habremos sido llevados
habrán sido llevados
habrán sido llevados

Para entonces los artículos robados ya habían sido llevados a otro país.

By then the stolen goods had already been taken to another country.

A principios del próximo siglo las muestras habrán sido llevadas a otro planeta en un laboratorio espacial.

At the beginning of the next century the samples will have been taken to another planet in a space laboratory.

Conditional perfect
habría sido llevado
habrías sido llevado
habría sido llevado
habríamos sido llevados
habrían sido llevados
habrían sido llevados

Nosotros no habríamos sido llevados en ese helicóptero si las autoridades hubieran insistido en realizar más pruebas.

We wouldn't have been taken in that helicopter if the authorities had insisted on carrying out more tests.

The passive construction in continuous tenses, e.g. **estoy siendo llevado**, is not very common.

Exercise 1

Change the sentences to the passive voice.

Example:

> **El alcalde inauguró la feria.**
> **La feria fue inaugurada por el alcalde.**
>
> **Destruyeron la muñeca.**
> **La muñeca fue destruida.**

1 **Construyeron la nueva autopista.**
2 **La municipalidad aplicó la multa.**
3 **El gobierno aprobó el presupuesto.**
4 **La tienda rebajó los precios.**
5 **Terminaron la obra.**
6 **La casa editorial habría publicado la obra.**
7 **Los llevarían a todos a la comisaría.**
8 **El juez habrá interrogado a todos.**
9 **Nos han engañado.**
10 **Un gran número de personas leería el libro.**

Dialogue 2 🔊

Se sabe

Juan is explaining the virtues of a new material in the product he sells

JUAN: Se sabe que este material dura años sin perder color.
ALICIA: ¿Qué se tiene que hacer para mantenerlo limpio?
JUAN: Sólo se necesita pasar un trapo húmedo para limpiarlo y
         ya está.
ALICIA: ¿No se necesita también utilizar un limpiador abrasivo?
JUAN: No es necesario. Un trapo húmedo es suficiente.
ALICIA: Lo probaré.

Language point

The impersonal se

Se is used in spoken Spanish to replace the passive construction
learned above, which is mainly used in written language.

Se sabe que no funciona.	It is known that it doesn't work.
Se espera que compren nuestros productos.	It is expected that they will buy our products.
Se decía que no tenía la información.	It was said that she did not have the information.
Finalmente se ha establecido por qué lo hicieron.	Finally it has been established why they did it.
Creo que se ha decidido que no asistirán al Congreso.	I think it has been decided that they will not attend the conference.

Exercise 2

Give a Spanish equivalent for the following sentences.

1 It has been decided that you will represent the company at the fair.
2 It is said that the competitors are demoralized.
3 It is explained in the leaflet.
4 It was accepted in the end.
5 It has been repeated for the third time.
6 It is known that this product affects the skin.
7 It is sent by post.
8 It is offered to members of the organization.
9 They are given in advance.
10 They will be returned the next day.

Exercise 3

Give an English equivalent for the following sentences.

1 **Se piensa que no habrá aumento de sueldos.**
2 **Se sabe que no llegarán hasta mañana.**
3 **Creo que ahora se entiende la idea.**
4 **Se ha terminado la sesión.**
5 **Primero, el producto se coloca en el interior de la máquina.**
6 **Se acordó durante la última reunión.**
7 **Se simplificarían trámites de exportadores para pagar impuestos.**
8 **El préstamo no se invertirá en obras públicas.**
9 **Se introducirá un nuevo sistema de clasificación.**
10 **La próxima semana se publicarán los nuevos precios del gas industrial.**

Language point

The passive with the subject performing the action

Although the passive construction and the impersonal **se** are interchangeable in the cases introduced above, only the passive construction can be used when the subject who performs the action is mentioned.

La noticia fue revelada a la prensa por el presidente de la comisión.	The news was revealed to the press by the president of the committee.
La mayor inversión fue realizada por el sector de la construcción.	The biggest investment was made by the construction sector.

Exercise 4

Change the sentences from the active to the passive construction.

Examples:

El Rector clausuró el año académico.
El año académico fue clausurado por el Rector.

Los alumnos han organizado la reunión de mañana.
La reunión de mañana ha sido organizada por los alumnos.

1 **La Directora inauguró la exposición sobre comercio exterior.**
2 **Los comerciantes del centro publicarán una nueva revista.**
3 **El distribuidor reemplazará la máquina.**
4 **El Ministerio de Transportes reconstruirá más de cien kilómetros de la carretera al Norte.**
5 **La Compañía de Teléfonos introducirá una nueva gama de productos.**
6 **El Ministerio del Interior ha distribuido la nueva tarjeta de identificación.**
7 **La policía detuvo al delincuente.**
8 **Las empresas extranjeras entregaron el donativo.**
9 **El dueño de la tienda donó una computadora.**
10 **Los hinchas llevaron en hombros al entrenador.**

Dialogue 3 ▣

La puerta estaba abierta

CARLOS: Cuando llegué la puerta ya estaba abierta.
SANDRA: Yo llegué unos momentos antes cuando un empleado estaba abriendo la puerta.
CARLOS: ¿Compraste algo?
SANDRA: Sí la ropa estaba bien rebajada. Compré una blusa para mi hermana y dos para mí.
CARLOS: Estaba convencido de que encontraría algo para Celia, pero al final no compré nada para ella.

Language point

Estaba abierta

When you use the passive with **estar** you usually refer to a state which is the result of an action; the agent of the action (i.e the person who performs the action) is usually not included: e.g. **La puerta estaba abierta** 'The door was open'. When you use the passive with **ser**, you describe the action itself and you can add the agent: **La puerta fue abierta (por el vigilante)** 'The door was opened (by the guard)'.

Exercise 5

Give an English equivalent for the following phrases.

1 **El libro estaba destinado a ser un éxito.**
2 **El libro fue destinado al mercado exterior.**
3 **Julián estaba castigado por no terminar sus deberes.**
4 **Julián fue castigado por su madre.**
5 **Este material es procesado en una máquina muy moderna.**
6 **El alimento ya estaba procesado.**
7 **Los soldados eran instruidos cada mañana.**
8 **Las flores eran cortadas cuidadosamente por las mujeres que trabajaban allí.**
9 **Las flores estaban cortadas.**
10 **La capital fue atacada por tropas extranjeras.**

Dialogue 4 🔘

Es cara, pero es buena

Cecilia and Rosa are discussing the washing instructions on a label

CECILIA: Esta blusa es cara, pero el material es bueno.
ROSA: Es un material muy durable, pero también delicado. Cuando se ensucie no lo pongas en la lavadora sino lávalo a mano.
CECILIA: ¿Por qué?
ROSA: Acá dice en la etiqueta: 'Lavarse a mano'. Lo que pasa es que si no lo lavas a mano puede perder su forma o color en la lavadora.
CECILIA: Muy bien. Habrá que lavarlo a mano.

Language point

Pero/sino

The two words **pero** and **sino** mean 'but' in English. It is important to understand the difference in Spanish.

Sabe nadar, pero no va a la piscina muy seguido.	She can swim, but she doesn't go to the swimming pool very often.
No quiere nadar, sino bucear.	He doesn't want to swim, he wants to dive.

Pero is used to contrast the first statement but it does not contradict it. **Sino**, however, contradicts the first statement. Here are some more examples:

Quisiera ir a la fiesta, pero no puedo.	I would like to go to the party, but I can't.
No pedí vino tinto, sino blanco.	I did not order red wine, but white.

Exercise 6

Give a Spanish equivalent for the following phrases:

1 I do not want cheese, but ham.
2 She doesn't have a house now, but perhaps next year she will.
3 They do not have a cat, but a dog.

4 We do not want a single, but a return ticket.
5 He has gone to Mexico, but I do not know when he will be back.

Language point

Si no

This expression – written as two words – must not be confused with
the one discussed above. In this case the meaning is 'if not', as in the
following examples:

Debes pagar la cuenta de la luz, si no te la cortan.	You must pay the electricity bill, if not you will be cut off.
Tiene que cuidarse, si no se va a enfermar.	You have to look after yourself, if not you'll fall ill.

Reading 📟

Argentina

Argentina cuenta con una población de más de 30 millones de habitantes. Es uno de los países con el más alto ingreso por habitante en Latinoamérica. El índice de alfabetismo (94%) es el más alto de América Latina. El país está situado en la zona templada, pero es posible hallar todo tipo de climas, desde el tropical en el norte, hasta el muy frío en las zonas altas andinas, en la Patagonia y en la Tierra del Fuego. La mayoría de la población argentina vive en las ciudades y casi la mitad del total de la población vive en la Provincia de Buenos Aires.

ingreso	income	**la mayoría**	most of, the majority
índice de alfabetismo	literacy rate		

Exercise 7

Based on the reading passage above, say if the following statements are **verdadero** (true) or **falso** (false).

1 **Argentina es uno de los países más pobres de América Latina.**
2 **Tiene el mayor número de alfabetos en América Latina.**
3 **Sólo hay clima templado en su territorio.**
4 **La mayoría de la población es rural.**
5 **Casi un cincuenta por ciento de la población vive en la Provincia de Buenos Aires.**

20 Repaso

Review

Dialogue 1 📼

Fui al cine

Sara and Pablo are talking about what they like to do

SARA: ¿Qué hiciste ayer?

PABLO: Fui al cine a ver una película francesa. Luego compré una revista para leer en el tren mientras volvía a casa.

SARA: ¿De qué se trata la revista?

PABLO: Trata de asuntos de actualidad.

SARA: ¿Es interesante?

PABLO: Sí. La compro todas las semanas. ¿Tú lees mientras viajas?

SARA: Sí, pero prefiero escuchar la radio.

PABLO: ¿Qué programas te gustan?

SARA: Me gusta un programa periodístico que se llama 'Primera Plana', otro que se llama 'Competencia' y es de deportes. También escucho el programa 'De noche' que es cultural, educativo y de servicio. El programa que más me gusta es 'Los 40 mejores'.

PABLO: ¿Qué tipo de programa es?

SARA: Es de música del momento.

PABLO: Sí, claro. Yo a veces lo escucho.

Exercise 1

Change these sentences to the preterite using the information in brackets.

Example:

Compro una revista de deportes. (ayer)
Ayer compré una revista de deportes.

1 Veo un programa de televisión. (anoche)
2 Marcelo y Estela diseñan interiores para una firma conocida. (el año pasado)
3 Cecilia imita a varios personajes en la tele. (el sábado pasado)
4 La telenovela 'Adoración' se transmite los viernes. (ayer)
5 El servicio de limpieza es criticado siempre. (ayer)
6 Siempre pierde las carreras. (el sábado pasado)
7 Pochita juega todos los domingos. (ayer y anteayer)
8 Leonardo no come en casa. (anoche)
9 El líder sindical organiza una reunión de trabajadores todos los meses. (el viernes pasado)
10 Steven viaja los lunes. (hace dos horas)

Exercise 2

Match the phrases 1 to 10 with the phrases (a) to (j).

1 El Código Alimentario establece . . .
2 En la foto de grupo . . .
3 La jueza . . .
4 Un coche-bomba . . .
5 Parecen iguales, . . .
6 Lo que necesitan los estudiantes . . .
7 El multimillonario pagó . . .
8 Hay un automóvil . . .
9 La comida que preparó Karina . . .
10 Ha bajado . . .

(a) cuatro kilos.
(b) denunció al ministro.
(c) pero no lo son.
(d) que hay tres clases de agua para el consumo humano.
(e) fue deliciosa.
(f) explotó en el museo.
(g) como primer premio.
(h) aparece junto a sus compañeros de escuela.
(i) para sus trabajos de investigación.
(j) muchos millones de dólares por el cuadro del pintor holandés.

Dialogue 2 🔲

¿Vas a ir al teatro?

While reading the dialogue below, see if you can find answers to these questions:

> Do both want to go to the same place?
> Why does Estela refuse Germán's invitation to go to the movies?

Estela and Germán are talking about going to the theater or movies

ESTELA:	¿Vas a ir al teatro?
GERMÁN:	No. No me gusta la obra. Creo que iré al cine.
ESTELA:	Pero tú dijiste que querías ir al teatro.
GERMÁN:	No dije cuándo. Hoy no puedo. Quizás el próximo fin de semana.
ESTELA:	Quizás yo no pueda el próximo fin de semana.
GERMÁN:	¿Por qué no vas al cine conmigo?
ESTELA:	¿Esta noche?
GERMÁN:	Sí. Esta noche. Es una película francesa.
ESTELA:	Creo que no. Va a venir Irene y creo que ella también quiere ir al teatro. Iremos juntas.
GERMÁN:	Bueno. Nos vemos luego.
ESTELA:	Chao.

Exercise 3

Match the phrases in 1 to 5 with the phrases (a) to (e).

1 **Voy a llegar tarde a la reunión.**
2 **Estaremos en el centro mañana.**
3 **Ayer compramos un nuevo juego de muebles.**
4 **Se ha dislocado el brazo.**
5 **Hace frío.**

(a) **Hay que llevarla al hospital.**
(b) **Ponte una chaqueta.**
(c) **No hay problema. Se ha postergado para mañana.**
(d) **¿Es de roble o caoba?**
(e) **Yo también. Tengo que hacer compras.**

Exercise 4

Give Spanish equivalents for the following sentences:

1 I wish you had not brought that book.
2 Let's hope Sharon has brought the same one.
3 If I were you I would send the money tomorrow.
4 If I were Sharon I would go there tonight.
5 If only I had enough time to visit all the museums and exhibitions in this city.

Dialogue 3 🔊

¿Qué software tienes?

Irene is asking Fernando about the software he has in his computer. Do they both have to pay to access the Internet?

IRENE: ¿Qué software tienes?

FERNANDO: Tengo precesador de texto, hoja de cálculo, gráficos, microedición, base de datos, paquete de presentación. Si hago click aquí, hay un enlace directo a mi correo electrónico. Por este atajo llego a la página *web* para mandar tarjetas virtuales.

IRENE: O sea, ya tienes Internet.

FERNANDO: Ahora sí tengo porque hay tarifa plana de teléfono.

Además, mi acceso a Internet por este portal es gratuito.

IRENE: Yo, en cambio, pago unos 15 dólares al mes por el servicio.

Exercise 5

Choose the correct form of the verb in brackets.

1 **Es posible que (vendrá/venga) mañana.**
2 **Le han recomendado que (viva/vive) en el campo.**
3 **¿Le (guste/gustaría) ir al cine esta noche o preferiría (quedarse/quedará) en casa?**
4 **Es importante que (coma/comería) fruta.**
5 **Me parece que no (tiene/tenga) plata para comprar el helado.**
6 **El televisor (no funciona/no funcione).**
7 **No creo que (coman/comen) en un restaurante de mariscos porque son vegetarianos.**
8 **Ojalá (llega/llegue) pronto.**
9 **Si (viene/venga) dale este dinero.**
10 **El médico le ha recomendado que (viajará/viaje) al campo.**

Exercise 6

Choose the correct form of the verb in brackets.

1 **Si (estaba/estuviera) en Cancún (estaría/estaré) en la playa y no en la cocina preparando la comida.**
2 **Mañana (estaremos/estuviéramos) en Río de Janeiro. Parece un sueño.**
3 **Ojalá (haya traído/trajo) el programa de actividades.**
4 **Caroline (trajo/trajese) el manual ayer, pero no sé dónde lo dejó.**
5 **Si la tienda (estuvo/estuviese) en el centro iríamos a pie en vez de ir en carro.**
6 **Quisiera (ser/fuese) diplomático para conocer varios países.**
7 **Quisiera que (ser/fuese) sábado, no lunes entonces no tendría que ir a trabajar.**
8 **Le dije que no podía continuar con el trabajo, a menos que (comiera/comerá) algo primero.**
9 **Esteban no (saldrá/saliera) al extranjero este mes porque tiene mucho que hacer en la empresa. Quizás (saliera/salga) el mes**

que viene.
10 Si (podría/pudiera) te visitaría.

Exercise 7

Choose the phrase in the group (a) to (j) that best completes the
sentence started in the group 1 to 10.

1 **Ralph tiene un suéter . . .**
2 **La revista dedica . . .**
3 **Muchos padres invierten . . .**
4 **La década del 90 . . .**
5 **El secretario se llama . . .**
6 **Los colegios no dicen . . .**
7 **El próximo mes . . .**
8 **Yo . . . es todo.**
9 **Estas son las obras . . .**
10 **Hay mucha preocupación . . .**

(a) **. . . tiempo y dinero en la educación de sus hijos.**
(b) **. . . de teatro más vistas este año.**
(c) **. . . tejido de lana de alpaca.**
(d) **. . . sus páginas al automovilismo.**
(e) **. . . Antonio Suárez.**
(f) **. . . por el medio ambiente.**
(g) **. . . creo que saldremos de vacaciones.**
(h) **. . . creo que eso**
(i) **. . . cuándo empezará el año escolar.**
(j) **. . . fue la última de este siglo.**

Exercise 8

Complete the sentence with a preposition from the list, if it is necessary.

| desde | a | para | de | en |
| por | hasta | abajo de/debajo de | durante |

1 **Se casaron _____ el mes pasado.**
2 **Hoy estamos a 21 _____ septiembre.**
3 **Voy a la escuela _____ la mañana.**
4 **Caracas, 22 _____ enero _____ 1994.**
5 **La tienda abre _____ las diez _____ las siete.**

6 Terminarán el edificio _____ fines de mes.
7 Faltan muchos días _____ el fin _____ año.
8 No estaba sobre la mesa sino _____ de ésta.
9 He trabajado _____ dos días seguidos y necesito un descanso.
10 Estaré con ustedes _____ verano.

Exercise 9

Rearrange the following words in three groups under the headings
fruta (fruit), **viajes** (travelling) and **colores** (colors).

bicicleta	**azul**	**negro**
manzana	**barco**	**amarillo**
ciclomotor	**plátano**	**sandía**
verde	**vuelo**	**carro**
frutilla	**piña**	**rojo**

Exercise 10

Match each of the questions 1 to 5 with the most suitable reply (a)
to (e).

1 ¿Adónde vas tan apurada?
2 ¿Quién es esa persona que te dio la llave?
3 ¿Cómo piensas ir a la universidad esta tarde?
4 ¿No te parece que ya es demasiado tarde para ir al teatro?
5 ¿Cuándo llegan tus padres?

(a) **Creo que Marcelo va a llevarme en su auto; de lo contrario iré
en el metro.**
(b) **La Sra Taboada. Ella es la dueña del hotel. Es un negocio de
familia.**
(c) **Hay dos posibilidades: una es a fines de este mes. Otra, a media-
dos del próximo.**
(d) **Esta noche la función empieza media hora más tarde que de
costumbre, así que llegaremos a tiempo.**
(e) **Al colegio a recoger a los chicos.**

Reading

Read the following text from an advertisement for a private ambu-
lance service.

MEDIC-MOVIL

Medic es un servicio de atención médica especializada. Sus unidades móviles cuentan con equipos de atención y resucitación que operan en toda la capital.

Si usted o uno de sus trabajadores sufre una emergencia médica, llame a nuestro teléfono y de inmediato un operador u operadora con conocimientos médicos se pondrá en comunicación por radio a la unidad móvil más cercana al lugar donde se encuentre el paciente.

Si está interesado llámenos por teléfono y nuestro representante lo visitará a la brevedad posible para darle mayor información.

Informes: 442255

Exercise 11

Based on the reading text above, say if the following statements are **verdadero** (true) or **falso** (false).

1 **Medic es un servicio de ambulancias que opera en todo el país.**
2 **El servicio es sólo para ejecutivos.**
3 **Los operadores se comunican por radio con las unidades móviles.**
4 **Los operadores tratan de ubicar la unidad móvil más cercana al paciente.**
5 **Para mayor información hay que ir personalmente a Médic-móvil.**

Exercise 12

Complete the sentences with the correct form of **ser** or **estar**.

1 **El taller _____ en la calle Emancipación.**
2 **_____ abogado (yo).**
3 **La niña _____ molesta.**
4 **¿_____ (ustedes) en la casa de mi hermana?**
5 **Estela y Lucrecia _____ obreras.**
6 **Guayaquil _____ en Ecuador.**
7 **El autor del libro _____ en Colombia.**
8 **El banco _____ cerrado.**
9 **No _____ representantes sino distribuidores (nosotros).**
10 **No _____ en su despacho (ella).**

Exercise 13

Change these commands to the negative.

Example:

Compren frutillas.
No compren frutillas.

1 **Vayan a la reunión.**
2 **Llama por teléfono a tu jefe.**
3 **Trata de vender tu carro.**
4 **Abra el archivo para ver.**
5 **Copien el documento en diskette.**
6 **Pide diez cuadernos.**
7 **Ven con tu novio.**
8 **Tome fotos.**
9 **Prepare el plato que le recomendé.**
10 **Instala la antena.**

Exercise 14

Rewrite these sentences in the imperative. Follow the examples.

Examples:

Ustedes deben venir mañana.
Vengan mañana.

Tienes que decir cuál es el problema.
Di cuál es el problema.

1 **Ustedes deben comprar una nueva máquina.**
2 **Tienes que oir lo que dice este señor.**
3 **Tiene que venir el próximo sábado.**
4 **Usted debe mandar el paquete por correo.**
5 **Debes escribir pronto.**
6 **Tienes que comer menos grasas.**
7 **Ustedes deben estudiar este contrato.**
8 **Tienes que hacer esto.**
9 **Usted debe ser más paciente.**
10 **Tienes que subir al tercer piso.**

Reading 🔲

Read the information about Maribel Hernández and then fill in the form which follows.

Maribel Hernández tiene 39 años. Está separada de su esposo. Es profesora en una escuela primaria en las afueras de Quito. Maribel tiene dos hijos que se llaman Alberto y Estela. Alberto tiene 11 años y Estela tiene 8 años. Viven en un departamento en la calle Iglesias 341 – C. El departamento tiene dos dormitorios. Uno es de Maribel, los niños comparten el otro. Alberto y Estela ayudan a su mami en las tareas de la casa.

Nombre:	
Edad:	
Estado civil:	
Ocupación:	
Nº de hijos:	
Nombre de los hijos:	
Edad de los hijos:	
Domicilio:	

Exercise 15

Based on the passage above, say if the following statements are **verdadero** (true) or **falso** (false).

1 **Estela no tiene hermanos.**
2 **Los niños no ayudan a Maribel en las tareas de la casa.**
3 **Estela es menor que Alberto.**
4 **Viven en la capital ecuatoriana.**
5 **Tienen un departamento de dos dormitorios.**

HORIZONTAL

1 Primer nivel de educación.
6 Aplicación de las ciencias prácticas o mecánicas en la industria y el comercio.
8 País latinoamericano.
9 Uno diferente. Uno más.

VERTICAL

1 Fruta.
2 Lo contrario de activo.
3 Lo contrario de bajo.
4 Hay muchos en las calles, carreteras y autopistas.
5 País latinoamericano de la zona andina.
6 Normalmente hay mucha en el centro de una ciudad.

Grammar summary

The Spanish alphabet

a	a	**n**	ene
b	be (alta, grande)	**ñ**	eñe
c	ce	**o**	o
ch	che	**p**	pe
d	de	**q**	cu
e	e	**r**	erre
f	efe	**s**	ese
g	ge	**t**	te
h	hache	**u**	u
i	i (latina)	**v**	ve (corta, chica)
j	jota	**w**	ve doble
k	ka	**x**	equis
l	ele	**y**	y griega
ll	elle	**z**	zeta
m	eme		

Stress and written accent

If the word ends in a vowel, **-n** or **-s** the stress is on the penultimate syllable, i.e. the syllable before the last one.

tra*ba*jo
es*cri*bes
dele*ga*do
***Car*men**

If the word ends in a consonant, except **-n** or **-s**, the stress is on the final syllable.

pa*pel*
co*lor*
ciu*dad*

When there is a deviation from these rules an acute accent is written on the vowel of the stressed syllable.

ac*á*
lat*ón*
pac*í***fico**

Word order

Word order (position of the subject in relation to the object of a sentence) is not as rigid in Spanish as it is in English. The most common patterns are:

subject + verb + object
Mariela vendió la casa.

object + verb + subject
La casa la vendió Mariela.

object + subject + verb
La casa Mariela la vendió.

In most cases adjectives are placed after the noun they qualify. In negative sentences **no** always precedes the verb.

Nouns and gender

Nouns in Spanish are either masculine or feminine. Not only people and animals are included in this classification, but things as well.

masc.		*fem.*	
hombre	man	**mujer**	woman
gato	male cat	**gata**	female cat
sol	sun	**luna**	moon

Generally speaking, the ending of a noun tells you whether it is masculine or feminine. The following are the most common endings.

Masculine: **-o**, **-l**, **-r**, **-y**; e.g. **alumno**, **papel**, **actor**, **rey**.

Feminine: **-a**, **-ión**, **-dad**, **-tad**, **-tud**, **-itis**; e.g. **alumna**, **canción**, **ciudad**, **libertad**, **altitud**, **artritis**.

Usually when the masculine ends in **-o**, you form the feminine by changing it to **-a**.

alumno   **alumna**

Usually when the masculine ends in a consonant, you form the feminine by adding **-a**.

vendedor   **vendedora**

Some nouns are both masculine and feminine but with a difference in meaning, as in the following examples:

el capital the capital (money)   **la capital** the capital (city)

el policía the police officer   **la policía** the police

Plural of nouns

When a noun ends in an **unstressed vowel** or a stressed **-e**, an **-s** is added

Examples:

niña   niñas
café   cafés

When a noun ends in a **consonant**, **-y** or a **stressed vowel** (except **-e**), **-es** is added

Examples:

pared   pared**es**
cuy   cuy**es**
rubí   rubí**es**

Note: There are exceptions to this third case (stressed vowel, other than **-e**). The most common exceptions are: mamá–mamás; papá–papás

Nouns ending in **-z** change the -z to **-e**, before adding **-es**

Examples:

luz   luc**es**
cruz   cruc**es**

Articles

The definite article

	masc.	fem.	
sing.	**el**	**la**	the
pl.	**los**	**las**	the

The definite article agrees in gender and number with the noun it precedes.

el carro	the car	**los carros**	the cars
la casa	the house	**las casas**	the houses

Note: if the definite article precedes a singular feminine noun which starts with a stressed a- or ha-, then **el** is used instead of **la**.

el agua	the water
el haba	the broad bean

The indefinite article

	masc.	fem.	
sing.	**un**	**una**	a/an
pl.	**unos**	**unas**	some

The indefinite article agrees in gender and number with the noun it precedes.

un gato	a cat	**una gata**	a jack
unos libros	some books	**unas libras**	some pounds

The neuter article

The neuter article **lo** never precedes a noun. Its main use is to form abstract nouns. In this case it is followed by an adjective or a past participle.

lo interesante	what is interesting
lo dicho	what has been said

Adjectives

Almost all adjectives agree in gender and number with the noun or pronoun they refer to.

When the adjective ends in -**o** the feminine is usually formed by changing the final letter to -**a**.

distribuidor exclusivo	sole distributor
moda exclusiva	exclusive fashion

Adjectives ending in a consonant usually add -**a**.

activador	**activadora**	activating
francés	**francesa**	French

Although the usual position of the adjective in a sentence is after the noun, it can appear before it.

una casa nueva	**una nueva casa**	a new house

Plural of adjectives

When an adjective ends in a vowel you add -**s** to form the plural, unless the final vowel is stressed, in which case you add -**es**.
When it ends in a consonant you add -**es**.

un médico peruano	a Peruvian doctor
médicos peruanos	Peruvian doctors
una palabra guaraní	a Guarani word
dos palabras guaraníes	two Guarani words
una solución fácil	an easy solution
soluciones fáciles	easy solutions

Demonstrative adjectives

These adjectives agree in number and in gender with the noun and usually precede it.

	masc.	*fem.*	
sing.	**este**	**esta**	this
	ese	**esa**	that
	aquel	**aquella**	that (distant)

pl.	estos	estas	these
	esos	esas	those
	aquellos	aquellas	those (distant)

Possessive adjectives

Possessive adjectives agree in number with the noun which they precede. Only **nuestro** (our) has a feminine form, **nuestra**, which agrees in number and gender with the noun.

mi	my
tu	your (sing.)
su	his, her, its, your (formal)
nuestro	our (masc.)
nuestra	our (fem.)
su	your (pl.)
su	their

Examples:

mi cuaderno de ejercicios	my exercise book
su diccionario bilingüe	her bilingual dictionary

If the noun possessed is in the plural you add an -**s** to the possessive adjective.

Mis amigos no han llegado.	My friends haven't arrived.
Nuestras empresas firmaron el contrato.	Our companies signed the contract.

Personal pronouns

These pronouns are used far less than their equivalents in English. Sometimes they are used for emphasis or to avoid confusion.

Singular		Plural	
yo	I	**nosotros**	we (masc.)
tú	you (informal)	**nosotras**	we (fem.)
usted	you (formal)	**ustedes**	you
él	he	**ellos**	they (masc.)
ella	she	**ellas**	they (fem.)

Adverbs

These are usually formed by adding the ending -**mente** to the feminine adjective. Note that adjectives ending in -**e** have the same form in the masculine and the feminine.

lento	**lentamente**	slowly
sincero	**sinceramente**	sincerely
urgente	**urgentemente**	urgently

When an adverb appears with a verb in the same sentence, it usually follows the verb. It can precede the verb for emphasis.

| **Se dirigieron a la escuela lentamente.** | They made their way to school slowly. |
| **Lentamente pasaron uno por uno.** | They slowly went past one by one. |

Prepositions

These link parts of a sentence and usually express manner, time or place:

a	to, at	**ante**	before
en	in, on, at	**bajo**	under
de	of, from	**delante de**	in front of
desde	from	**detrás de**	behind
hacia	towards	**encima**	over
por	for, by, through	**entre**	between
para	for	**sobre**	on

Verbs

The infinitive

The infinitive is the form of a verb given in a dictionary. It is also the form that you will find in the glossary of this book. According to the ending of the infinitive there are three types of verbs in Spanish:

verbs ending in -**ar**	also called verbs of the first conjugation
verbs ending in -**er**	also called verbs of the second conjugation
verbs ending in -**ir**	also called verbs of the third conjugation

Examples:

-ar	**comprar**	to buy
	trabajar	to work
	estudiar	to study
-er	**comer**	to eat
	vender	to sell
	comprender	to understand
-ir	**vivir**	to live
	escribir	to write
	subir	to go up

The present tense indicative

The present tense indicative is used with actions which are habitual or timeless.

Examples:

Siempre voy en tren.	I always go by train.
Martha es peruana.	Martha is Peruvian.

Here are three examples of regular verbs in the present tense indicative: **trabajar** (to work), **comer** (to eat) and **escribir** (to write).

trabajo	I work
trabajas	you work (informal)
trabaja	you work (formal); he/she works
trabajamos	we work
trabajan	you work (formal and informal)
trabajan	they work

como	**comemos**	**escribo**	**escribimos**
comes	**comen**	**escribes**	**escriben**
come	**comen**	**escribe**	**escriben**

Irregular verbs

Some verbs do not follow the pattern or rule of regular verbs. For that reason they are called *irregular*. Here is one example: **tener**.

tengo	I have
tienes	you have (informal)

tiene	you have (formal); he/she/it has
tenemos	we have
tienen	you have
tienen	they have

Forming questions

Both regular and irregular verbs form questions by adding question marks to affirmative and negative statements. When speaking you sound as if you are asking a question. Unlike English, you do not need an auxiliary word like 'do'.

Trabajan mucho.	They work hard.
¿Trabajan mucho?	Do they work hard?
No tienes tiempo.	You do not have time.
¿No tienes tiempo?	Don't you have time?

Radical changing verbs

These are verbs in Spanish which undergo a change of the stem vowel (i.e. the vowel in the part of the verb that remains the same when it is conjugated) when you conjugate them. In these verbs the vowel -**e**- in the stem becomes -**ie**-, and the vowel -**o**- becomes -**ue**-. The exception is the first person plural.

Examples:

-**e**- → -**ie**-	-**o**- → -**ue**-
preferir	**dormir**
prefiero	**duermo**
prefieres	**duermes**
prefiere	**duerme**
preferimos	**dormimos**
prefieren	**duermen**
prefieren	**duermen**

The present continuous tense

The present continuous tense is formed by using **estar** + the gerund form of the verb. The gerund ends in -**ando** or -**iendo** (-**ando** for -**ar** verbs; **-iendo** for **-er** and **-ir** verbs.) The forms correspond to the English ending '-ing', as in 'eating', 'running', etc.

estoy estudiando	I am studying
estás estudiando	you are studying (informal)
está estudiando	you are studying (formal); he/she is studying
estamos estudiando	we are studying
están estudiando	you are studying (formal and informal)
están estudiando	they are studying

The present continuous refers to an action which is in progress at the time of speaking.

The present perfect tense

The present perfect tense is formed by the auxiliary verb **haber** and the past participle of the main verb of the sentence.

Example:

He perdido mi maletín.   I have lost my briefcase.

The forms of **haber** are:

he	I have
has	you have (informal)
ha	you have (formal); he/she has
hemos	we have
han	you have (plural)
han	they have

You form the past participle of a verb by replacing the infinitive ending **-ar** by the ending **-ado**, and the endings **-er** and **-ir** by **-ido**.

trabajar	**trabajado**
comer	**comido**
vivir	**vivido**

The most common irregular past participles are:

abrir (to open)	**abierto**
decir (to say)	**dicho**
escribir (to write)	**escrito**
hacer (to do, to make)	**hecho**
morir (to die)	**muerto**

poner (to put)	**puesto**
romper (to break)	**roto**
ver (to see)	**visto**
volver (to return)	**vuelto**

The present perfect is used to indicate that an event has happened in a period of time in the past but which includes the present or whose effects still bear on the present.

The present perfect continuous

This tense is used to indicate that an action has been in progress over a period of time and continues to be in progress at the time of speaking. It is formed by using **haber** plus the past participle plus the gerund, i.e. the verb showing action in progress, (e.g. **escribiendo** 'writing', **viajando** 'traveling'.

Example:

Hemos estado trabajando	We have been working on this
todo el día en este asunto.	matter all day.

ir a + infinitive

One way of expressing the future is by using the present tense of the verb **ir** (to go) followed by **a** plus the infinitive expressing the intended action. This is similar to the English structure 'to be going to + infinitive'.

Example:

Vamos a visitar el museo.	We are going to visit the museum.

Here are all the forms of the verb **ir + a**:

voy a	I am going to
vas a	you are going to (informal)
va a	you are going to (formal) he/she/it is going to
vamos a	we are going to
van a	you are going to
van a	they are going to

The past tense or preterite

The past tense, or preterite, is used to express an action in the past already complete at the time of speaking.

Example:

Ayer comimos en un   Yesterday we went to a restaurant
restaurante.   for a meal.

The past tense of regular verbs is formed as follows:
-**ar** verbs: **terminar** (to finish)

termin*é*	I finished
terminaste	you finished (informal)
termin*ó*	you finished (formal); he/she/it finished
terminamos	we finished
terminaron	you finished
terminaron	they finished

-**er** verbs: **comer**

com*í*	**comimos**
comiste	**comieron**
com*ió*	**comieron**

-**ir** verbs: **vivir**

viv*í*	**vivimos**
viviste	**vivieron**
viv*ió*	**vivieron**

Here are some examples of irregular verbs in the past:

hacer	**ir**	**tener**	**dar**
hice	**fui**	**tuve**	**di**
hiciste	**fuiste**	**tuviste**	**diste**
hizo	**fue**	**tuvo**	**dio**
hicimos	**fuimos**	**tuvimos**	**dimos**
hicieron	**fueron**	**tuvieron**	**dieron**
hicieron	**fueron**	**tuvieron**	**dieron**

The future tense

To form the future of regular verbs you add the same endings to the infinitive of all -**ar**, -**er** or -**ir** verbs.

trabajar	comer	vivir
trabajaré	comeré	viviré
trabajarás	comerás	vivirás
trabajará	comerá	vivirá
trabajaremos	comeremos	viviremos
trabajarán	comerán	vivirán
trabajarán	comerán	vivirán

The future tense is used mainly in written language. In conversation the future tense is less common than its equivalent in English. Spanish speakers tend to prefer the '**ir** + **a** + verb' structure to express ideas in the future.

Here are some irregular verbs in the future:

decir	hacer	salir	venir
diré	haré	saldré	vendré
dirás	harás	saldrás	vendrás
dirá	hará	saldré	vendrá
diremos	haremos	saldremos	vendremos
dirán	harán	saldrán	vendrán
dirán	harán	saldrán	vendrán

The imperfect indicative tense

The imperfect tense is used to indicate a habitual or repeated action in the past. It is the equivalent of verbs with 'used to' or 'was' in English.

Example:

Los fines de semana nos reuníamos en grupos.   We used to gather in groups at the weekends.

It is also used to describe characteristics in the past when such characteristics continued to exist for a period of time.

Example:

La gata se llamaba Magdalena.   The cat used to be called/was called Magdalena.

Regular verbs have their forms in the imperfect indicative as follows:

comprar	vender	vivir
compraba	vendía	vivía
comprabas	vendías	vivías
compraba	vendía	vivía
comprábamos	vendíamos	vivíamos
compraban	vendían	vivían
compraban	vendían	vivían

There are only three verbs which are irregular in the imperfect indicative:

ir	ser	ver
iba	era	veía
ibas	eras	veías
iba	era	veía
íbamos	éramos	veíamos
iban	eran	veían
·iban	eran	veían

The imperfect continuous tense

This tense is used to refer to an action already in progress in the past when something else happened, interrupting the first action.

Example:

Estaba escuchando música cuando sonó el timbre.   I was listening to music when the bell rang.

In the imperfect continuous you use the verb **estar** in the imperfect indicative together with the continuous form of the main verb.

trabajar

estaba trabajando	I was working
estabas trabajando	you were working (informal)
estaba trabajando	you were working (formal); he/she was working
estábamos trabajando	we were working

| estaban trabajando | you were working (formal and informal) |
| estaban trabajando | they were working |

The present subjunctive

The subjunctive is a verb form used in Spanish to express attitude, such as wishing, hoping, doubting, etc., and to indicate actions which are only hypothetical or a possibility in the future, at the moment of speaking. It is little used in English.

Examples:

| **Espero que puedas venir a la fiesta.** | I hope you can make it to the party. |
| **Quisiera que ayudes a Isabel.** | I would like you to help Isabel. |

The present subjunctive of regular verbs is formed as follows:

trabajar	comer	vivir
trabaje	coma	viva
trabajes	comas	vivas
trabaje	coma	viva
trabajemos	comamos	vivamos
trabajen	coman	vivan
trabajen	coman	vivan

The conditional tense

The conditional tense (in English 'I would go', etc.) is formed by adding the following endings to the infinitive: -ía, -ías, -ía, -íamos, -ían. The same endings are used with the three conjugations.

trabajar	comer	vivir
trabajaría	comería	viviría
trabajarías	comerías	vivirías
trabajaría	comería	viviría
trabajaríamos	comeríamos	viviríamos
trabajarían	comerían	vivirían
trabajarían	comerían	vivirían

Here is a list of the main irregular verbs in the conditional tense:

decir	haber	hacer
diría	habría	haría
dirías	habrías	harías
diría	habría	haría
diríamos	habríamos	haríamos
dirían	habrían	harían
dirían	habrían	harían

poder	poner	querer
podría	pondría	querría
podrías	pondrías	querrías
podría	pondría	querría
podríamos	pondríamos	querríamos
podrían	pondrían	querrían
podrían	pondrían	querrían

salir	tener	venir
saldría	tendría	vendría
saldrías	tendrías	vendrías
saldría	tendría	vendría
saldríamos	tendríamos	vendríamos
saldrían	tendrían	vendrían
saldrían	tendrían	vendrían

The imperative

The imperative form is used to give commands, orders or instructions.

Examples:

| **Prepare un informe para mañana. (usted)** | Prepare a report for tomorrow. |
| **Toma estas pastillas. (tú)** | Take these tablets. |

The imperative for the second person singular informal (**tú**) is the same as the form for the third person singular in the present indicative, in the case of regular verbs.

preparar	**prepar*a***
comer	**com*e***
subir	**sub*e***

The most frequently used irregular verbs in the imperative for the second person informal (**tú**) are:

decir	**di**	**salir**	**sal**
estar	**está**	**ser**	**sé**
hacer	**haz**	**tener**	**ten**
ir	**ve**	**venir**	**ven**
oír	**oye**		

The imperative for the second person singular formal (**usted**) is the same as the present subjunctive for **usted**, **él** or **ella**.

preparar	**prepare**
comer	**coma**
subir	**suba**

The imperative for the second person plural (**ustedes**) is the same as the present subjunctive for **ustedes**, **ellos** or **ellas**.

preparar	**preparen**
comer	**coman**
subir	**suban**

The imperfect subjunctive

The imperfect subjunctive indicates actions which are hypothetical and also remote possibilities at the time of speaking. Compared to the present subjunctive, the action is less likely to take place. One use of the imperfect subjunctive is for sentences expressing hope. Another is in hypothetical conditional sentences.

Ojalá llamase.

The imperfect subjunctive has two alternative conjugations, which are interchangeable. Here is an example of a regular verb, **trabajar**, in the two forms of the imperfect subjunctive:

trabajara	**trabajase**
trabajaras	**trabajases**
trabajara	**trabajase**
trabajáramos	**trabajásemos**
trabajaran	**trabajasen**
trabajaran	**trabajasen**

The conditional perfect tense

The verb **haber** in the conditional tense (**habría**, **habrías**, etc.) together with the past participle of the main verb are used to form the conditional perfect tense. Here are the forms of **trabajar** in the conditional perfect:

habría trabajado	I would have worked
habrías trabajado	you would have worked (informal)
habría trabajado	you would have worked (formal); he/she would have worked
habríamos trabajado	we would have worked
habrían trabajado	you would have worked
habrían trabajado	they would have worked

The pluperfect subjunctive

To form the pluperfect subjunctive, you use the imperfect subjunctive of **haber** together with the past participle of the verb. Here are the forms of **comprar** in the pluperfect subjunctive:

hubiera comprado	I would have bought
hubieras comprado	you would have bought (informal)
hubiera comprado	you would have bought (formal); he/she would have bought
hubiéramos comprado	we would have bought
hubieran comprado	you would have bought
hubieran comprado	they would have bought

As in the case of the imperfect subjunctive, it is possible to use the alternative form **-se**. They are interchangeable.

The passive voice

The verb **ser** is used with the past participle to form the passive voice. There is agreement in number and gender with the subject of the verb **ser**. The passive voice is used to put the emphasis on the action taking place rather than on the subject performing the action (as in sentences in the active voice).

Example:

Los expedientes han sido devueltos.	The dossiers have been returned.

The following are examples of the passive voice in various tenses.

Present	*Imperfect*
soy llevado	**era llevado**
eres llevado	**eras llevado**
es llevado	**era llevado**
somos llevados	**éramos llevados**
son llevados	**eran llevados**
son llevados	**eran llevados**

Preterite	*Future*
fui llevado	**seré llevado**
fuiste llevado	**serás llevado**
fue llevado	**será llevado**
fuimos llevados	**seremos llevados**
fueron llevados	**serán llevados**
fueron llevados	**serán llevados**

Conditional	*Present perfect*
sería llevado	**he sido llevado**
serías llevado	**has sido llevado**
sería llevado	**ha sido llevado**
seríamos llevados	**hemos sido llevados**
serían llevados	**han sido llevados**
serían llevados	**han sido llevados**

Pluperfect	*Future perfect*
había sido llevado	**habré sido llevado**
habías sido llevado	**habrás sido llevado**
había sido llevado	**habrá sido llevado**
habíamos sido llevados	**habremos sido llevados**
habían sido llevados	**habrán sido llevados**
habían sido llevados	**habrán sido llevados**

Conditional perfect
habría sido llevado
habrías sido llevado
habría sido llevado
habríamos sido llevados
habrían sido llevados
habrían sido llevados

The impersonal se

Se is used in spoken Spanish to replace the passive construction learned above, which is mainly used in written language.

Examples:

Se sabe que no funciona.	It is known that it doesn't work.
Se espera que compren nuestros productos.	It is expected that they will buy our products.

Key to exercises

Please note that with open-ended exercises, answers will not always appear in the Key.

Chapter 1

Exercise 1

(c)	1	(d)	34
(j)	7	(k)	62
(h)	12	(l)	79
(e)	13	(b)	93
(g)	15	(i)	94
(f)	27	(a)	100

Exercise 2

(a)	25	**veinticinco**	(d)	13	**trece**
(b)	68	**sesenta y ocho**	(e)	44	**cuarenta y cuatro**
(c)	76	**setenta y seis**			

Exercise 3

Carlos veinte años
Luisa veintitres años
Milagros cincuenta y cinco años
Carolina veintisiete
Esteban noventa y ocho años

Exercise 4

(a) **Buenos días** (d) **Buenas noches**
(b) **Buenas tardes** (e) **Buenas noches**
(c) **Buenos días**

Exercise 5

1 **Arturo tiene carro/auto.**
2 **Lupe trabaja en Méjico/México.**
3 **La agencia de viaje tiene fax.**
4 **¿Trabajas? ¿Trabaja (ud.)?**

Exercise 6

1 **tengo . . . tiene** 4 **tiene**
2 **tenemos** 5 **tienen**
3 **tienen**

Chapter 2

Exercise 1

1 **viene** 4 **hace**
2 **Salgo** 5 **decimos**
3 **va**

Exercise 2

¿A qué hora sale el avión a Caracas?
Sale a las trece cuarenta y cinco.

¿A qué hora sale el avión a Lima?
Sale a las nueve veinte.

¿A qué hora sale el avión a Quito?
Sale a las seis (horas).

¿A qué hora llega el avión de Madrid?
Llega a las once cuarenta y cinco.

¿A qué hora llega el avión de Santiago?
Llega a las once cincuenta.

¿A qué hora llega el avión de México D.F.?
Llega a las diez veinte.

Exercise 3

Camisas	treinta y seis
Blusas	veintiocho
Abrigos	noventa y cuatro, cinco
Pañuelos	cinco, cuarenta
Pantalones	treinta y ocho, cuarenta
Camisetas	diez, ochenta

Exercise 4

Hombres	Mujeres	Ambos
corbata	medias	zapatos
calzoncillo	lápiz labial	suéter
	aretes	pañuelo
	blusa	camisa
	falda	
	vestido	

Exercise 5

1
3
4

Exercise 6

Páguese a Viajes El Sol la suma de doscientos cuarenta y cinco dólares.

Chapter 3

Exercise 1

1	los	6	el
2	la	7	la
3	el	8	el/la
4	los	9	los
5	el/la	10	el

Exercise 2

1 (j)	6 (i)
2 (d)	7 (e)
3 (b)	8 (g)
4 (a)	9 (h)
5 (f)	10 (c)

Exercise 4

VENTAJAS

piscina
aire acondicionado
caja fuerte individual

DESVENTAJAS

céntrico
desayuno incluido
calefacción central
cambio de moneda
restaurante
teléfono en la habitación

Exercise 5

Mi plan para el martes es leer una guía turística y comprar un mapa.
Mi plan para el miércoles es buscar información y navegar en Internet.
Mi plan para el jueves es estudiar el informe y escribir comentarios.
Mi plan para el viernes es preparar documentos y hacer las maletas.
Mi plan para el sábado el llegar al aeropuerto a las 2.30 y comprar una novela.
Mi plan para el domingo es descansar.

Exercise 6

1 **Hasta el lunes**
2 **Hasta el sábado**
3 **Hasta el domingo**
4 **Hasta el martes**
5 **Hasta mañana**

Exercise 7

1 **25 de diciembre**
3 **1 de enero**

Exercise 8

1 **individual con baño**
2 **el viernes**

Exercise 9

TELEFAX
Dirigido a Señora Urrutia
Hotel Embajador

Estimada señora:
Le ruego reservar una habitación doble con baño y teléfono para
3 noches a partir del sábado próximo.

Atentamente

Chapter 4

Exercise 2

1 (e)	4 (c)
2 (d)	5 (a)
3 (b)	

Exercise 3

1 **soy**	4 **es**
2 **son**	5 **son**
3 **somos**	

Exercise 4

1 **está**	6 **está**
2 **soy**	7 **es**
3 **está**	8 **está**
4 **Estamos**	9 **Somos**
5 **son**	10 **está**

Exercise 5

(a)
¿Dónde está la librería?
La librería está a la izquierda.

¿Dónde está la comisaría?
La comisaría está a la izquierda.

¿Dónde está el cine?
El cine está a la izquierda.

¿Dónde está el hotel?
El hotel está a la derecha.

¿Dónde está el banco?
El banco está a la derecha.

¿Dónde está el supermercado?
El supermercado está a la derecha.

¿Dónde está la panadería?
La panadería está a la derecha.

(b)
¿Dónde está la librería?
La librería está a la izquierda, enfrente del banco.

¿Dónde está la comisaría?
La comisaría está a la izquierda, enfrente del supermercado.

¿Dónde está el cine?
El cine está a la izquierda, enfrente de la panadería.

¿Dónde está el hotel?
El hotel está a la derecha, enfrente del bar.

¿Dónde está el banco?
El banco está a la derecha, enfrente de la librería.

¿Dónde está el supermercado?
El supermercado está a la derecha, enfrente de la comisaría.

¿Dónde está la panadería?
La panadería está a la derecha, enfrente del cine.

(c)
¿Dónde está la librería?
La librería está a la izquierda, enfrente del banco, al lado del bar/al lado de
la comisaría.

¿Dónde está la comisaría?
La comisaría está a la izquierda, enfrente del supermercado, al lado de la
librería/del cine.

¿Dónde está el cine?
El cine está a la izquierda, enfrente de la panadería, al lado de la comisaría.

¿Dónde está el hotel?
El hotel está a la derecha, enfrente del bar, al lado del banco.

¿Dónde está el banco?
El banco está a la derecha, enfrente de la librería, al lado del hotel/del supermercado.

¿Dónde está el supermercado?
El supermercado está a la derecha, enfrente de la comisaría, al lado del banco/de la panadería.

¿Dónde está la panadería?
La panadería está a la derecha, enfrente del cine, al lado del supermercado.

Exercise 6

1 (b)	5 (a)
2 (c)	6 (f), (g)
3 (b), (e)	7 (h)
4 (d)	8 (f), (h)

Exercise 7

1 V	4 V
2 F	5 V
3 F	

Chapter 5

Exercise 1

(Answers may vary according to individual choice or circumstances.)

1 **diario**	4 **mensual**
2 **anual**	5 **semanal**
3 **trimestral**	

Exercise 2

(Answers may vary according to individual choice or circumstances.)

1 **una vez por semana.**
2 **todos los días.**
3 **tres veces por semana.**
4 **dos veces por año.**
5 **una o dos veces por año.**

Exercise 3

(Answers may vary according to individual choice or circumstances.)

1 **Hago las compras**
2 **Voy de vacaciones**
3 **Limpio las ventanas**
4 **Desayuno**
5 **Voy a la iglesia**

Exercise 5

1 **Quisiera comprar un periódico.**
2 **Quisiéramos visitar el museo.**
3 **Quisiéramos dos habitaciones individuales.**
4 **Quisiera un libro nuevo.**
5 **Quisiera ir a Uruguay.**

Exercise 6

(a) **Por/en la mañana**
(b) **En la madrugada**
(c) **Por/en la noche**
(d) **En/por la tarde**
(e) **En/por la noche**

Exercise 7

(Answers may vary according to individual choice or circumstances.)

POR LA MAÑANA	POR LA TARDE	POR LA NOCHE
despertarse: 7.00 a.m.	**trabajar**: 2.00 p.m.	**cenar**: 9.00 p.m.
desayunar: 7.45	**jugar al tenis**: 4.00 p.m.	**mirar la tele**: 22.00
vestirse: 8.15	**conversar/platicar**: 5.30 p.m.	**acostarse**: 23.45

Exercise 8

1 lejos	4 rápido
2 allá	5 subir
3 barato	

Exercise 9

1 V	4 V
2 F	5 F
3 F	

Chapter 6

Exercise 1

1 empieza	4 mueren
2 recuerdo	5 recuerda
3 cerramos	

Exercise 2

1 F	4 F
2 F	5 V
3 F	

Exercise 3

1 La chica más inteligente en el/del grupo.
2 Es la peor película del festival.
3 Los modelos más funcionales están acá/aquí.
4 Me gustaría el producto más barato.
5 Es el problema más difícil.

Exercise 4

1 puedo	4 puede
2 Podemos	5 puedo
3 Puede	

Exercise 7

1 F
2 V
3 V

4 V
5 F

Chapter 7

Exercise 1

1 Está estudiando.
2 Están escribiendo.
3 Estoy trabajando en la oficina.
4 Estamos arreglando el jardín.
5 Están practicando el baile.

Exercise 2

1 The telephone company apologizes for the inconvenience.
2 They are installing new telephone lines.

Exercise 3

1 We are interviewing candidates for two positions.
2 The group is making inroads into the international market.
3 The economic recovery is beginning.
4 I am looking for an alternative to this product.
5 Genaro is working on a new project.

Exercise 4

1 **Sus**
2 **Su**
3 **Su**

4 **Mi**
5 **Su**

Exercise 6

A: **haciendo**
M: **preparando**
A: **haciendo**
M: **escribiendo**

Exercise 7

1 Estoy
2 está
3 están

4 está
5 está

Exercise 8

1 Maribel
2 Asunción y Genaro
3 Usted . . . tú
4 Yo
5 La radio

Chapter 8

Exercise 1

(Answers may vary according to individual choice.)

1 En el trabajo tengo que abrir la correspondencia.
2 En el trabajo tengo que enviar faxes.
3 En el trabajo tengo que escribir cartas.
4 En el trabajo tengo que supervisar la producción.
5 En el trabajo tengo que trabajar hasta tarde.
6 En el trabajo tengo que presentar informes.
7 En el trabajo tengo que llamar por teléfono.
8 En el trabajo tengo que tratar con el público.
9 En el trabajo tengo que utilizar la computadora.

1 En casa tengo que preparar la comida.
2 En casa tengo que limpiar.
3 En casa tengo que pasar la aspiradora.
4 En casa tengo que planchar.
5 En casa tengo que ayudar a los niños con sus tareas.
6 En casa tengo que contestar el teléfono.
7 En casa tengo que atender el jardín.
8 En casa tengo que hacer reparaciones.

Exercise 2

1 en contra
2 en favor
3 en contra

Exercise 3

(Answers may vary according to individual choice.)

Primero tiene que preparar un informe, después tiene que visitar la fábrica. Entonces tiene que ver muestras y probar el producto. Más tarde tiene que discutir precios. Por último tiene que estudiar el contrato.

Exercise 5

1 (b)	3 (c)
2 (d)	4 (a)

Exercise 6

1 (e)	5 (c)	9 (i)
2 (j)	6 (f)	10 (d)
3 (b)	7 (h)	
4 (g)	8 (a)	

Exercise 8

1 **Quiero ir contigo.**
2 **La Sra Rosas vive en una casita/casa chica con ellas.**
3 **Ven conmigo.**
4 **Quieren una reunión contigo.**
5 **Siempre llega con ellos.**

Chapter 9

Exercise 1

1 **He terminado mi trabajo.**
2 **He estado escribiendo esta carta desde hace 2 horas.**
3 **Elena y yo hemos escrito una carta al periódico.**
4 **Roger está en Cali desde hace una semana.**
5 **Carlos Fuentes ha publicado un libro nuevo/otro libro.**
6 **Has/ha vivido en Paraguay desde hace mucho tiempo.**
7 **El banco ha abierto una sucursal nueva.**
8 **No hemos visto a Lorena desde esta mañana.**
9 **Han llegado.**
10 **¿No has/ha terminado?**

Exercise 3

1	para	4	por
2	Por	5	por
3	para		

Chapter 10

Exercise 1

1	(c)	4	(f)
2	(b)	5	(d)
3	(e)	6	(a)

Exercise 2

El martes voy a asistir a la reunión y también voy a comer en un restaurante céntrico.

El miércoles voy a estudiar el reglamento y también voy a escribir cartas.

El jueves voy a probar el equipo nuevo y también voy a entrevistar al posible jefe de ventas.

El viernes voy a recoger la nueva impresora láser y también voy a compar 'compact discs'.

El sábado voy a descansar.

El domingo también voy a descansar.

Exercise 4

1 Sí es posible.
2 No es posible.
3 No es posible.
4 Sí es posible.
5 Sí es posible.

Exercise 5

1	V	4	V
2	F	5	F
3	F		

Exercise 6

1 (c)   4 (b)
2 (d)   5 (e)
3 (a)

Exercise 7

Clásico

Chapter 11

Exercise 1

1 **Se abre temprano.**
2 **Se fabrican carros aquí.**
3 **Se arreglan computadoras.**
4 **Se prepara un informe cada día.**
5 **Se dice que está muy enfermo.**

Exercise 2

Hotel	Nº de noches	desayuno	piscina	pasaje	asistencia médica
Amsterdam	7	sí	sí	sí	sí
Central	5	sí	no	sí	sí
Apartamento	7	no	no	sí	sí

Exercise 4

1 **Graciela no vive tan cerca como Carlos.**
2 **Carolina es tan alta como José.**
3 **La rosa es tan linda como el clavel.**
4 **Mi televisor no es tan grande como el (televisor) de mi novia.**
5 **Esta impresora no es tan rápida como la otra (impresora).**

Exercise 5

1 (c)   4 (d)
2 (b)   5 (e)
3 (a)

Exercise 6

1 **más de**	4 **menos de**
2 **más de**	5 **más de**
3 **menos de**	

Exercise 7

1 F	6 V
2 F	7 F
3 V	8 V
4 V	9 V
5 F	10 F

Exercise 8

1 F	4 V
2 F	5 F
3 V	

Chapter 12

Exercise 1

(Other answers are possible depending on what you 'chose to do'.)

Compré la revista Quehacer y después visité la exposición de pintura en la galería Forum. Luego llamé por teléfono a una amiga y más tarde bailamos en la discoteca.

Exercise 2

1 (e)	4 (d)
2 (a)	5 (b)
3 (c)	

Exercise 3

1 **fui**	6 **llegó**
2 **Vimos**	7 **Aprendí**
3 **visitaron**	8 **estuvimos**

4 **Compré**	9 **Vimos**
5 **Visitaste**	10 **Escribió**

Exercise 4

En la primera semana estudió el sistema operativo. Escribió texto y fórmulas. Imprimió la hoja de trabajo, diseñó pantallas y alimentó datos. En la segunda semana analizó economía empresarial y preparó estrategias financieras. Entonces, aplicó estadísticas y probabilidades. Por fin, desarrolló métodos de valuación de proyectos.

Exercise 5

1 Anoche escuché un programa de radio.
2 El año pasado Marcelo y Estela diseñaron ropa para una firma extranjera.
3 El sábado pasado Carlos imitó a Elvis Presley en la tele.
4 Ayer salió la revista 'Decoración'.
5 Ayer fue criticado el servicio médico.
6 El sábado pasado ganó las carreras.
7 Ayer y anteayer entrenó Pochita.
8 Anoche Leonardo comió en casa.
9 El viernes pasado el jefe organizó una reunión de ejecutivos.
10 Hace dos horas (que) volvió Steven.

Chapter 13

Exercise 1

1 Comeremos juntos.
2 Marcelo preparará la comida mañana.
3 Esteban y yo escribiremos el informe.
4 Esperaremos hasta que llegue la nueva computadora.
5 Abrirán a las 9.30 en vez de las 10.00.
6 Vendrás mañana temprano, ¿no?
7 Se llevarán todo.
8 Elena empezará a trabajar el lunes.
9 La reunión será en mi despacho.
10 Dejaré a mi hija en la escuela.

Exercise 2

1 Ann y yo iremos a la agencia de viajes el martes próximo/que viene.
2 Viajaré a Guatemala y Nicaragua el año que viene/próximo.
3 Discutiremos precios en nuestra próxima reunión.
4 La compañía crecerá en los próximos años.
5 Se anunciarán nuevos precios para el gas la semana que viene.

Exercise 3

1 La semana que viene saldremos de paseo al campo.
2 El lunes que viene firmaremos el contrato.
3 El semestre que viene será decisivo para la empresa.
4 El mes que viene terminamos el proyecto.
5 La entrevista que viene será con el Director.

Exercise 4

El lunes irá/va a ir a la feria de informática. Comprará/va a comprar un
nuevo equipo.
El martes visitará/va a visitar la tienda de repuestos.
El miércoles enviará/va a enviar fax a las sucursales. Informará/va a infor-
mar sobre cambios en el horario.
El jueves terminará/va a terminar el informe anual.
El viernes empezará/va a empezar las negociaciones con el nuevo socio.

Exercise 5

1 V	4 F
2 V	5 V
3 F	

Exercise 6

1 vendrán	6 celebrará
2 empezará	7 aparecerá
3 regresaremos	8 presentará
4 pondrá	9 hablará
5 establecerán	10 veremos

Exercise 7

1 (c)   4 (a)
2 (e)   5 (b)
3 (d)

Exercise 8

1 F   4 F
2 V   5 V
3 V

Chapter 14

Exercise 1

1 **trabajaba**   6 **fueron . . . volvieron**
2 **iba**   7 **compró**
3 **llegó**   8 **tenía**
4 **costaba**   9 **tenía**
5 **llamé**   10 **volvió**

Exercise 2

1 Iris was working/worked/used to work in a travel agency.
2 We used to study in the evening.
3 We were watching television when Rosana arrived.
4 Every Sunday he used to come and visit his grandparents.
5 The computers were available to the students.

Exercise 3

1 **¿Qué estabas haciendo cuando sonó el teléfono?**
2 **El avión estaba aterrizando cuando oímos la explosión.**
3 **Viajaba mucho.**
4 **La comida era barata en esos días.**
5 **La oficina estaba en la segunda planta.**

Exercise 4

1 **Se llamaba Colegio San Antonio.**
2 **Estaba en Avenida de la Montaña 2759.**
3 **Tenía un laboratorio de idiomas.**
4 **Hacían viajes estudiantiles a Brasil, EE. UU, Canadá, Inglaterra, España y Japón.**
5 **Aconsejaban a los alumnos con orientación personal.**
6 **Practicaban atletismo, tenis y natación.**
7 **Sí, era grande.**
8 **Ofrecía también bachillerato internacional.**
9 **Había 4 canchas.**
10 **Sí, había pista de atletismo.**

Exercise 5

1 Nobody has anything.
2 He/she never buys any presents.
3 Estela does not eat meat or eggs.
4 Nobody learns a language in one day.
5 The museum is very near.

Exercise 6

1 Sigue igual		6	Ha subido
2 Ha bajado		7	Ha subido
3 Ha subido		8	Ha bajado
4 Ha bajado		9	Ha subido
5 Ha bajado		10	Sigue igual

Chapter 15

Exercise 1

1 I do not believe he will finish everything.
2 How interesting that he is including this in his book.
3 It is probable that he is going out tonight.
4 I want you to go to the doctor.
5 I am asking you to continue in your job.
6 It does not seem to them that it offers possibilities.
7 It annoys us that she does not arrive early.

8 It is important that we eat vegetables and fruit.
9 We doubt that she will write from Ecuador.
10 I am sorry that you cannot come to the meeting.

Exercise 2

1 **Es necesario que comas menos.**
2 **Es interesante que responda en español.**
3 **Busco algo que ayude a todos.**
4 **(Te) aconsejamos que lo hagas.**
5 **Piden que contestes pronto.**

Exercise 3

1 **vendrá**	6 **esté**
2 **venga**	7 **encuentre**
3 **prepare**	8 **sea**
4 **trajo**	9 **escuchará . . . hable**
5 **compre**	10 **empezarán**

Exercise 4

1 **Quiero que tenga capacidad para cinco pasajeros.**
2 **Quiero que sea económico con el combustible.**
3 **Quiero que sea de tamaño mediano.**
4 **Quiero que incluya cierre electrónico de puertas.**
5 **Quiero que cuente con motor de 1300 o 1400 centímetros cúbicos.**
6 **Quiero que venga con caja de cambios de cinco velocidades.**
7 **Quiero que sea de un precio razonable.**
8 **Quiero que funcione con gasolina sin plomo.**
9 **Quiero que ofrezca fiabilidad.**
10 **Quiero que esté entre los líderes del mercado.**

Exercise 5

1 (b)	6 (g)
2 (e)	7 (a)
3 (j)	8 (f)
4 (c)	9 (h)
5 (i)	10 (d)

Exercise 6

1 tengas	6 devuelvas
2 sea	7 llegará
3 tiene	8 traigan
4 dice	9 ayuden
5 prepare	10 será

Chapter 16

Exercise 2

1 (f)	6 (d)
2 (g)	7 (a)
3 (i)	8 (c)
4 (h)	9 (e)
5 (j)	10 (b)

Exercise 3

1 No vengan a la fiesta.
2 No llames a tu novia.
3 No compres cigarrillos.
4 No abras la ventana.
5 No copien el documento en diskette.
6 No pidas diez cuadernos.
7 No vengas con tu novio.
8 No tomes fotos.
9 No prepare el plato que le recomendé.
10 No instales la antena.

Exercise 4

1 Baja al primer piso.
2 Sea más eficiente.
3 Toma esto.
4 Revisen este contrato.
5 Regresa pronto.
6 Come más proteínas.
7 Envíe el paquete por vía aérea.
8 Vaya el próximo domingo.

9 **Haz lo que dice esta señorita.**
10 **Vendan la máquina.**

Chapter 17

Exercise 2

1 If I could I would travel more.
2 If Marcelo was better organized, he would have better results.
3 Since you are coming by car, you will arrive before Alberto.
4 If you are writing a check, spell the name correctly.
5 If they gave me the opportunity, I would work in Uruguay.
6 I would visit the capital if I had more time, but I will only be here for two days.
7 I would bring it on floppy disk, if it was compatible.
8 If the figures indicated the opposite, we would have to carry out an investigation.
9 If the novel was shorter, I would have more success.
10 If you know the answer, why don't you say it?

Exercise 3

1 **Si hay un problema te envío un fax.**
2 **No creo que Helen vaya al trabajo/a trabajar mañana.**
3 **Si tuviese la oportunidad, ¿volvería/regresaría?**
4 **Como tiene/tienes sólo uno, llévese/llévate estos otros dos.**
5 **Si llama, le damos los detalles.**

Exercise 4

1 (b), (c)   4 (e)
2 (c), (b)   5 (d)
3 (a)

Exercise 5

1 **Si tuviéramos/tuviésemos más personal podríamos obtener mejores resultados.**
2 **Necesitamos pedir ayuda a una consultoría.**
3 **Nuestra empresa se extendería mercados extranjeros si tuviéramos/ tuviésemos una mejor política de exportación.**

4 Su enfoque no es muy profesional.
5 Creo/Pienso que no es muy buena idea.

Exercise 6

1	V	6	V
2	F	7	F
3	F	8	F
4	V	9	F
5	F	10	V

Chapter 18

Exercise 1

1 Si hubiera tenido tiempo habría terminado la pintura.
2 Si hubiéramos tenido las entradas habríamos ido al teatro.
3 Si hubieras tenido suficiente dinero habrías comprado el regalo.
4 Si hubieran tenido una invitación habrían venido a la fiesta.
5 Si hubiera tenido los datos necesarios habría preparado el informe.

Exercise 2

1	(b)	6	(a)
2	(i)	7	(e)
3	(j)	8	(h)
4	(d)	9	(g)
5	(c)	10	(f)

Exercise 3

1 Aunque no tenía licencia de conducir, manejó el auto.
2 Aunque tenía tarjetas de crédito, pagó al contado.
3 Aunque el supermercado está cerca, compro en una tiendecita.
4 Aunque no se afeita, le regaló una loción para después de afeitarse.
5 Aunque recibió su carta, no contestó.
6 Aunque llegaba de madrugada, organizó una reunión para la mañana siguiente.
7 Aunque la computadora es nueva, no es compatible con las demás de la oficina.
8 Aunque es latinoamericano, no le gusta la comida picante.

9 **Aunque es el archivo más grande del país, no tiene sistema computarizado.**

10 **Aunque estuvo a dieta todo el año pasado, no bajó de peso.**

Exercise 4

1 **Hay demasiados estudiantes en esta sala/aula/habitación.**
2 **Todo es demasiado caliente.**
3 **La temperatura es demasiado fría para esta época del año.**
4 **Está demasiado alto. No puede alcanzar.**
5 **Puse demasiadas monedas en la máquina. No funciona.**

Exercise 5

1 Even though he did not have any money, he ordered expensive food.
2 We finished, even though the conditions were negative.
3 In spite of his complaints, he is not receiving help.
4 He visits his grandchildren very often, in spite of being very old.
5 In spite of the opportunities that he had, he never triumphed/succeeded.
6 In spite of having a great cast, this film is not good.
7 In spite of problems with his health, he carries on playing football.
8 He does not go out, even though the doctor advised it.
9 In spite of the rain, they walked all afternoon.
10 In spite of having a very high salary, he always asks for loans.

Exercise 6

1 He will not answer the questions, even if he is tortured.
2 She will wait for her son, even if he arrives very late.
3 We will go, even if it rains all night.
4 We would tell you, even if it is very late.
5 In my case, I would have rung you, even if it had been Sunday.

Chapter 19

Exercise 1

1 **La nueva autopista fue construida.**
2 **La multa fue aplicada por la municipalidad.**
3 **El presupuesto fue aprobado por el gobierno.**
4 **Los precios fueron rebajados por la tienda.**

5 La obra fue terminada.
6 La obra habría sido publicada por la casa editorial.
7 Todos serían llevados a la comisaría.
8 Todos habrán sido interrogados por el juez.
9 Hemos sido engañados.
10 El libro sería leído por un gran número de personas.

Exercise 2

1 Se ha decidido que representarás a la empresa en la feria.
2 Se dice que los competidores están desmoralizados.
3 Se explica en el folleto.
4 Al final se aceptó.
5 Se ha repetido por tercera vez.
6 Se sabe que el producto afecta la piel.
7 Se manda/envía por correo.
8 Se ofrece a los socios de la organización.
9 Se dan por adelantado.
10 Se devolverán el próximo día/al día siguiente.

Exercise 3

1 It is thought that there will not be an increase in salaries.
2 It is known that they will not arrive until tomorrow.
3 I believe that the idea is understood now.
4 The session has finished.
5 First, the product is placed inside the machine.
6 It was agreed upon during the last meeting.
7 Procedures for paying export taxes could/would be simplified.
8 The loan will not be invested in public services.
9 A new system of classification will be introduced.
10 The new prices of industrial gas will be published next week.

Exercise 4

1 La exposición sobre comercio exterior fue inaugurada por la Directora.
2 Una nueva revista será publicada por los comerciantes del centro.
3 La máquina será reemplazada por el distribuidor.
4 Más de cien kilómetros de la carretera al norte serán reconstruidos por el Ministerio de Transportes.
5 Una nueva gama de productos será introducida por la Compañía de Teléfonos.

6 **La nueva tarjeta de identificación ha sido distribuida por el Ministerio del Interior.**
7 **El delincuente fue detenido por la policía.**
8 **El donativo fue entregado por las empresas extranjeras.**
9 **Una computadora fue donada por el dueño de la tienda.**
10 **El entrenador fue llevado en hombros por los hinchas.**

Exercise 5

1 The book was destined to be a success.
2 The book was destined for the external market.
3 Julián was punished for not finishing his homework.
4 Julián was punished by his mother.
5 This material is processed on a very modern machine.
6 The food was already processed.
7 The soldiers were instructed every morning.
8 The flowers were cut carefully by the women working there.
9 The flowers were cut.
10 The capital was attacked by foreign troops.

Exercise 6

1 **No quiero queso, sino quiero jamón.**
2 **No tiene una casa ahora, pero quizás tenga una el año próximo.**
3 **No tienen (un) gato, sino (un) perro.**
4 **No queremos un boleto de ida, sino uno de ida y vuelta.**
5 **Ha ido a México, pero no sé cuando vuelve.**

Exercise 7

1 F 4 F
2 V 5 V
3 F

Chapter 20

Exercise 1

1 **Anoche vi un programa de televisión.**
2 **El año pasado Marcelo y Estela diseñaron interiores para una firma conocida.**

3 El sábado pasado Cecilia imitó a varios peronajes en la tele.

4 Ayer se transmitió la telenovela 'Adoración'.

5 Ayer criticaron al servicio de limpieza.

6 El sábado pasado perdió las carreras.

 7 Ayer y anteayer jugó Pochita.

 8 Anoche Leonardo no comió en casa.

 9 El viernes pasado el líder sindical organizó una reunión de trabajadores.

10 Hace dos horas (que) viajó Steven.

Exercise 2

1	(d)	6	(i)
2	(h)	7	(j)
3	(b)	8	(g)
4	(f)	9	(e)
5	(c)	10	(a)

Exercise 3

1	(c)	4	(a)
2	(e)	5	(b)
3	(d)		

Exercise 4

1 Ojalá no hubieras/hubieses traído ese libro.

2 Ojalá Sharon haya traído el mismo.

3 Yo que tú, mandaría el dinero/la plata mañana.

4 Yo que Sharon, iría allá esta noche.

5 Ojalá tuviera/tuviese tiempo para visitar todos los museos y exposiciones en esta ciudad.

Exercise 5

1	venga	6	no funciona
2	viva	7	coman
3	gustaría . . . quedarse	8	llegue
4	coma	9	viene
5	tiene	10	viaje

Exercise 6

1 estuviera ... estaría
2 estaremos
3 haya traído
4 trajo
5 estuviese

6 ser
7 fuese
8 comiera
9 saldrá. ... salga
10 pudiera

Exercise 7

1 (c)
2 (d)
3 (a)
4 (j)
5 (e)

6 (i)
7 (g)
8 (h)
9 (b)
10 (f)

Exercise 8

1 –
2 de
3 en/por
4 de ... de
5 desde ... hasta

6 a
7 para ... de
8 abajo de/debajo de
9 durante
10 en

Exercise 9

FRUTA	VIAJES	COLORES
manzana	bicicleta	verde
frutilla	ciclomotor	azul
plátano	barco	negro
piña	vuelo	amarillo
sandía	carro	rojo

Exercise 10

1 (e)
2 (b)
3 (a)

4 (d)
5 (c)

Exercise 11

1 F	4 V
2 F	5 F
3 V	

Exercise 12

1 está	6 está
2 Soy	7 está
3 está	8 está
4 están	9 somos
5 son	10 está

Exercise 13

1 No vayan a la reunión.
2 No llames por teléfono a tu jefe.
3 No trates de vender tu carro.
4 No abra el archivo para ver.
5 No copien el documento en diskette.
6 No pida diez cuadernos.
7 No vengas con tu novio.
8 No tome fotos.
9 No prepare el plato que le recomendé.
10 No instales la antena.

Exercise 14

1 Compren una nueva máquina.
2 Oye lo que dice este señor.
3 Venga el próximo sábado.
4 Mande el paquete por correo.
5 Escribe pronto.
6 Come menos grasas.
7 Estudien este contrato.
8 Haz esto.
9 Sea más paciente.
10 Sube al tercer piso.

Exercise 15

1 F	4 F
2 F	5 V
3 V	

CRUCIGRAMA

Dialogue translations

Lesson 7
Dialogue 1

MARITZA: Nice photographs! What are you doing in that photograph?
ERNESTO: I'm celebrating my birthday.
MARITZA: And in this one?
ERNESTO: Julia and I are dancing. Here everybody is making a toast.
MARITZA: You're reading a speech.
ERNESTO: Yes, something funny.

Dialogue 2

ERNESTO: In this photo I'm reading my cards.
MARITZA: Look, here you are with a huge serving on your plate.
ERNESTO: And in this one Rosana is posing for the photographer. She's looking at the flowers.
MARITZA: She looks great.
ERNESTO: Yes, she does.

Lesson 8
Dialogue 1

MARK: I have to change some traveler's checks. I need some more money. Let's go to the Bureau de Change.
CARMEN: The bank would be better.
MARK: Why?
CARMEN: The bank charges less commission and pays more per dollar.
MARK: Then let's go to the bank.
CARMEN: We have to rush. The bank closes at three. Hurry up! We've got ten minutes.

Dialogue 2

INTERVIEWER: What sort of housework do you have to do, Mrs Huertas?
MRS HUERTAS: I have to do the washing, I have to do the washing up, I have to clean the house, I have to prepare breakfast, I have to take the children to school . . .

Dialogue 3

ANA MARÍA: Adela? What are you doing?
ADELA: I am listening to my compact discs. Shall we listen to music together?
ANA MARÍA: Alright.
ADELA: Come round, then.
ANA MARÍA: Yes, I'll come round straight away.

Lesson 9
Dialogue 1

JAIME: What's the matter?
CATHERINE: I've lost my passport.
JAIME: Where? How?
CATHERINE: I don't know. I'm not sure. Perhaps in the market.
JAIME: We must go to the police station and then to the consulate.
CATHERINE: Yes. I need a replacement.

Dialogue 2

POLICEMAN: Good afternoon.
MARK: I've lost my briefcase with all my documents in it.
POLICEMAN: Your name, please.
MARK: Mark Williams.
POLICEMAN: What is in the briefcase?
MARK: Just a moment, please. I've made a list. Here it is. My passport, flight ticket, traveler's checks, a guide to Latin America, a list of hotels and a diary.
POLICEMAN: I'll write down the details.

MARK: I would like a copy of the police report. It's for the insurance.
POLICEMAN: Yes, of course.

Dialogue 3

DELIA: Why are you sad?
MARK: Because I've lost my briefcase with my diary in it.
DELIA: When?
MARK: The other day. I've been to the police station, but they haven't found the briefcase.
DELIA: Why don't you buy another diary?
MARK: I've got a new one. But I've lost the names and addresses of important contacts.

Lesson 10
Dialogue 1

TOURIST: What are we going to do today?
GUIDE: First, we are going to visit the Archaeological Museum. Apart from the exhibition, you are going to watch a ten-minute video and then we are going to have lunch in a typical restaurant. In the afternoon we are going to go round the old churches in the capital and we are going to buy souvenirs. The guide is going to explain . . .

Dialogue 2

CUSTOMER: What is 'lenguado'?
Meat? Fish? Vegetable?
WAITER: It's fish. It's very nice.
CUSTOMER: A steak for me. For my husband, sole with ginger.
WAITER: Something to drink?
CUSTOMER: White wine, please.

Lesson 11

Dialogue 1

INTERVIEWER: This year tourism has shown an increase of 30 per cent. How was this achieved?
MAYOR: We are working for growth. We allocate 25 per cent of resources to public works annually. Staff have been reduced by 35 per cent. Cleanliness is improved continuously in squares, promenades and streets. We have to attract tourists.
INTERVIEWER: What other plans are there?
MAYOR: Sport and cultural venues will be built. Tourism is linked to sport and culture.

Dialogue 2

SON: Dad, I want a bike. A mountain bike.
FATHER: You'll have to wait until Christmas. Besides, mountain bikes are more expensive than ordinary bicycles.
SON: But they are on special offer until Saturday.
FATHER: Riding a bike can be dangerous.

SON: Yes, but I'm going to wear a helmet. I've seen a yellow one I like. It's not as big as the one you need to go on a motorbike.

Note: **Bici** is short for *bicycle*.

Lesson 12

Dialogue 1

CAROLA: Hello! Tell me about your weekend.
ELSA: On Friday evening we had a meal in a typical restaurant. We danced 'landó' and then we went back to the apartment. On Saturday morning we went to town and bought a few things. Later we bought some take-away food and had lunch in the apartment. In the afternoon we saw a film at the cinema and then we saw the play *Don't Play That Waltz* in a little theater on Avenida Brasil. A beautiful play.
CAROLA: And on Sunday?
ELSA: On Sunday, we had a rest.

Note: **Landó** is a type of Afro-Peruvian music.

Dialogue 2

JOURNALIST: Where were you born?
COLLAR: I was born in Itauguá Guazú in 1964.
JOURNALIST: Where did you spend the first years of your life?
COLLAR: I was with my maternal grandmother. I learned Guarani as my first language. Later I got used to speaking Spanish.
JOURNALIST: Did you have a happy childhood?

COLLAR: I had to work from the age of ten. First in a chemist's and then as an apprentice in a printing workshop. After that I had my own graphic design studio.

JOURNALIST: How did your work as a painter start?

COLLAR: I studied in the School of Fine Arts. Gradually I took part in individual and group exhibitions.

JOURNALIST: Have you won any awards?

COLLAR: I recently won the Martel Prize for the Arts.

Lesson 13
Dialogue 1

CARMEN: What are you going to do this afternoon? Will you go to the town center or will you come to the university?

SANTIAGO: I'll go to the university and we'll put the finishing touches to the work we are preparing. The other students in our group will want to know how this project is coming on. We'll have a meeting at seven in the cafeteria. What do you think?

CARMEN: Fine. What are you going to do after the meeting?

SANTIAGO: Raúl, Silvia and I will go to the cinema. Do you want to go, too?

CARMEN: Yes, of course.

Lesson 14
Dialogue 1

RAMÓN: At that time, I was studying at the university. It was an old mansion with courtyards and balconies. The lessons were from four in the afternoon until ten at night. Many of the students worked, so the evening lessons were convenient.

JULIA: Was it difficult to study and work?

RAMÓN: Yes. We used to arrive at the university half asleep. We were tired due to our work during the day. Sometimes we would miss the first hour and would only start to attend from the second lesson.

JULIA: How did you manage to keep up to date?

RAMÓN: We used to gather in groups at weekends and try to catch up with work on our course.

Dialogue 2

JULIA: How did you travel to the university?

RAMÓN: It was difficult to reach the campus. In my group nobody had a car. None of us had enough money to afford even a small used car. We all had to go by bus, which used to take one hour to cover ten kilometers. Nothing was more irritating for me than having to travel standing for one hour. Although I was 20, I already had rheumatoid arthritis.

Lesson 15
Dialogue 1

TANIA: I'm looking for somebody who can give me some guidance regarding the consultancy project.
LAURA: I don't think you need to look any further. I know a person with a lot of experience in this matter. It's Iris Vidal, head of a Business Consultancy and Advice Bureau.
TANIA: Could you give me her telephone number?
LAURA: Sure. I have it here in my diary.

Dialogue 2

LOLA: It's a shame that José is not at home.
MIRTHA: Yes. I think we need to give him a ring.
LOLA: Perhaps I have his number in my handbag. Let's see . . . Yes. Here it is. I don't think he will be surprised to hear my voice. But you never know.
MIRTHA: When did you talk to him last?
LOLA: Three or four days ago. Sara and I were in the town center and he came up to us.
MIRTHA: When will he be back?
LOLA: I don't think it will be this week.

Dialogue 3

GENARO: Well. I'm off. I have to be at the airport in twenty minutes.
LUISA: Yes, hurry up. Don't forget anything.
GENARO: Everything is in the suitcase.
LUISA: I hope everything goes well! Have a good time!
GENARO: Thanks. I'll be back on Sunday.

Dialogue 4

ELISA: What's the matter?
OLGA: I don't feel well. I've got a bad headache.
ELISA: Take a tablet to relieve the pain.
OLGA: I've already taken one and the pain is still there. I think I'll go to bed.
ELISA: Yes. It'll do you good.
OLGA: If the pain doesn't go, I'll go to the doctor tomorrow.
ELISA: Let me know and I'll go with you.
OLGA: Thanks. I'll give you a ring tomorrow at ten.
ELISA: Bye.
OLGA: Bye.

Lesson 16
Dialogue 1

INTERVIEWER: Would you like a tram service around here?

PASSER-BY 1: No. It would be a waste of public money and it would destroy the atmosphere of the main street which goes back to the colonial days.

INTERVIEWER: Would you support a tram service around here?

PASSER-BY 2: Yes. First, because it would be faster than buses and second, because it would be cleaner. Less pollution. Mind you, I guess it would be dearer.

INTERVIEWER: Would you say that it is a good idea to have a tram service running here, along the main street?

PASSER-BY 3: Yes, of course. We need fast transport. Years ago we used to have trams. It was great.

Dialogue 2

ADELA: Squeeze the four lemons and after chopping the onions marinate them in this juice. Boil the potatoes and then peel them.

MARIANA: Do you mash them?

ADELA: Yes, mash the potatoes, onions and lemon juice. Add oil if necessary. Put the mixture in a mould and garnish with boiled eggs, olives and cheese.

Lesson 17
Dialogue 1

GENARO: If I had some extra income, I would buy something for the house.

ALAN: What would you buy?

GENARO: I would buy a new vacuum cleaner, because the one we have is very old, and also a writing desk for the kids.

ALAN: Would you buy on credit?

GENARO: Yes. There are good offers on 24-month interest-free credit.

Dialogue 2

ALBERTO: If you come this afternoon, we can go to the cinema.

EMILIA: All right. Since you insist.

ALBERTO: What time are you coming?

EMILIA: I don't know. It depends. Perhaps I'll come by car or perhaps I'll walk. Since you live so close.

ALBERTO: If you come by car you'll be here soon and we can go to the first show. If you want, we can go and have a drink afterwards.

EMILIA: That's fine. I'll come by car.

Dialogue 3

JOSÉ LUIS: If I had the money, I would buy the computer we want.

MARCELO: Never mind. Dad says that perhaps we might pay for it in instalments.

JOSÉ LUIS: But mum didn't think my dad could afford the monthly payments since he also has to pay for the car.

MARCELO: If we had the chance to work this summer during the holidays, we could help with the monthly payments.

JOSÉ LUIS: Let's have a word with Antonio.

MARCELO: Yes, let's.

Dialogue 4

ENRIQUE: If I could I would buy it immediately.

ROSARIO: It would be a rushed decision.

ENRIQUE: If it was you, you would possibly do the same.

ROSARIO: You're right.

Dialogue 5

ELENA: If I had more time, I would prepare the database we need. I think we will have to ask for help from a consultancy.

JORGE: I agree. We cannot carry on without having all our information properly organized before discussing our expansion plans.

ELENA: Last year when we had production problems two consultants from an international firm came to give us guidance and they did it very well. I think we could contact them again.

JORGE: Yes, they had a very professional approach and dealt with the problem very efficiently. Let's contact them again.

ELENA: I've got their telephone number here. I'll give them a ring.

Lesson 18
Dialogue 1

JUAN: If you had sent the letter, you would have had the necessary information. Then you wouldn't have had to come back this morning with all the documents.

MARIELA: What happened was that I did not have the full address. If you had given me all the information, then I would have been able to send the letter. But the name of the street was missing! Anyway, it doesn't matter now.

JUAN: I'm sorry. If I had noticed that something was missing, I would have sent you a fax or would have given you a ring.

MARIELA: It's all right. It's all sorted out now.

Dialogue 2

SIMÓN: If I were you I would not accept those conditions.

TERESA: I have no choice. I need the loan. If I was somebody with a steady job I would be able to go to the bank to ask for a loan.

SIMÓN: You're right. When you get a full-time job you will have more financial security.

TERESA: I do hope it is soon.

Dialogue 3

MR MÉNDEZ: What do you think about the publicity for the product?

MR SOSA: Although the graphics are very good, I think the text is too long. It has to be shortened.

MR MÉNDEZ: It may be long, but even if we shorten the text, we would have to include enough information on the technical specifications of the product. It is a very important point to attract potential customers. It is here that we have an edge over our competitors.

Mr Sosa: I believe it is a matter of opinion. For me, the picture is worth more than the words. I would like you to consider the possibility of shortening the text, let's say by 15 to 20 per cent.

Mr Méndez: All right, despite the fact that the deadline for submission of material to the advertising department of the magazine has passed, I'll find out if we can make some changes.

Dialogue 4

Juan: Supposing they don't arrive, what shall we do?

María: Nothing. We have to wait and then we will see.

Juan: I thought you wanted to solve things quickly. I thought you were not going to wait.

María: I changed my mind.

Juan: Even if they arrive late, it would be better than not arriving at all.

Lesson 19
Dialogue 1

Laura: What do you know about this matter?

Eduardo: Only what is in the newspaper. Listen. Two of the three dossiers which went missing have been returned. The directors have been interviewed by the police. The documents have been returned this morning. It is not known who handed them back.

Laura: It's a mystery. Let's go and ask your brother. He may have more news.

Eduardo: Yes, let's go.

Dialogue 2

Juan: It is known that this material lasts for years without fading.

Alicia: What is needed to keep it clean?

Juan: You only need to wipe it clean with a damp cloth and that's it.

Alicia: Don't you also need to use an abrasive cleaner?

Juan: It's not necessary. A damp cloth is enough.

Alicia: I'll try it.

Dialogue 3

Carlos: When I arrived the door was already open.

Sandra: I arrived a few moments earlier when a shop assistant was opening the door.

Carlos: Did you buy anything?

Sandra: Yes, clothes were reduced. I bought a blouse for my sister and two for me.

Carlos: I was sure I would find something for Celia, but in the end I didn't buy anything for her.

Dialogue 4

Cecilia: This is an expensive blouse, but the material is good.

Rosa: It is a durable material, but it is a delicate fabric as well. When it gets dirty don't put it in the washing machine, but wash it by hand.

Cecilia: Why?

Rosa: It says here on the label, 'Hand Wash'. If you don't wash it by hand, what happens is that it may lose its shape or fade in the washing machine.

Cecilia: All right. It will have to be washed by hand.

Lesson 20

Dialogue 1

SARA: What did you do yesterday?
PABLO: I went to the movies to see a French film. Then I bought a magazine to read on the train on the way home.
SARA: What kind of magazine is it?
PABLO: It deals with current affairs.
SARA: Is it interesting?
PABLO: Yes. I buy it every week. Do you read while you travel?
SARA: Yes. But I prefer to listen to the radio.
PABLO: What programs do you like?
SARA: I like a news program called 'Primera Plana', another called 'Competencia' which is about sport. I also listen to the program 'De noche'. It is cultural, educational and serves the community. The program I like most is 'Los 40 mejores'.
PABLO: What kind of program is it?
SARA: It plays the latest music.
PABLO: That's right. I sometimes listen to it as well.

Dialogue 2

ESTELA: Are you going to go to the theater?
GERMÁN: No. I don't like the play. I think I'll go to the movies.

ESTELA: But you said you wanted to go to the theater.
GERMÁN: I didn't say when. I can't today. Perhaps next week.
ESTELA: I may not be able to go next weekend.
GERMÁN: Why don't you come to the movies with me?
ESTELA: Tonight?
GERMÁN: Yes, tonight. It's a French film.
ESTELA: I don't think so. Irene is coming and I think she also wants to go to the theater. We'll go together.
GERMÁN: All right. See you later.
ESTELA: Bye.

Dialogue 3

IRENE: What software have you got?
FERNANDO: I have a word processor, spreadsheet, graphics, desktop publishing, database, presentation software. If I click here, there is a direct link to my e-mail. Using this shortcut I can go to a web page which sends virtual greeting cards.
IRENE: So, you are now connected to Internet.
FERNANDO: I am now, because there is a flat payment plan for the telephone line. Besides, my Internet provider gives me free access.

Spanish–English glossary

Abbreviations

(adj.)	adjective
(Ar.)	Argentina
(aux.)	auxiliary
(Bo.)	Bolivia
(Ch.)	Chile
(Col.)	Colombia
(conj.)	conjunction
(Ec.)	Ecuador
(f.)	feminine noun
(for.)	formal
(inf.)	informal
(m.)	masculine noun
(Méx.)	Mexico
(Pe.)	Peru
(pl.)	plural
(prep.)	preposition
(pron.)	pronoun
(sing.)	singular
(Sp.)	equivalent in Spain
(Uru.)	Uruguay

a	to; at
a continuación	now follows
a fin de	in order to
a menos que	unless
a partir de	from, as from
a pesar de	despite
a pie	on foot
a tiempo completo	full-time
a tiempo parcial	part-time
a veces	sometimes
a vuelta de correo	by return of post
abajo de (Sp. **debajo de**)	under
abierto	open
abrasivo	abrasive
abrigo (m.)	coat
abril (m.)	April
abrir	to open
abuela (f.)	grandmother
abuelo (m.)	grandfather
abuelos (m. pl.)	grandparents
acá (Sp. **aquí**)	here
acabar	to finish
académico	academic
acceso (m.)	access
aceite (m.)	oil
aceituna (f.)	olive
aceleradamente	fast
aceptable	acceptable
aceptar	to accept
acerca de	about
acercarse	to get near
acero (m.)	steel
acompañar	to go with
aconsejar	to advise
acordar	to agree
acordarse	to remember
acostarse	to go to bed
actividad (f.)	activity
acto (m.)	act; ceremony; event

actor (m.)	actor	**ahí**	there
actriz (f.)	actress	**ahora**	now
actual	present, current	**ahorita**	straight away
actualidad (f.)	current affairs	(Sp. **enseguida**)	
actualizado	updated	**ahorros** (m. pl.)	savings
actualizar	to update	**aire** (m.)	air
actualmente	at present	**aire**	air conditioning
acuerdo (m.)	agreement	**acondicionado**	
acusado (m.)	accused, defendant	(m.)	
adelgazar	to slim	**ajustar**	to adjust
además	besides	**al aire libre**	in the open air
adentro	inside	**al contrario**	on the contrary
(Sp. **dentro**)		**al día**	up to date
adiós (for.)	goodbye	**al final**	in the end
(Sp. for.		**al lado de**	next to
and inf.)		**alberca** (m.)	swimming pool
adjuntar	to enclose	**alcalde** (m.)	mayor
adolescente	teenager	**alcanzar**	to reach
(m., f.)		**alegre**	cheerful, glad
adonde, adónde	where (to)	**alfabeto** (m.)	alphabet, literate
adorno (m.)	ornament	**algo**	something
aeróbicos	aerobics	**algodón** (m.)	cotton
(m. pl.)		**alguien**	somebody
aeropuerto (m.)	airport	**alguno**	some; someone
afectar	to affect	**alimentación** (f.)	feeding
afeitarse	to shave	**alimentar**	to feed
África (f.)	Africa	**alimento** (m.)	food
afueras (f. pl.)	outskirts	**aliviar**	to relieve
agarrar	to take	**almorzar**	to have lunch
(Sp. **coger**)		**aló** (Sp. **dígame**)	hello (answering
agencia de	travel agent		the phone)
viajes (f.)		**alta resolución**	high resolution
agenda (f.)	diary	(f.)	
agosto (m.)	August	**alternativa** (f.)	alternative
agradable	pleasant	**alto**	tall, high
agradecer	to thank	**altura** (f.)	height
aghregar	add	**alumno** (m.)	pupil
agregar	to add	**allá**	there
(Sp. **añadir**)		**allí**	there
agua (f.)	water	**amar**	to love
aguacate (m.)	avocado	**amarillo**	yellow
aguaitar (Sp.	to watch	**amarrar** (Sp. **atar**)	to tie, to tie up
acechar, mirar)		**ambiente** (m.)	atmosphere

ambos	both	**apartado de correos** (m.)	PO box
amenazar	to threaten	**aparte**	apart
América (f.)	the Americas	**aparte de**	apart from
América Central (f.)	Central America	**apellido** (m.)	surname
América Latina (f.)	Latin America	**aplicar**	to apply
		aportar	to afford
americano	Latin American; American	**apoyar**	to support
		apoyo (m.)	support
amigo (m.)	friend	**aprender**	to learn
ampliar	to extend	**aprendizaje** (m.)	learning
amplio	ample, large	**aprobar**	to approve
analfabeto (m.)	illiterate	**apropiado**	appropriate, suitable
analizar	to analyze		
andar	to walk	**apuntes** (m. pl.)	notes
ándele, ándale (Méx.) (Sp. **venga**)	come on!	**apurado** (m. pl.) (Sp. **apresurado**)	rushed
angosto (Sp. **estrecho**)	narrow	**apurarse** (Sp. **darse prisa**)	to hurry up
animal (m.)	animal	**aquel, aquellos**	that, those
animal doméstico (m.)	pet	**aquél, aquéllos**	that one, those ones
anoche	last night	**aquella, aquellas**	that, those
anteayer	the day before yesterday	**aquélla, aquéllas**	that one, those ones
antena (f.)	aerial	**aquí**	here
anteojos (m.) (Sp. **gafas**)	glasses, spectacles	**árbol** (m.)	tree
		archivo (m.)	archive(s)
antepasado (m.)	ancestor	**aretes** (m. pl.) (Sp. **pendientes**)	earrings
anterior	previous	**Argentina** (f.)	Argentina
antes	before	**argentino**	Argentinian
anticuado	old-fashioned	**aroma** (f.)	smell
antiguo	old	**arquitecto** (m.)	architect
antojitos (m. pl.) (Sp. **tapas**)	snacks	**arquitectura** (f.)	architecture
		arrancar	to start up
anual	yearly	**arreglar**	to tidy up
anunciar	to announce	**arroz** (m.)	rice
anuncio (m.)	advertisement	**arte** (m.)	art
año (m.)	year	**artesanía** (f.)	handicraft
Año Nuevo (m.)	New Year	**artículo** (m.)	article
apagar	to blow out; to turn off	**artículos de tocador** (m. pl.)	toiletries

artículos para el hogar (m. pl.)	household goods
artificial	artificial, man-made
asado	roasted
ascensor (m.)	lift
así	even if; so, thus
asiento (m.)	seat
asistencia médica (f.)	medical assistance
asistir	to be present, to attend
aspiradora (f.)	vacuum cleaner
astronomía (f.)	astronomy
asunto (m.)	matter
atacar	to attack
ataque (m.)	attack
ataúd (m.)	coffin
atender	to attend to
atentamente	sincerely (end of letter)
atento	attentive
aterrizar	to land
atletismo (m.)	athletics
atracción (f.)	attraction
atractivo	attractive
atraer	to attract
atrás de (Sp. **detrás de**)	behind
auditorio (m.)	auditorium
aula (f.)	classroom
aumentar	to increase
aumento (m.)	increase
aunque	although
ausencia (f.)	absence
Australia (f.)	Australia
australiano	australian
auténtico	authentic
auto, automóvil (m.)	car, motorcar
autopista (f.)	motorway
autor (m.)	author
autoridad (f.)	authority
autorizar	to authorize
aventura (f.)	adventure
averiguar	to find out
avión (m.)	aeroplane
avisar	to warn, to advise
ayer	yesterday
aymara (m.)	indigenous language spoken in Peru and Bolivia
ayuda (f.)	assistance, help
ayudante (m., f.)	assistant, helper
ayudar	to help
azafata (f.)	air hostess
azafate (m.) (Sp. **bandeja**)	tray
azúcar (f.) (Sp. m.)	sugar
azul	blue
azul marino	navy blue
bachillerato internacional (m.)	baccalaureate, school-leaving examination
bailar	to dance
bailarina (f.)	ballerina
baile (m.)	dance
bajar	to go down
bajar de peso	to lose weight
bajo	short (height)
balcón (m.)	balcony
banco (m.)	bank
bandera (f.)	flag
banqueta (f.) (Méx.) (Sp. **acera**)	pavement
baño (m.) (Sp. **servicio**, **aseo** = toilet)	bath; bathroom; toilet
bar (m.)	bar
barato	cheap
barba (f.)	beard
barco (m.)	ship

barrio (m.)	neighborhood; residential area
base (f.)	base
base de datos (f.)	database
básico	basic
bastante	fairly
batería (f.)	battery (for a car)
beber	to drink
bebida (f.)	drink
bebida gaseosa (f.)	soft drink
beneficio (m.)	benefit
berenjena (f.)	aubergine
biblioteca (f.)	library
bicicleta (f.)	bicycle
bien	well
bienvenida (f.)	welcome
bienvenido	(to be) welcome
bigote (m.)	moustache
bilingüe	bilingual
billete (m.)	banknote
billetera (f.)	wallet
bizcochuelo (m.)	cake
blanco	white
blanco y negro	black and white
blando	soft
blusa (f.)	blouse
bocaditos (m. pl.)	snacks
boletería (f.) (Sp. **taquilla**)	ticket office
boleto (m.) (Sp. **billete**)	ticket
boleto de avión (m.)	air ticket
Bolivia (f.)	Bolivia
boliviano	Bolivian
bolsa (f.)	bag
bolsa de dormir (f.) (Sp. **saco de dormir**)	sleeping bag
bombero (m.)	firefighter
bonito	nice
botar (Sp. **tirar**)	to throw away
botella (f.)	bottle
Brasil (m.)	Brazil
brasileño	Brazilian
brazo (m.)	arm
brillo (m.)	brightness
brindar	to drink a toast to
británico	British
broqueta (f.)	brochette
bucear	to dive
buceo (m.)	diving
budín (m.)	bread pudding
buen	good
buenas	short for **buenos días**
buenas noches	good evening; good night
buenas tardes	good afternoon
bueno	good
buenos días	good morning
buscar	to look for
buzón (m.)	postbox
caballero (m.)	gentleman
caballeros (m. pl.)	gentlemen (sign on toilets)
cabeza (f.)	head
cacao (m.)	cacao
cada	each; every
café (m.)	coffee
cafetería (f.)	café
caja (f.)	box
caja de cambios (f.)	gear box
caja fuerte (f.)	safe
cajero (m.)	cashier
cajero automático (m.)	cash dispensing machine
calato (Sp. **desnudo**)	naked
calavera (f.)	skull

calefacción (f.)	heating	**cancha** (f.)	sports court *or* field
calefacción central (f.)	central heating	**canción** (f.)	song
calentar	to warm up	**canillita** (Sp. **vendedor de periódicos**)	news-vendor
calidad (f.)	quality		
cálido	hot (climate)		
caliente	hot	**cansado**	tired
calor (m.)	heat	**cantante** (m., f.)	singer
caloría (f.)	calorie	**cantar**	to sing
calzado (m.)	footwear	**cantidad** (f.)	quantity
calzón (m.)	knickers	**cantina** (f.) (Sp. **taberna**)	bar
calzoncillo (m.)	men's under-pants		
calle (f.)	street	**caña de azúcar** (f.)	sugar cane
calle principal (f.)	main street	**caoba** (f.)	mahogany
cama (f.)	bed	**capacidad** (f.)	capacity
cámara (f.)	camera	**capital** (m., f.)	capital (m. = sum of money) (f. = city)
cambiar	to change, to exchange		
cambio (m.)	change; exchange	**capitalista**	capitalist
		capítulo (m.)	chapter
caminar	to walk	**cara** (f.)	face
camino (m.)	way, road	**característica** (f.)	characteristic
camión (m.)	lorry	**carapulcra** (f.)	Peruvian dish made with dried potatoes
camión (m.) (Méx.) (Sp. **autobús**)	bus		
		cargo (m.)	position (job)
camioneta (f.)	light van; station wagon	**cariño** (m.)	affection
		carne (f.)	meat
camisa (f.)	shirt	**carnicería** (f.)	butcher's
camiseta (f.)	vest, T-shirt	**caro**	expensive
campamentismo (m.)	camping	**carpeta** (f.) (Sp. **pupitre**)	desk
campeón (m.)	champion	**carrera** (f.)	career; run; race; avenue (Col.)
campeonato (m.)	championship		
campesino (m.)	peasant	**carretera** (f.)	road
camping (m.)	campsite	**carro** (Sp. **coche**)	car
campo (m.)	field	**carta** (f.)	letter
campo de deportes (m.)	sports field	**cartelera** (f.)	list of cinemas and theaters
canadiense	Canadian	**cartera** (f.)	purse, handbag, wallet
cáncer (m.)	cancer		

cartero (m.)	postman, mailman	**cerrado**	closed
cartón (m.)	cardboard	**cerrar**	to close
casa (f.)	house, home	**cerveza** (f.)	beer
casa editorial (f.)	publishing house	**chequear**	to check
casado	married	**chiquito**	small
casarse	to get married	**ciclomotor** (m.)	moped
casi	almost	**cielo** (m.)	sky, heaven
casilla de mensajes (f.)	voice mail	**ciencia** (f.)	science
		cierre (m.)	locking device
casona (f.)	large old house	**cierto**	certain
cassette (m.)	cassette	**cifra** (f.)	figure
castellano (Sp. **español**)	Spanish (language)	**cigarrillo** (m.)	cigarette
		cine, cinema (m.)	cinema
castigado	punished	**cine de estreno** (m.)	cinema which shows new films
castigar	to punish		
castigo (m.)	punishment		
catedral (f.)	cathedral	**cinta** (f.)	tape, ribbon
categoría (f.)	category	**círculo** (m.)	circle
católico	catholic	**cita** (f.)	date
causar	to cause	**ciudad** (f.)	city
cebiche (m.)	dish made with raw fish marinated in lemon	**ciudadano** (m.)	citizen
		clase (f.)	lesson, class
		clasificación (f.)	classification
celebración (f.)	celebration	**clausurar**	to bring to a close
celebrar	to celebrate		
celular (m.)	mobile phone	**clavel** (m.)	carnation
cena (f.)	evening meal, supper	**cliente** (m.)	client, customer
		clima (m.)	climate
cenar	to have an evening meal, to have supper	**climatizado**	air-conditioned
		clínica (f.)	private hospital
		club (m.)	club
centígrado (m.)	centigrade	**cobrar**	to charge (money)
céntrico	central		
centro (m.)	center	**cobre** (m.)	copper
Centroamérica (f.)	Central America	**cocina** (f.)	kitchen
		coctel (m.)	cocktail
centro comercial (m.)	shopping center	**coche-bomba** (m.)	car bomb
		coger	to take (in Ar., Méx., Uru. it has sexual connotations)
cerca	near		
cercano	nearby		
cerdo (m.)	pig		
cerebro (m.)	brain	**colegio** (m.)	school

colgar — to hang up (phone)
colocar — to place
colocarse — to place oneself
Colombia (f.) — Colombia
colombiano (m.) — Colombian
colonia (f.) (Ch., Méx.) (Sp. **barrio**, **urbanización**) — residential suburb
colonia proletaria (f.) (Méx.) (Sp. **chabolas**) — shanty town
color (m.) — color
combinación (f.) — combination
combustible (m.) — fuel
comedor (m.) — dining room
comentario (m.) — comment
comenzar — to start, to begin
comer — to eat
comercial — commercial
comerciante (m., f.) — trader, shopkeeper
comercio (m.) — commerce
cómico — comic(al)
comida (f.) — meal
comisaría (f.) — police station
comisión (f.) — committee, commission
cómo — how
cómodo — comfortable
como siempre — as always
compañero (m.) — classmate, workmate
compañía (f.) — company
comparación (f.) — comparison
compatible — compatible
competencia (f.) — competititon
competidor (m.) — competitor
competitivo — competitive
completo — complete, comprehensive

complicado — complicated
compra (f.); **compras** (f. pl.) — purchase; shopping
comprar — to buy
comprender — to understand
comprobar — to check
compromiso (m.) — commitment
computador (m.), **computadora** (f.) (Sp. **ordenador**) — computer
comunicación (f.) — communication
comunista — communist
con — with
con tal que — provided that
concejo (m.) — council
concierto (m.) — concert
concurrido — well attended, busy
concursante (m., f.) — contestant
concurso (m.) — contest, competition
condición (f.) — condition
conducir — to drive
conferencia (f.) — conference
confianza (f.) — confidence
confirmación (f.) — confirmation
confirmar — to confirm
confundir — to confuse
congreso (m.) — congress, conference
conmigo — with me
contraste (m.) — contrast
conocer — to know
conseguir — to obtain
consejo (m.) — advice
conservación (f.) — conservation
conservar — to preserve
construcción (f.) — construction
construir — to build

cónsul (m., f.)	consul	**costar**	to cost
consulado (m.)	consulate	**costarricense,**	Costa Rican
consultar	to consult	**costariqueño**	
consultor (m.)	consultant	**costo** (m.)	cost
consultoría (f.)	consultancy	(Sp. **coste**)	
consumidor (m.)	consumer	**costumbre** (f.)	custom
consumir	to consume	**crecer**	to grow
consumo (m.)	consumption	**crédito** (m.)	credit
contabilidad (f.)	accountancy	**creer**	to believe
contacto (m.)	contact	**criollo** (m.)	creole
contador (m.)	accountant	**criticar**	to criticize
(Sp. **contable**)		**cruzar**	to cross
contaminación	contamination,	**cuaderno** (m.)	exercise book,
(f.)	pollution		notebook
contaminante	polluting	**cuadra** (f.)	block (of houses)
contar	to count; to tell	(Sp. **manzana**)	
contar con	to have	**cuadrado**	square
contento	contented,	**cuadro** (m.)	frame, painting,
	happy		chart
contestar	to answer	**cuadro**	statistics chart
contigo	with you	**estadístico** (m.)	
continuar	to continue	**cuál**	which
contra	against	**cualquier**	any
contrario	opposite	**cualquiera**	any, anyone,
contraste (m.)	contrast		whichever
contrato (m.)	contract	**cuándo, cuando**	when
convencer	to convince	**cuánto, cuánta**	how much
convenio (m.)	agreement	**cuántos, cuántas**	how many
corazón (m.)	heart	**cuarto** (m.)	fourth; bedroom
corbata (f.)	tie	**Cuba** (f.)	Cuba
corregir	to correct	**cubano** (m.)	Cuban
correo (m.)	post office	**cubiertos** (m. pl.)	cutlery
correr	to run	**cuchara** (f.)	spoon
correspondencia	correspondence;	**cucharada** (f.)	spoonful
(f.)	post	**cucharita** (f.)	teaspoon
corresponsal	correspondent	**cuenta** (f.)	check
(m., f.)		**cuenta corriente**	current account
corte (f.)	cut; court	(f.)	
corto	short	**cuento**	short story
cosa (f.)	thing	**cuero** (m.)	leather
costa (f.)	coast	**cuidado** (m.)	care; be careful!
Costa Rica (f.)	Costa Rica	**cuidadosamente**	carefully

cuidar	to look after	**dañino**	harmful
cultivar	to cultivate	**dar**	to give
cultivo (m.)	cultivation	**datos** (m. pl.)	information, data
cultural	cultural	**de**	of; from; than
cumpleaños (m.)	birthday	**de acuerdo**	agreed!, I agree!
cuota mensual	monthly	**de lo contrario**	otherwise
(f.)	payment	**de nada**	you're welcome
cupón (m.)	coupon, voucher	**Debajo debajo**	underneath
curso (m.)	course	**deber** (m.)	duty
champiñón (m.)	mushroom	**deberes** (m. pl.)	homework
chancho (m.)	pig, pork	**débil**	weak
(Sp. **cerdo**)		**década** (f.)	decade
chao, chau (inf.)	bye	**decidir**	to decide
chaqueta (f.)	jacket	**décimo** (m.)	tenth
charla (f.)	talk	**decir**	to say
che (Ar., Uru.)	hey!	**decisión** (f.)	decision
(Sp. **oiga, oye**)		**decisivo**	decisive
cheque (m.)	check	**declarar**	to declare
(Sp. **talón**)		**decorar**	to decorate
cheque de	traveler's check	**dedicarse**	to devote oneself
viaje/viajero			to
(m.)		**defecto** (m.)	defect
chequeas	to check	**defender**	to defend
chica (f.)	girl	**dejar**	to leave
chicano (m.)	Mexican working	**delante de**	in front of
	in the USA	**deletrear**	to spell
chico (m.); (adj.)	boy; small	**delgado**	thin
(Sp. **pequeño**)		**delicado**	delicate
chiquito	small	**delicioso**	delicious
Chile (m.)	Chile	**delincuente**	delinquent,
chileno	Chilean	(m., f.)	criminal
chipa (f.)	Paraguayan dish	**demasiado**	too much/many;
	made with corn		too
chiste (m.)	joke	**democracia** (f.)	democracy
chistoso	funny	**democrático**	democratic
chocolate (m.)	chocolate	**demorar**	to take (time)
chompa (f.) (Pe.)	jumper; sweater;	(Sp. **tardar**)	
(Sp. **jersey**)	cardigan	**denunciar**	to denounce
dama (f.)	lady	**dentro de**	inside
damas (f. pl.)	ladies (sign on	**depender**	to depend
	toilets)	**deporte** (m.)	sport
danza (f.)	dance	**deportivo**	sporty

derecha   right
derecho (m.)   law; right
derechos   human rights
   humanos
   (m. pl.)
derroche (m.)   waste (of money)
desacuerdo (m.)   disagreement
desaparecer   to disappear
desarrollar   to develop
desastre (m.)   disaster
desayunar   to have breakfast
desayuno (m.)   breakfast
descansar   to rest
descanso (m.)   rest
descartable   disposable
descolgar   to take the
     phone off the
     hook
descuento (m.)   discount
desde   from; since
desear   to want, to wish
desempleo (m.)   unemployment
   (Sp. **paro**)
desgraciada-   unfortunately
   mente
desilusión (f.)   disappointment
desilusionado   disappointed
desmoralizado   demoralized
despacio   slowly
despacho (m.)   office
despedida (f.)   farewell
despedirse   to say goodbye
despertador (m.)   alarm clock
despertarse   to wake up
después   afterwards
destinar   to destine, to
     assign
destruir   to destroy
desventaja (f.)   disadvantage
desvestir   to undress
   (Sp. **desnudar**)
detalle (m.)   detail

detrás de   behind
devolver   to give back
día (m.)   day
diálogo (m.)   dialogue
diario,   daily
   diariamente
dibujos   cartoons
   animados (m. pl.)
diccionario (m.)   dictionary
diciembre (m.)   December
dictadura (f.)   dictatorship
dietético   healthy (food)
diferencia (f.)   difference
diferente   different
difícil   difficult
dificultad (f.)   difficulty
dinero (m.)   money
diputado (m.)   deputy (in
     Parliament)
dirección (f.)   address;
     direction
dirigido   planned, directed
disco (m.)   record (music)
disco compacto   compact disc
   (m.)
disco duro (m.)   hard disk
discoteca (f.)   discoteque
disculpar   to excuse
disculparse   to apologize
discurso (m.)   speech
discusión (f.)   discussion
discutir   to discuss
diseño (m.)   design
diskette (m.)   diskette, data
     disk
dislocar   to dislocate
disminuir   to reduce, to go
     down
disponible   available
distinción (f.)   distinction
distinguido   distinguished
distinto   different

distribuidor (m.)	distributor	**ecológico**	ecological, 'green'
Distrito Federal (m.)	Federal District (Méx.)	**economía** (f.)	economy
		económico	economical
diurno	daytime (adj.)	**ecuador** (m.)	equator
diversión (f.)	entertainment	**Ecuador** (m.)	Ecuador
diverso	diverse	**ecuatoriano**	Ecuadorean
divertido	entertaining, funny	**edad** (f.)	age
		edición (f.)	edition
divertirse	to have a good time	**edificio** (m.)	building
		educación (f.)	education
divisa (f.)	foreign currency	**educativo**	educational
divorciado	divorced	**efectivizar**	to implement
divorcio (m.)	divorce	**efectivo** (m.)	cash
doblar	to turn	**ejecutivo** (m.)	executive
doble	double	**ejército** (m.)	army
docena (f.)	dozen	**el; él**	the (m. sing.); he
doctor (m.)	doctor	**el otro día**	the other day
documental (m.)	documentary	**El Salvador** (m.)	El Salvador
documento (m.)	document		
dólar (m.)	dollar	**elaborar**	to make
doler	to hurt	**elección** (f.)	election
dolor (m.)	pain	**electo**	elected
domicilio (m.)	address	(Sp. **elegido**)	
domingo (m.)	Sunday	**electricidad** (f.)	electricity
dominicano	Dominican	**eléctrico**	electric
donativo (m.)	donation	**electrónico**	electronic
dónde; donde	where	**elegante**	elegant
dormido	asleep	**elegido**	elected
dormir	to sleep	**elegir**	to elect
dormitorio (m.)	bedroom	**ella**	she
dudar	to doubt	**ellas**	they (f.)
dueño (m.)	owner	**ellos**	they (m.)
dulce (m.; adj.)	sweet	**embajada** (f.)	embassy
duplicado (m.)	duplicate	**embajador** (m.)	ambassador
durable	durable	**embarcar**	to board
duración (f.)	duration	**embarque** (m.)	boarding
durante	during	**emigrar**	to emigrate
durar	to last	**empanada** (f.)	pasty
duro	hard	**empatar**	to draw
e	and (only before words beginning with **i**-)	**empezar**	to start
		empleado (m.)	employee
		empresa (f.)	firm, company

empresario (m.)	businessman	**entrevista** (f.)	interview
empujar	to push	**entrevistar**	to interview
en	in, on, at	**envase**	packet, container
enamorado (m.);	boyfriend;	**en vez de**	instead of
enamorada (f.)	girlfriend	**enviar**	to send
encantado	pleased to meet you	**época de lluvias** (f.)	rainy season
encargado (m.)	person in charge	**época del año** (f.)	time of the year
en cartelera	on at the theater or at the cinema	**equipaje** (m.)	luggage
		equipo (m.)	team
		equivalente	equivalent
encender	to light, to turn on	**equivocarse**	to be mistaken
		error (m.)	mistake, error
encima	over	**esa, esas**	that, those (f.)
encontrar	to find	**ésa, ésas**	that one, those ones (f.)
encuesta (f.)	survey		
enero (m.)	January	**escalera** (f.)	stairs, ladder
enfermera (f.)	nurse	**escaso**	scarce
enfermo	ill	**escocés**	Scottish
enfrente de	opposite	**Escocia** (f.)	Scotland
engañar	to deceive	**escoger**	to choose
engaño (m.)	deception	**esconder**	to hide
en peligro	endangered	**escribir**	to write
ensalada (f.)	salad	**escrito**	written
enseguida	straight away	**escritor** (m.)	writer
enseñar	to show; to teach	**escritorio** (m.)	desk
entender	to understand	**escritura jeroglífica** (f.)	hieroglyphic writing
entonces	then		
entorno (m.)	environment	**escuchar**	to listen
entrada (f.)	admission ticket; entrance	**escuela** (f.)	school (primary)
		ese, esos	that, those (m.)
entrar	to enter	**ése, ésos**	that one, those ones (m.)
entre	between, among		
entrega (f.)	delivery	**espacio** (m.)	space
entregado	handed over	**espalda** (f.)	back (part of the body)
entregar	to give, to deliver		
		España (f.)	Spain
entrenador (m.)	coach, manager (of a sports team)	**español** (m.)	Spanish (person and language)
		especial	special
entrenar	to train	**especializada**	specialized
entretener	to entertain	**especie** (f.)	species

especificaciones (f. pl.)	specification	**estrategia** (f.)	strategy
espectador (m.)	spectator	**estratégica**	strategic
esperar	to wait	**estudiante** (m., f.)	student
espinaca (f.)	spinach	**estudiar**	to study
esposo (m.); **esposa** (f.)	husband; wife	**estudios** (m. pl.)	studies
esquí (m.)	ski	**etiqueta** (f.)	label
esquina (f.)	corner	**Europa** (f.)	Europe
esta, estas	this, these (f.)	**europeo** (m.)	European
ésta, éstas	this one, these ones (f.)	**evento** (m.)	event
		evitar	to avoid
establecer	to establish	**exacto**	exact
estación (f.)	station, season	**examen** (m.)	exam
estacionamiento	car parking (m.)	**examinar**	to examine
estacionar	to park	**excelente**	excellent
estadía (f.) (Sp. **estancia**)	stay	**exceso** (m.)	excess
		exclusivo	exclusive
estadio (m.)	stadium	**excursión** (f.)	excursion
estadística (f.)	statistics	**exigir**	to demand
estado (m.)	state	**éxito** (m.)	success
estado civil (m.)	marital status	**expansión** (f.)	expansion
Estados Unidos (m. pl.)	United States	**expectativa** (f.) (Sp. **expectación**)	expectation
estadounidense	from the United States	**expediente** (m.)	dossier, process
		experiencia (f.)	experience
estampilla (f.) (Sp. **sello**)	stamp (postage)	**experimentar**	to experiment, to experience
estante (m.)	shelf	**explicación** (f.)	explanation
estantería (f.)	shelving	**explicar**	to explain
estar	to be	**explosión** (f.)	explosion
estatura (f.)	height (of a person)	**explotar**	to exploit
		exportación (f.)	export
estatuto (m.)	statute	**exportador** (m.)	exporter
este	east	**exportar**	to export
este, estos	this, these (m.)	**exposición** (f.)	exhibition
éste, éstos	this one, these ones (m.)	**expresar**	to express
		exprimir	to extract
estéreo	stereo	**extranjero** (m.)	foreign, foreigner; abroad
estilo (m.)	style		
estimado	dear (in a letter)	**extrañar** (Sp. **echar de menos**)	to miss (to feel the absence of)
estómago (m.)	stomach		

fábrica (f.)	factory	**flor** (f.)	flower
fabricar	to manufacture	**folklórico** (m.)	folk
fácil	easy	**folleto** (m.)	leaflet
facsímil (m.)	facsimile	**fondo** (m.)	bottom
factura (f.)	invoice	**formar**	to form
falda (f.)	skirt	**fórmula** (f.)	formula
falso	false	**formulario** (m.)	form
falta (f.)	lack	**Forum**	well-known art
faltar	to lack		gallery in Lima
falla (f.)	failure, fault	**fósforo** (m.)	match
(Sp. **fallo**)		(Sp. **cerilla**)	
familia (f.)	family	**foto(grafía)** (f.)	photo(graph)
familiares (m. pl.)	relatives	**fracasar**	to fail
famoso	famous	**fracaso** (m.)	failure
farmacia (f.)	chemist's	**frambuesa** (f.)	raspberry
fauna (f.)	fauna	**francés**	French
favor (m.)	favor	**Francia** (f.)	France
febrero (m.)	February	**frazada** (f.)	blanket
fecha (f.)	date	(Sp. **manta**)	
felicitaciones	congratulations	**frecuente**	frequent
(f. pl.) (Sp.		**freir**	to fry
enhorabuena)		**frío**	cold
felicitar	to congratulate	**frito**	fried
feliz	happy	**frontera** (f.)	border, frontier
femenino	feminine; women's	**fruta** (f.)	fruit
feria (f.)	fair	**frutal**	fruity
festival (m.)	festival	**frutería** (f.)	fruit shop
fiabilidad (f.)	reliability	**frutilla** (f.)	strawberry
fibra (f.)	fiber	(Sp. **fresa**)	
fibra de vidrio (f.)	glass fiber	**fuente** (f.)	source
fiebre (f.)	fever	**fuente de divisas**	source of foreign
fiesta (f.)	party, festival	(f.)	exchange
fin (m.)	end	**fuerte**	strong
fin de semana	weekend	**fumador** (m.)	smoker
(m.)		**fumar**	to smoke
final (m.)	end	**función** (f.)	show (in a
finalmente	finally, lastly		cinema,
financiero	financial		theater)
fino	fine (quality)	**funcional**	functional
firma (f.)	signature	**funcionar**	to work
firmar	to sign	**funcionario** (m.)	official
flexible	flexible	**fútbol** (m.)	football

futuro (m.)	future	**grupo** (m.)	group
galería (f.)	gallery	**guacamole** (m.)	typical Mexican sauce or dip
Gales (m.)	Wales		
galés	Welsh	**guaraní** (m.)	language spoken in Paraguay
gama (f.)	range		
ganador (m.)	winner	**guardar**	to keep
ganar	to win	**Guatemala** (f.)	Guatemala
garaje (m.)	garage	**guatemalteco**	Guatemalan
garantía (f.)	guarantee	**guerra** (f.)	war
garantizar	to guarantee	**guía turística** (f.)	tourist guide
garbanzo (m.)	chickpea	**gustar**	to like
garganta (f.)	throat	**haber**	to have (aux.)
garrafa (f.)	carafe	**habitación** (f.)	room
gas (m.)	gas (fuel)	**habitante** (m.)	inhabitant
gasolina (f.)	gas	**habla castellana** (f.)	Spanish speaking
gasolina sin plomo (f.)	lead-free gas		
		hablar	to speak
gastar	to spend (money)	**hace**	ago
		hacer; hace (frío/ viento/etc.)	to do, to make; it's (cold/ windy/etc.)
gasto (m.)	expense		
gato (m.)	cat		
general (m.)	general	**hacia**	towards
generalmente	generally	**hallar**	to find
gente (f.)	people	**hambre** (f.); **tener hambre**	hunger; to be hungry
geografía (f.)	geography		
gimnasio (m.)	gymnasium	**hasta**	until
gimnasio cubierto (m.)	indoor gymnasium	**hasta luego**	see you later
		hay	there is/are
gobierno (m.)	government	**hecho** (m.)	fact
gordo	fat	**helado** (m.)	ice cream
grabar	to record on tape	**helicóptero** (m.)	helicopter
		hermano (m.); **hermana** (f.)	brother; sister
gracias	thanks, thank you		
		hervir	to boil
grado (m.)	degree	**hielo** (m.)	ice
gráfico (m.)	graphic	**hijo** (m.), **hija** (f.)	son; daughter
grande	big, large	**hijos** (m. pl.)	children
grasa (f.)	fat	**hincha** (m.)	football fan
gratis	free	**hispánica**	Hispanic
gripe (f.)	influenza, cold	**historia** (f.)	history
grueso	thick	**historial** (m.)	record, history
grupal	in groups	**hoja** (f.)	sheet

hoja de cálculo (f.)	spreadsheet	**impresora matricial** (f.)	dot matrix printer
hoja de ruta (f.)	route plan	**imprimir**	to print
hola	hello	**impuesto** (m.)	tax
hombre (m.)	man	**inauguración** (f.)	opening,
hombro (m.)	shoulder		inauguration
Honduras (f.)	Honduras	**inaugurar**	to inaugurate
hondureño	Honduran	**incendio** (m.)	fire
hora (f.)	hour	**incentivo** (m.)	incentive
horario (m.)	opening hours	**incienso** (m.)	incense
hornalla, hornilla (f.)	burner (in a cooker)	**incluido**	included
hospital (m.)	hospital	**incómodo**	uncomfortable
hospitalidad (f.)	hospitality	**inconveniente**	inconvenient
hotel (m.)	hotel	**increible**	incredible
hoy	today	**incremento** (m.)	increase
huevo (m.)	egg	**incursionar**	to make inroads
humano	human	**indicar**	to indicate
húmedo	wet, damp	**índice de alfabetismo**	literacy rate
ida (f.)	single (trip, journey)	**indígena** (m., f.)	indigenous person
ida y vuelta (f.)	return (trip, journey)	**individual**	individual
ideal	ideal	**industria** (f.)	industry
identificación (f.)	identification	**industrial**	industrial
idioma (m.)	language	**infancia** (f.)	infancy
iglesia (f.)	church	**infantil**	children's
igual	equal, the same	**inferior**	inferior
igualdad (f.)	equality	**inflación** (f.)	inflation
ilegal	ilegal	**información** (f.)	information
iluminado	illuminated, lit	**informar**	to inform
imagen (f.)	picture (TV)	**informática** (f.)	computing
impedir	to prevent	**informativo** (m.)	news program
imperfecto	imperfect	**informe** (m.)	report
importación (f.)	import	**ingeniero** (m.)	engineer
importador (m.)	importer	**Inglaterra** (f.)	England
importante	important	**inglés**	English
importar	to import	**ingreso** (m.)	income
imposible	impossible	**iniciar**	to begin
imprenta (f.)	printing works	**iniciativa** (f.)	initiative
impresora (f.)	printer	**inmediato**	immediate
		inmenso	huge

inmigración (f.)	immigration
inmigrante (m., f.)	immigrant
inmigrar	immigrate
inocente	innocent
insistir	to insist
inspirar	to inspire
instalar	to install
instruir	to instruct
instrumento (m.)	instrument
inteligente	intelligent
intentar	to attempt
interés (m.)	interest
interesado	interested
interesante	interesting
internacional	international
interno	internal
interpretar	to sing; to interpret
intérprete (m., f.)	singer; interpreter
interrogar	to interrogate
interrumpir	to interrupt
interrupción (f.)	interruption
inversión (f.)	investment
invertir	to invest
investigación (f.)	investigation, research
invierno (m.)	winter
invitación (f.)	invitation
invitado (m.)	guest
ir	to go
ir de compras	to go shopping
Irlanda (f.)	Ireland
irlandés	Irish
isla (f.)	island
itinerario (m.)	itinerary
izquierda (f.)	left
jabón (m.)	soap
Jamaica (f.)	Jamaica
jamaiquino	Jamaican
jamás	never
jamón (m.)	ham

Japón (m.)	Japan
japonés	Japanese
jardín (m.)	garden
jefe (m.)	boss, head
jefe de ventas (m.)	head of sales
jenjibre (m.)	ginger
joven	young
juego (m.)	game
juego de muebles (m.)	suite of furniture
jueves (m.)	Thursday
juez (m.)	judge
jugar	to play (a game or sport)
jugo (m.)	juice
juguete (m.)	toy
julio (m.)	July
junio (m.)	June
junto a	next to
juntos	together
justo	fair, just
juventud (f.)	youth
kilo (m.)	kilo
kilómetro (m.)	kilometer
la, las	the (f. sing., f. pl.)
laboratorio de idiomas (m.)	language laboratory
lado (m.)	side
lago (m.)	lake
lágrima (f.)	tear
lamentablemente	regrettably
lamentar	to regret
lana (f.)	wool
langostino (m.)	prawn
lapicero (m.), **lapicera** (f.)	ball-point pen
lápiz labial (m.)	lipstick
largo	long
láser (f.)	laser
lástima (f.)	pity

lateral	lateral	**libro** (m.)	book
Latinoamérica (f.)	Latin America	**licencia de conducir** (f.)	driving licence
latinoamericano	Latin American	**licuado energético** (m.)	isotonic drink
lavadora (f.)	washing machine		
lavar	to wash	**líder** (m.)	leader
lavar en seco (Sp. **limpiar en seco**)	to dry clean	**líder sindical** (m.)	union leader
		ligero	light
le ruego	would you please	**limitar con**	to have borders with
lección (f.)	lesson	**limón** (m.)	lemon
lectura (f.)	reading	**limpiar**	to clean
leche (f.)	milk	**limpieza** (f.)	cleanliness
lechuga (f.)	lettuce	**lindo** (Sp. **bonito, majo**)	pretty
leer	to read		
legal	legal	**línea** (f.)	line
legalizar	to legalize	**línea aérea** (f.)	airline
lejos	far	**linterna** (f.)	torch
lengua (f.)	tongue	**lista** (f.)	list
lenguado (m.)	sole	**listo**	ready
lentes (m. pl.)	glasses, spectacles	**literatura** (f.)	literature
		liviano	light
lentes de contacto (m. pl.) (Sp. **lentillas**)	contact lenses	**llamada** (f.)	telephone call
		lo	it
lento	slow	**local** (m.)	premises
letrero (m.)	sign	**loción** (f.)	lotion
levantacristales eléctrico (m.)	electric window winder (car)	**loco**	mad
		lograr	to achieve
levantar	to lift	**lomo** (m.)	beefsteak
levantarse	to get up	**lona** (f.)	canvas
ley (f.)	law	**Londres** (m.)	London
libertad (f.)	freedom	**longitud** (f.)	length
libertad de expresión (f.)	freedom of expresion	**los**	the (m. pl.)
		lo siento	I'm sorry
libertad de prensa (f.)	freedom of the press	**luchar**	to fight
		luego	then, later
libra (f.)	pound	**lugar** (m.)	place
libra esterlina (f.)	pound sterling	**luna** (f.)	moon
		lunes (m.)	Monday
libre	free	**luz** (f.)	light
librería (f.)	bookshop	**llamada** (f.)	telephone call
		llamar	to call

llamarse	to be called	**máquina de**	typewriter
llave (f.)	key	**escribir** (m.)	
llavero (m.)	key-ring	**mar** (m.)	sea
llegada (f.)	arrival	**marca** (f.)	brand, make
llegar	to arrive	**marido** (m.)	husband
llenar	to fill	**marisco** (m.)	seafood
lleno	full	**mármol** (m.)	marble
llevar a cabo	to take place, to	**marrón**	brown
	carry out	**martes** (m.)	Tuesday
llover	to rain	**marzo** (m.)	March
lluvia (f.)	rain	**más**	more
lluviosa (**imagen**)	snowy (TV	**más adelante**	later
	picture)	**más adentro**	further inside
lluvioso	rainy	**más tarde**	later
macerar	to marinate	**matar**	to kill
machucar	to mash (food)	**mate** (m.)	infusion drunk
madera (f.)	wood		mainly in
madre (f.)	mother		Argentina
madrugada (f.)	early hours of	**materia prima** (f.)	raw material
	the morning	**material** (m.)	material
mal	badly	**máximo**	maximum
malecón (m.)	promenade	**mayo** (m.)	May
maleta (f.)	suitcase	**mayor**	elder; more
maletín (m.)	briefcase	**mayoría** (f.)	majority
malo	bad; poor	**mecánica** (f.)	mechanics
malla entera de	one-piece	**mecánico** (m.)	mechanic
baño (f.)	swimsuit	**mediano**	medium
mandar	to send	**medianoche** (f.)	midnight
¿mande?	pardon?	**medias** (f. pl.)	socks, stockings
(Sp. **¿cómo?**)		**medicina** (f.)	medicine
manejar	to drive	**médico** (m.)	doctor
manera (f.)	manner, way	**medida** (f.)	measurement,
mano (f.)	hand		measure
mantener	to maintain	**medio**	half a
manualidades	handicraft	**medio ambiente**	environment
(f. pl.)		(m.)	
manzana (f.)	apple	**mediodía** (m.)	midday
mañana (f.); (m.)	morning;	**medios de**	means of
	tomorrow	**transporte**	transport
mapa (m.)	map	(m. pl.)	
máquina (f.)	machine	**medir**	to measure
maquinaria (f.)	machinery	**mejor**	better; best

mejorar	to improve	**mínimo**	minimum
melón (m.)	melon	**ministerio** (m.)	ministry
memoria (f.)	memory	**ministro** (m.)	minister
menor	younger; less	**minusválido** (m.)	handicapped
menos	less		person
mensaje (m.)	message	**minuto** (m.)	minute
mensual	monthly	**mirar**	to look
mentira (f.)	lie	**mirar tiendas**	to go window
menú (m.)	menu		shopping
mercado (m.)	market	**misa** (f.)	mass (religion)
mercado de	currency	**mismo**	same
cambios (m.)	market	**mitad** (f.)	half
mercado	free rate	**mochila** (f.)	rucksack
paralelo (m.)	currency	**moda** (f.)	fashion
	market	**modales** (m. pl.)	manners
mes (m.)	month	**modelo** (m.)	model
mesa (f.)	table	**moderar**	to moderate
mestizo (m.)	person who has	**moderno**	modern
	one Spanish	**modo** (m.)	manner, way
	and one	**módulo** (m.)	module, unit
	indigenous	**molestar**	to annoy, to
	parent		bother
metal (m.)	metal	**molestia** (f.)	trouble,
metro (m.)	subway;		inconvenience
	meter	**molesto**	annoyed,
mexicano,	Mexican		bothered
mejicano		**momento** (m.)	moment
México, Méjico	Mexico	**moneda** (f.)	coin; currency
(m.)		**monitor** (m.)	monitor
mezcla (f.)	mixture	**montaña** (f.)	mountain
mi, mis	my	**montañismo** (m.)	mountaineering
mí	me (pron. after	**montañoso**	mountainous
	prep.)	**montar**	to ride
miedo (m.)	fear	**monumento** (m.)	monument
mientras	while	**morir**	to die
miércoles (m.)	Wednesday	**mostrar**	to show
mil	thousand	**motocicleta** (f.)	motorbike
milanesa (f.)	escalope	**mucho**	much
militar	military	**muchos**	many
millón (m.)	million	**muebles** (m. pl.)	furniture
mineral (m.)	mineral	**muela** (f.)	tooth
minería (f.)	mining	**muerte** (f.)	death

muerto	dead	**negro**	black
muestra (f.)	sample	**nervioso**	nervous
mujer (f.)	woman; wife	**neutro** (m.)	neutral
mulato (m.)	mulatto (person with one white and one black parent)	**nevar**	to snow
		ni	nor
		Nicaragua (f.)	Nicaragua
		nicaragüense	Nicaraguan
multa (f.)	fine	**niebla** (f.)	fog
mundo (m.)	world	**nieto** (m.);	grandson;
municipalidad (f.)	city/local council	**nieta** (f.)	granddaughter
(Sp. **ayunta-miento**)		**ninguno**	no one
muñeco (m.)	doll	**niño** (m.); **niña** (f.)	boy; girl
museo (m.)	museum	**niños** (m. pl.)	children
música (f.)	music	**ni siquiera**	not even
musical	musical	**nivel** (m.)	level
muy	very	**nivel de precios**	price range (m.)
nacer	to be born	**no**	no, not
nacimiento (m.)	birth	**nocturno**	nocturnal, in the evening
nación (f.)	nation		
nacional	national	**noche** (f.)	night
nacionalidad (f.)	nationality	**no fumador** (m.)	non-smoker
nada	nothing	**nogal** (m.)	walnut tree
nadar	to swim	**no hay de qué**	you're welcome
nadie	nobody	**no importa**	it doesn't matter
naranja (f.)	orange		
natación (f.)	swimming	**no más**	no more
natatorio (m.)	swimming pool	(Sp. **nada más**)	
(Ch., Ar. **piscina**)		**nombre** (m.)	name
		no precisa/no	don't know (in a
natural	natural	**responde**	survey)
navegar en Internet	to surf the Net	**norma de calidad** (f.)	quality standards
Navidad (f.)	Christmas	**normal**	normal
necesario	necessary	**normalmente**	normally
necesidad (f.)	need, necessity	**norte** (m.)	north
necesitar	to need	**norteamericano**	North American; American
negar	to deny		
negativo (m.)	negative	**nosotros**	we
negociación (f.)	negotiation	**nos vemos**	see you (inf.)
negociar	to negotiate	**nota** (f.)	note; grade, mark
negocio (m.)	business		

notar	to notice	**ocupado**	busy
noticia (f.)	news item	**ocupar**	to occupy
noticiero,	news bulletin	**ocurrir**	to occur
noticiario (m.)		**oeste** (m.)	west
novela (f.)	novel	**oferta** (f.)	reduced
noveno	ninth		merchandise
noviembre (m.)	November	**oficina** (f.)	office
novio (m.);	fiancé; fiancée	**ofrecer to**	offer
novia (f.)		**oído** (m.)	hearing, inner
nube (f.)	cloud		ear
nublado	cloudy	**oír**	to hear
nuestro/a,	our	**ojalá**	if only
nuestro/as		**ojo** (m.)	eye
Nueva York (f.)	New York	**ola** (f.)	wave (in the sea)
nuevamente	again	**olimpiadas**	school sports
nuevo	new	**estudiantiles**	festival
número (m.)	number	(f. pl.)	
nunca	never	**olvidar**	to forget
nutrición (f.)	nutrition	**omnibús** (m.)	bus
o	or	**operación** (f.)	operation
objetivo (m.)	target	**opinar**	to give an
objeto (m.)	object		opinion
obligación (f.)	obligation	**opinión** (f.)	opinion
obligar	to force, to	**oportunidad** (f.)	opportunity
	oblige	**óptimo**	optimum
obligatorio	obligatory,	**ordenar**	to tidy up
	compulsory	**oreja** (f.)	ear
obra cómica (f.)	comedy	**organización** (f.)	organization
obra de teatro (f.)	play (theater)	**organizar**	to organize
obras públicas	public works	**orientación** (f.)	guidance,
(f. pl.)			counselling
obrero (m.)	manual worker	**oro** (m.)	gold
obtener	to obtain	**orquesta** (f.)	orchestra
Oceanía (f.)	Australasia	**otoño** (m.)	autumn
océano (m.)	ocean	**otra época** (f.)	bygone era
Océano Atlántico	Atlantic Ocean	**otro**	another, other
(m.)		**paciente** (m., f.)	patient
Océano Pacífico	Pacific Ocean	**padre** (m.);	father; parents
(m.)		**padres** (m. pl.)	
octavo	eighth	**pagar**	to pay
octubre (m.)	October	**Página Web** (f.)	web page
ocupacíon (f.)	occupation	**página** (f.)	page

pago (m.)	payment	**parrillada** (f.)	grilled meats
páguese a	payable to	**parte** (f.)	part
país (m.)	country	**participación** (f.)	participation
paisaje (m.)	landscape	**participar**	to take part
palabra (f.)	word	**particular**	private;
palanca (f.)	lever		particular
pan (m.)	bread	**partido** (m.)	match; party
panadería (f.)	bread shop		(political)
Panamá (m.)	Panama	**pasado**	past; last
panameño	Panamanian	**pasaje** (f.)	fare
panqueque (m.)	pancake	**pasajero** (m.)	passenger
pantalón, (m.)	pants, (trousers)	**pasaporte** (m.)	passport
pantalones		**pasar**	to pass
(m. pl.)		**pasar la**	to vacuum
pantalla (f.)	screen	**aspiradora**	
pañuelo (m.)	handkerchief	**pasar las**	to spend your
papa (f.)	potato	**vacaciones**	holiday
(Sp. **patata**)		**pasatiempo** (m.)	pastime
papel (m.)	paper	**pasear**	to go for a walk
paquete (m.)	parcel	**paseo** (m.)	walk, stroll
par (m.)	pair	**pasillo** (m.)	aisle, corridor
para	for; to; in order	**paso** (m.)	step
	to	**paso a paso**	step by step
para llevar	to take away	**pastel** (m.)	pie, cake
parada (f.)	stop (bus)	**pastelería** (f.)	cake shop
paradero (m.)	stop (bus)	**pastilla** (f.)	tablet
(Col., Ec.,		**patio** (m.)	yard, courtyard
Pe., Bo., Ch.)		**patria** (f.)	fatherland
parado	standing	**paz** (f.)	peace
(Sp. **de pie**)		**pecho** (m.)	breast, chest
Paraguay (m.)	Paraguay	**pedido** (m.)	order
paraguayo	Paraguayan	**pedir**	to order (goods);
parar	to stop		to ask for
pararse (Sp.	to stand up	**pelar**	to peel
ponerse de pie)		**película** (f.)	movie
parecer	to seem	**película del**	western
parecerse	to resemble, to	**oeste** (f.)	
	look alike	**peligro** (m.)	danger
pared (f.)	wall	**pelirrojo**	red-haired
pareja (f.)	partner	**pelo** (m.)	hair
parientes (m. pl.)	relations	**peluquería** (f.)	hairdresser's
parque (m.)	park	**pensar**	to think

pensión (f.)	pension; boarding house	**pintor** (m.)	painter
peor	worse	**pintura** (f.)	painting; paint
pequeño	little; small	**piña** (f.)	pineapple
pera (f.)	pear	**pionero** (m.)	pioneer
perder	to lose	**piscina** (f.)	swimming pool
perderse	to get lost	**pista** (f.)	track
¡perdón! (m.)	sorry!	**plan** (m.)	plan
perdonar	to forgive	**planchar**	to iron
perfecto	perfect	**planta** (f.)	plant; floor level (in a building)
periódico (m.)	newspaper		
periodista (m., f.)	journalist	**planta alta** (f.)	upstairs
		planta baja (f.)	downstairs
período (m.)	period	**plástico** (m.)	plastic
permiso (m.)	permission	**plata** (f.) (Sp. **dinero**)	money
permitir	to allow		
pero	but	**plátano** (m.)	banana
perro (m.)	dog	**platicar**	to talk
perseguir	to pursue, to chase	**plato** (m.)	plate
		playa (f.)	beach
persona (f.)	person	**plaza** (f.)	square
personaje (m.)	character (theater, novel, etc.)	**plegable**	folding
		población (f.)	population
		poblado	populated
		pobre	poor
personal (m.)	personnel, staff	**pobreza** (f.)	poverty
personalidad (f.)	personality	**poco; pocos**	little/few
Perú	Peru	**poco a poco**	little by little
peruano	Peruvian	**poder**	can
pesado	heavy	**poesía** (f.)	poetry
pesca (f.)	fishing	**poeta** (m.); **poetisa** (f.)	poet
pescado (m.)	fish		
peso (m.)	weight	**policía** (f., m., f.)	police; policeman; policewoman
petróleo (m.)	oil; petroleum		
piano (m.)	piano		
picante	hot (spicy)	**policial**	police (adj.)
picar	to chop (food)	**política** (f.)	politics; policy
pie (m.)	foot	**polo** (m.) (Ch., Ar., Uru. **polera**)	T-shirt
piel (f.)	skin		
pierna (f.)	leg		
pila (f.)	battery	**pollo** (m.)	chicken
pileta (f.)	swimming pool	**poner**	to put
pintar	to paint	**popular**	popular

por	for; by; because of	**préstamo** (m.)	loan
por ahora	for the time being	**prestar**	to lend
por ciento	per cent	**presupuesto** (m.)	budget
(Sp. **por cien**)		**previo**	prior, previous
porción (f.)	portion, serving	**primaria** (f.)	primary (education)
por correo	by post	**primavera** (f.)	spring (season)
por ejemplo	for example	**primer/o**	first
por el momento	for the time being	**principal**	principal
		principio (m.)	beginning
por favor	please	**privado**	private
por fin	at last	**probabilidad** (f.)	probability
por otra parte	on the other hand	**probable**	probable
		probar	to try, to test
por qué	why	**problema** (m.)	problem
por si acaso	just in case	**procesamiento**	word processing
por supuesto	of course	**de texto** (m.)	
por todas partes	everywhere	**procesar**	to process
por último	lastly	**proceso** (m.)	process
porque	because	**procurar**	to try
portugués	Portuguese	**producción** (f.)	production
posibilidad (f.)	possibility	**producir**	to produce
posible	possible	**producto** (m.)	product
postal (f.)	postcard	**profesor** (m.)	teacher
postergar	to postpone	**profundo**	deep
(Sp. **aplazar**)		**programas de**	current affairs
postre (m.)	dessert	**actualidad**	
potente	powerful	**prohibición** (f.)	ban, prohibition
practicar	to practise	**prohibir**	to ban, to prohibit
precio (m.)	price		
preferir	to prefer	**promedio**	average
pregunta (f.)	question	**promesa** (f.)	promise
preguntar	to ask a question	**prometer**	to promise
premio (m.)	prize	**pronóstico del**	weather forecast
prensa (f.)	press	**tiempo** (m.)	
preocuparse	to worry	**pronto**	soon
preparar	to prepare	**pronunciación** (f.)	pronunciation
presentar	to present; to introduce	**pronunciado**	marked
		pronunciar	to pronounce
presidente (m.)	president	**propiedad** (f.)	property
presionar	to press	**propietario** (m.)	proprietor, owner
preso (m.)	prisoner		

propio	own		musical
proponer	to propose		instrument
protestante	protestant	**querer**	to want
provincia (f.)	province	**querido**	dear (e.g. to start
próximo	next		a letter)
proyecto (m.)	project	**queso** (m.)	cheese
publicación (f.)	publication	**quien; quién**	who
publicar	to publish	**quinto**	fifth
publicidad (f.)	advertising,	**quitar**	to take away
	publicity	**quizá, quizás**	perhaps
público (m.)	public; audience	**radio** (m.)	radio
pueblo (m.)	town, village;	**ranura** (f.)	slot
	people (of a	**rápido**	fast
	nation)	**rato** (m.)	while
puente (m.)	bridge	**ratón** (m.)	mouse
puente aéreo (m.)	shuttle service	**rayo** (m.)	lightning
puerta (f.)	door	**raza** (f.)	race
puesto (m.)	position (job);	**razón** (f.)	reason
	stall (market)	**razonable**	reasonable
puesto de	job	**realidad** (f.)	reality
trabajo (m.)		**realizar**	to carry out
puro (m.)	cigar	**rebajado**	reduced
puro	pure	**rebajar**	to reduce
que	that; than	**recepción** (f.)	reception
qué	what	**recepcionista** (f.)	receptionist
¿qué pasa?	what's happen-	**recesión** (f.)	recession
	ing, what's the	**receta** (f.)	receipt;
	matter?		prescription
¡qué pena!	what a pity!	**recibir**	to receive
que viene	next	**recibo** (m.)	receipt
quechua (m.)	indigenous	**recoger**	to pick up
	language	**recomendación**	recommendation
	spoken in the	(f.)	
	Andean	**recomendar**	to recommend
	countries	**reconocer**	to recognize
quedar	to stay; to be	**reconstruir**	to rebuild, to
	left		reconstruct
queja (f.)	complaint	**recordar**	to remember
quejarse	to complain	**recorrer**	to go through, to
quemar	to burn		travel
quena (f.)	traditional	**recortar**	to cut back, to
	Andean		trim

recreativo	leisure	**reservar**	reserve
rector (m.)	vice-chancellor	**residente** (m.)	resident
recuerdo (m.)	souvenir	**resolver**	to solve
recuperación (f.)	recovery	**respetar**	to respect
recuperar	to recover	**respeto** (m.)	respect
red (f.)	network	**responder**	to reply
reducir	to reduce	**respuesta** (f.)	reply
reemplazar	to replace	**restauración** (f.)	restoration
refresco (m.)	refreshing drink	**restaurante** (m.)	restaurant
regalar	to give (present), to give away	**restaurar**	to restore
regalo (m.)	gift, present	**resto** (m.)	rest, remainder
región (f.)	region	**resultado** (m.)	result
reglamento (m.)	regulation	**retirar**	to withdraw
regresar	to return	**retrato** (m.)	portrait
regular	regular; not too bad	**reunión** (f.)	meeting
regular	to adjust	**revelado** (m.)	development (photographs)
reir	to laugh	**revelar**	to reveal; to develop (a film)
religión (f.)	religion		
reloj (m.)	watch; clock	**revista** (f.)	magazine
reloj despertador (m.)	alarm clock	**revolución** (f.)	revolution
rellenar	to fill in	**rezar**	to pray
remedio (m.)	remedy	**rico**	tasty, delicious
remuneración (f.)	remuneration	**río** (m.)	river
renovar	to renew	**riqueza** (f.)	wealth
rentar	to rent	**rizado**	curly
renunciar	to resign	**robar**	to steal; to rob
reparación (f.)	repair	**roble** (m.)	oak
reparar	to repair	**robo** (m.)	robbery, burglary
reparto (m.)	delivery	**rojo**	red
repetir	to repeat	**romántico**	romantic
representante (m.)	representative	**romper**	to break
		ron (m.)	rum
República Dominicana (f.)	Dominican Republic	**ropa** (f.)	clothing
		ropero (m.)	wardrobe
		rosa (f.)	rose
repuesto (m.)	spare part	**ruido** (m.)	noise
requisito (m.)	requirement	**rural**	rural
rescatar	to rescue	**ruta** (f.)	route
reservación (f.)	reservation	**sábado** (m.)	Saturday

saber	to know	**semanal**	weekly
sabor (m.)	flavor, taste	**semestral**	six-monthly
sacar	to take out	**semestre** (m.)	semester
sala (f.)	living room; hall	**senador** (m.)	senator
salario (m.)	wage	**sentarse**	to sit down
salida (f.)	departure	**sentimiento** (m.)	feeling
salir	to leave; to go out	**sentir**	to feel
		señor	gentleman, mister
salsa (f.)	sauce		
saltar	to jump	**señora**	lady, Mrs
salud (f.)	health; cheers!	**señorita**	young lady, miss
saludable	healthy	**separado**	separated
saludar	to greet	**ser**	to be
saludo (m.); **saludos**	greeting; regards (at the end of a letter)	**servicio** (m.)	service
		servir	to serve
		sesión (f.)	session
salvado (m.)	bran	**setiembre, septiembre** (m.)	September
salvadoreño	Salvadorian		
sandía (f.)	watermelon	**sétimo, séptimo**	seventh
satisfecho	satisfied	**si**	if
se puede	one can	**sí**	yes
sección (f.)	section	**siempre**	always
seco	dry	**siglo** (m.)	century
secretario (m.), **secretaria** (f.)	secretary	**significar**	to mean
		silencio (m.)	silence
sector (m.)	sector	**silla** (f.)	chair
sector informal (m.)	the 'informal' sector (of the economy)	**simplificar**	to simplify
		sin	without
		sindicato (m.)	trade union
secundaria (f.)	secondary (education)	**sin duda**	no doubt
		sino	but
sed (f.)	thirst	**sistema** (m.)	system
seguido (Sp. **frecuentemente**)	frequently	**sitio** (m.)	site, place
		situación (f.)	situation, location
seguir	to carry on		
según	according to	**situar**	to locate
segundo	second	**sobre** (prep.); (m.)	on, over; envelope
seguridad (f.)	safety		
seguro (m.)	insurance	**socialista**	socialist
selva (f.)	jungle	**sociedad** (f.)	society
semana (f.)	week	**socio** (m.)	member; partner
Semana Santa (f.)	Easter	**soldado** (m.)	soldier

soledad (f.)	loneliness	**tabaco** (m.)	tobacco
solicitar	to request, to apply for	**talla** (f.)	size (clothes)
		tamaño (m.)	size
solidaridad (f.)	solidarity	**también**	also
sólido	solid	**tampoco**	neither
solo	alone	**tan . . . como**	as . . . as
sólo	only	**tapete** (m.)	tapestry
solución (f.)	solution	**tarde** (f.)	afternoon; late
somos	we are	**tarea** (f.)	homework
son	you are (for. and inf.); they are	**tarifa** (f.)	tariff
		tarjeta (f.)	card
sonido (m.)	sound	**tarjeta de débito** (f.)	debit card
sonrisa (f.)	smile		
soñar	to dream	**tarta** (f.)	pie
sorpresa (f.)	surprise	**taza** (f.)	cup
sorteo (m.)	draw, raffle	**té** (m.)	tea
sortija (f.)	ring	**teatro** (m.)	theater
Sr	Mr	**teclado** (m.)	keyboard
Sra	Mrs	**técnica** (f.)	tecnique
Srta	Miss	**técnico** (m.)	technician
su, sus	your (for. sing. and pl.); his; her	**tecnología** (f.)	technology
		tela (f.)	fabric
suave	soft	**telefonear**	to phone
subcomisión	subcommittee	**teléfono** (m.)	telephone
subir	to go up	**teléfono móvil** (m.)	mobile phone
subsidio (m.)	subsidy		
sucesor (m.)	successor	**telenovela** (f.)	soap opera
sucio	dirty	**televisión** (f.)	television
sucursal (m.)	branch	**Televisor** (m.)	TV set
Sudamérica (f.)	South America	**tema** (m.)	topic, theme, subject
sueldo (m.)	salary		
suelto	loose	**temperatura** (f.)	temperature
suéter (m.)	sweater	**templado**	warm
suficiente	enough	**temprano**	early
suma (f.)	amount, sum	**tener**	to have
supermercado (m.)	supermarket	**tener hambre**	to be hungry
		tener lugar	to take place
supervisar	to supervise	**tener razón**	to be right
suponer	to suppose	**tener sed**	to be thirsty
sur	south	**tener un aire de**	to have an air of
suyo	yours (for. sing. and pl.); his; hers;	**tenis** (m.)	tennis
		terminar	to end, to finish

termo (m.)	flask	**trabajo** (m.)	work
terrible	terrible	**traducción** (f.)	translation
territorio (m.)	territory	**traer**	to bring
terrorismo (m.)	terrorism	**trámites** (m. pl.)	paperwork, red tape
texto (m.)	text		
ti	you (pron. after prep.)	**tranquilo**	quiet
		transeunte (m.)	passer-by
tía (f.)	aunt	**transmitir**	to broadcast
tiempo (m.)	time; weather	**transporte** (m.)	transport
tienda (f.)	shop	**tranvía** (m.)	tram
tierra (m.)	earth; soil	**trapo** (m.)	cloth
timbre (m.)	bell	**tratar con/sobre**	deal with
timón (m.)	steering wheel	**tren** (m.)	train
(Sp. **volante**)		**tribu** (f.)	tribe
(Ch., Ar.		**tribunal** (m.)	court
manurio)		**trimestral**	quarterly
tinto (m.)	red wine; black coffee (Col.)	**triste**	sad
		triunfar	to succeed
tío (m.)	uncle	**tropa** (f.)	troop
tipo (m.)	type	**tropezar**	to stumble
titular (m.)	headline	**tropical**	tropical
tocar	to play (a musical instrument)	**tu, tus**	your (inf.)
		tú	you (inf.)
		turismo (m.)	tourism
todavía	still; yet	**turista** (m., f.)	tourist
todo	all; whole; every	**turno** (m.)	turn
todo-terreno	all-terrain	**u**	or (only before words beginning with **o-**)
todos	all; everybody		
tolerancia (f.)	tolerance		
tomar	to take; to eat; to drink	**ubicar** (Sp. **localizar**, **situar**)	to locate
tomate (m.)	tomato	**último**	last; latest
tonto (m.)	silly, stupid	**un, uno, una**	a; one
tormenta (f.)	storm	**único**	unique; single
torta (f.)	cake	**unidad** (f.)	unit
(Sp. **tarta**)		**universidad** (f.)	university
tortilla (f.)	omelette; maize pancake (Méx.)	**urgente**	urgent
		Uruguay (m.)	Uruguay
		uruguayo	Uruguayan
torturar	to torture	**usado**	used
trabajador (m.)	worker	**usar**	to use
trabajar	to work	**usted**	you (for.)

ustedes (Sp. **vosotros** = inf.)	you (for. and inf.)	**vespertino**	in the afternoon
usuario (m.)	user	**vestido** (m.)	dress; clothing
útil, útiles	useful	**vestirse**	to get dressed
utilizar	to use	**vez** (f.)	time, occasion
vacaciones	holidays (f. pl.)	**viaje** (m.)	trip
valer	to be worth	**viajero** (m.)	traveler
válido	valid	**vida** (f.)	life
valor (m.)	value	**video** (m.)	video
vamos	let's go!	**vidrio** (m.)	glass
variada	varied	**viento** (m.)	wind
varios (pl.)	several	**viernes** (m.)	Friday
vaso (m.)	glass, tumbler	**vino** (m.)	wine
vecino (m.)	neighbor	**visa** (f.) (Sp. **visado**)	visa
vela (f.)	candle		
velocidad (f.)	speed	**visita** (f.)	visit
vendedor (m.)	seller; salesman	**visitar**	to visit
vendedor ambulante (m.)	street seller	**viuda** (f.)	widow
		viudo (m.)	widower
		vivienda (f.)	housing
vender	to sell	**vivir**	to live
venezolano	Venezuelan	**vocear**	to shout
Venezuela (f.)	Venezuela	**vocero** (m.)	spokesperson
venir	to come	**volar**	to fly
venta (f.)	sale	**volver**	to return
ventaja (f.)	advantage	**voz** (f.)	voice
ventana (f.)	window	**vuelo** (m.)	flight
ventanilla (f.)	counter	**vuelta** (f.)	return
ventanilla (f.)	window (at a bank)	**y**	and
		ya	already
ver	to see; to watch	**yo**	I
verano (m.)	summer	**zambo** (m.)	person with one black and one Indian parent
verdad (f.)	truth; right		
verdadero	true		
verde	green		
verdulería (f.)	vegetable shop	**zapatilla** (f.)	sports shoe; trainer
verdura (f.)	vegetable		
vereda (f.) (Sp. **acera**)	pavement	**zapato** (m.)	shoe
		zona (f.)	zone, area

English–Spanish glossary

English	Spanish	English	Spanish
a	**un, uno, una**	apologize, to	**disculparse**
able to, to be	**poder**	apple	**manzana** (f.)
abroad	**extranjero**	area	**zona** (f.)
add	**agregar**	arm	**brazo** (m.)
address	**dirección** (f.)	arrival	**llegada** (f.)
advise, to	**avisar**	article	**artículo** (m.)
airplane	**avión** (m.)	artificial	**artificial**
afternoon	**tarde** (f.)	as	**como**
afterwards	**después**	at	**en**
against	**contra**	back (part of	**espalda** (f.)
age	**edad** (f.)	the body)	
ago	**hace**	bad	**malo**
agreed, I agree	**de acuerdo**	badly	**mal**
aim	**fin** (m.)	ball-point pen	**lapicero** (m.);
air	**aire** (m.)		**lapicera** (f.)
air-conditioned	**climatizado**	bank	**banco** (m.)
air ticket	**boleto de avión**	banknote	**billete** (m.)
	(m.)	bar	**bar** (m.)
all	**todo**	bath; bathroom	**baño** (m.)
alone	**solo**	be, to	**ser; estar**
already	**ya**	beach	**playa** (f.)
also	**también**	beard	**barba** (f.)
always	**siempre**	because of	**por**
among	**entre**	bed	**cama** (f.)
ancestor	**antepasado** (m.)	bedroom	**cuarto** (m.)
and	**y**	beer	**cerveza** (f.)
animal	**animal** (m.)	begin, to	**comenzar**
another	**otro**	behind	**atrás de**
answer, to	**contestar**		(Sp. **detrás de**)
any	**cualquier**	better	**mejor**
anyone	**cualquiera**	best	**el/la/lo mejor**

between	**entre**	cash dispensing	**cajero**
big	**grande**	machine	**automático** (m.)
bill	**cuenta** (f.)	cat	**gato** (m.)
birthday	**cumpleaños** (m.)	cathedral	**catedral** (f.)
blouse	**blusa** (f.)	Central America	**Centroamérica**
blow out, to	**apagar**		(f.)
blue	**azul**	center	**centro** (m.)
book	**libro** (m.)	chair	**silla** (f.)
bookshop	**librería** (f.)	change, to	**cambiar**
bottle	**botella** (f.)	chapter	**capítulo** (m.)
box	**caja** (f.)	cheap	**barato**
boy	**chico** (m.); **niño**	cheers!	**salud**
	(m.)	cheese	**queso** (m.)
branch	**sucursal** (m.)	chemist's	**farmacia** (f.)
bread	**pan** (m.)	check	**cheque** (m.)
breakfast	**desayuno** (m.)		(Sp. **talón**)
breast	**pecho** (m.)	check, to	**chequear**
bridge	**puente** (m.)	chest	**pecho** (m.)
bring, to	**traer**	children	**hijos** (m. pl.);
British	**británico**		**niños** (m. pl.)
brother	**hermano** (m.)	church	**iglesia** (f.)
brown	**marrón**	cigar	**puro** (m.)
building	**edificio** (m.)	cinema	**cine**, **cinema**
burglary	**robo** (m.)		(m.)
bus	**omnibús** (m.),	city	**ciudad** (f.)
	camión (m.)	classroom	**aula** (f.)
	(Méx.)	clean, to	**limpiar**
	(Sp. **autobús**)	climate	**clima** (m.)
businessman	**empresario**	clock	**reloj** (m.)
	(m.)	close, to	**cerrar**
but	**pero**	closed	**cerrado**
buy, to	**comprar**	clothing	**vestido** (m.)
by	**por**	coast	**costa** (f.)
café	**cafetería** (f.)	coffee	**café** (m.)
call, to	**llamar**	cold (illness)	**gripe** (f.)
car	**auto** (m.),	cold	**frío**
	automóvil (m.),	(temperature)	
	carro (m.)	color	**color** (m.)
	(Sp. **coche**)	come, to	**venir**
car parking	**estacionamiento**	comfortable	**cómodo**
	(m.)	comment	**comentario** (m.)
cash	**efectivo** (m.)	commerce	**comercio** (m.)

commercial	**comercial**	difference	**diferencia** (f.)
company	**compañía** (f.);	difficult	**difícil**
	empresa (f.)	dining room	**comedor** (m.)
computer	**computador**	direction	**dirección** (f.)
	(m.), **computa-**	dirty	**sucio**
	dora (f.) (Sp.	discussion	**discusión** (f.)
	ordenador)	do, to	**hacer**
condition	**condición** (f.)	doctor	**médico** (m.);
confuse, to	**confundir**		**doctor** (m.)
consulate	**consulado** (m.)	document	**documento**
contact	**contacto** (m.)		(m.)
contented	**contento**	dog	**perro** (m.)
continue, to	**continuar**	dollar	**dólar** (m.)
contract	**contrato** (m.)	door	**puerta** (f.)
contrast	**contraste** (m.)	down, to go	**bajar**
cost	**costo** (m.)	dress	**vestido** (m.)
	(Sp. **coste**)	drink (a)	**bebida** (f.)
cost, to	**costar**	drink, to	**beber; tomar**
counter	**ventanilla** (f.)	drive, to	**conducir;**
country	**país** (m.)		**manejar**
court	**tribunal** (m.)	each	**cada**
current affairs	**programas de**	early	**temprano**
	actualidad	east	**este**
dance, to	**bailar**	easy	**fácil**
date	**fecha** (f.)	eat, to	**comer; tomar**
date	**cita** (f.)	electricity	**electricidad** (f.)
(appointment)		embassy	**embajada** (f.)
daughter	**hija** (f.)	end	**fin** (m.)
day	**día** (m.)	end, to	**terminar**
day before	**anteayer**	England	**Inglaterra** (f.)
yesterday, the		English	**inglés**
dear (in a letter)	**estimado**	enough	**suficiente**
debit card	**tarjeta de débito**	enter, to	**entrar**
	(f.)	error	**error** (m.)
December	**diciembre** (m.)	Europe	**Europa** (f.)
decision	**decisión** (f.)	European	**europeo** (m.)
declare, to	**declarar**	even if	**así**
deliver, to	**entregar**	every	**cada; todo**
departure	**salida** (f.)	exchange, to	**cambiar**
dessert	**postre** (m.)	exit	**salida** (f.)
dictionary	**diccionario** (m.)	expect, to	**esperar**
die, to	**morir**	expensive	**caro**

export, to	**exportar**	go up, to	**subir**
exporter	**exportador** (m.)	good afternoon	**buenas tardes**
eye	**ojo** (m.)	good evening,	**buenas noches**
face	**cara** (f.)	good night	
fair	**justo**	good morning	**buenos días**
family	**familia** (f.)	goodbye (inf.)	**chao, chau**
far	**lejos**	granddaughter	**nieta** (f.)
fare	**pasaje** (f.)	grandson	**nieto** (m.)
fast	**rápido**	green	**verde**
father	**padre** (m.)	hair	**pelo** (m.)
February	**febrero** (m.)	ham	**jamón** (m.)
fever	**fiebre** (f.)	hand	**mano** (f.)
film	**película** (f.)	handbag	**cartera** (f.)
find, to	**encontrar**	handicraft	**artesanía** (f.)
fine	**multa** (f.)	handkerchief	**pañuelo** (m.)
finish, to	**terminar**	happy	**contento**
fire (accidental)	**incendio** (m.)	have, to	**tener**
firm	**firma** (f.);	he	**él**
	empresa (f.)	head	**cabeza** (f.)
first	**primer/o**	health	**salud** (f.)
fish	**pescado** (m.)	hear, to	**oír**
flight	**vuelo** (m.)	hearing, inner ear	**oído** (m.)
food	**alimento** (m.)	heart	**corazón** (m.)
foot	**pie** (m.)	heat	**calor** (m.)
for	**para; por**	heating	**calefacción** (f.)
foreign, foreigner	**extranjero** (m.)	height (of a	**estatura** (f.)
forget, to	**olvidar**	person)	
form	**formulario** (m.)	hello (answering	**aló** (Sp. **dígame**)
free	**libre**	the phone)	
Friday	**viernes** (m.)	hello	**hola**
from	**desde; de**	help, to	**ayudar**
fruit	**fruta** (f.)	here	**acá, aquí**
fuel	**combustible** (m.)	high	**alto**
functional	**funcional**	Hispanic	**hispánica**
gentleman	**señor**	holidays	**vacaciones**
gentlemen (sign	**caballeros**		(f. pl.)
on toilets)	(m. pl.)	home	**casa** (f.)
get up, to	**levantarse**	hope, to	**esperar**
girl	**chica** (f.); **niña**	hospital	**hospital** (m.)
	(f.)	hot	**caliente**
give, to	**dar; entregar**	hotel	**hotel** (f.)
go, to	**ir**	hour	**hora** (f.)

house	**casa** (f.)	ladies (sign on	**damas** (f. pl.)
how	**cómo**	toilets)	
how many	**cuántos, cuántas**	language	**idioma** (m.)
how much	**cuánto, cuánta**	large	**grande**
hunger	**hambre** (f.)	last night	**anoche**
hungry, to be	**tener hambre**	late	**tarde**
husband	**esposo** (m.);	later	**luego**
	marido (f.)	Latin America	**Latinoamérica**
I	**yo**		(f.)
identification	**identificación** (f.)	Latin American	**latinoamericano**
if	**si**	leaflet	**folleto** (m.)
ill	**enfermo**	learn, to	**aprender**
import, to	**importar**	left	**izquierda**
important	**importante**	leg	**pierna** (f.)
in	**en**	less	**menos**
in front of	**delante de**	lesson, class	**clase** (f.)
in order to	**para**	letter	**carta** (f.)
industry	**industria** (f.)	lift	**ascensor** (m.)
influenza	**gripe** (f.)	light	**luz** (f.)
information	**información** (f.)	light, to	**encender**
innocent	**inocente**	like, to	**gustar**
insurance	**seguro** (m.)	listen, to	**escuchar**
interesting	**interesante**	little	**pequeño**
international	**internacional**	little by little	**poco a poco**
interview	**entrevista** (f.)	live, to	**vivir**
invest, to	**invertir**	London	**Londres** (m.)
investigation	**investigación** (f.)	long	**largo**
investment	**inversión** (f.)	look, to	**mirar**
invoice	**factura** (f.)	lorry	**camión** (m.)
Ireland	**Irlanda** (f.)	luggage	**equipaje** (m.)
Irish	**irlandés**	lunch, to have	**almorzar**
it's cold/windy/	**hace frío/viento/**	make, to	**hacer**
hot, etc.	**calor, etc.**	man	**hombre** (m.)
January	**enero** (m.)	man-made	**artificial**
July	**julio** (m.)	many	**muchos**
June	**junio** (m.)	map	**mapa** (f.)
just	**justo**	March	**marzo** (m.)
key	**llave** (f.)	market	**mercado** (m.)
kilo	**kilo** (m.)	married	**casado**
kilometer	**kilómetro** (m.)	mass (religion)	**misa** (f.)
kitchen	**cocina** (f.)	material	**material** (m.)
ladder	**escalera** (f.)	matter	**asunto** (m.)

matter, it doesn't	**no importa**	neither (conj.)	**tampoco**
meal	**comida** (f.)	network	**red** (f.)
meat	**carne** (f.)	never	**nunca**
medium	**mediano**	new	**nuevo**
meeting	**reunión** (f.)	news item	**noticia** (f.)
menu	**menú** (m.)	newspaper	**periódico** (m.)
meter	**metro** (m.)	next	**próximo**
midday	**mediodía** (m.)	next to	**junto a; al lado**
midnight	**medianoche**		**de**
	(f.)	nice	**bonito**
milk	**leche** (f.)	no	**no**
million	**millón** (m.)	no one	**ninguno**
minute	**minuto** (m.)	no, not	**no**
miss	**señorita**	nobody	**nadie**
mistake	**error** (m.)	noise	**ruido** (m.)
Miss	**Srta**	non-smoker	**no fumador**
mobile phone	**celular** (m.);		(m.)
	teléfono	normal	**normal**
	móvil (m.)	normally	**normalmente**
moment	**momento** (m.)	north	**norte**
Monday	**lunes** (m.)	North American,	**norteamericano**
money	**dinero** (m.);	American	
	plata (f.)	November	**noviembre** (m.)
	(Sp. **dinero**)	now	**ahora**
month	**mes** (m.)	number	**número** (m.)
more	**más**	nurse	**enfermera** (f.)
morning	**mañana** (f.)	occasion	**vez** (f.), **ocasión**
mother	**madre** (f.)		(f.)
motorbike	**motocicleta** (f.)	occupation	**ocupación** (f.)
mountain	**montaña** (f.)	October	**octubre** (m.)
mustache	**bigote** (m.)	of	**de**
movies	**cine**	office	**oficina** (f.)
Mr	**Sr**	on	**en**
Mrs	**Sra**	one	**un, uno, una**
much	**mucho**	only	**sólo, solamente**
museum	**museo** (m.)	opposite	**enfrente de**
music	**música** (f.)	or	**o**
my	**mi**, **mis**	orange	**naranja** (f.)
name	**nombre** (m.)	other	**otro**
navy blue	**azul marino**	over	**encima**
near	**cerca**	pain	**dolor** (m.)
necessary	**necesario**	partner	**pareja** (f.)

pants	**pantalón** (m.)	purse	**cartera** (f.)
	pantalones (m. pl.)	put, to	**poner**
		question	**pregunta** (f.)
paper	**papel** (m.)	quiet	**tranquilo**
paperwork	**trámite** (m.)	rain	**lluvia** (f.)
parcel	**paquete** (m.)	raspberry	**frambuesa** (f.)
parents	**padres** (m.)	read, to	**leer**
park, to	**estacionar**	red tape	**trámite** (m.)
partner	**pareja** (f.)	refreshing drink	**refresco** (m.)
passenger	**pasajero** (m.)	relieve, to	**aliviar**
passport	**pasaporte** (m.)	repair, to	**reparar**
pasty	**empanada** (f.)	repeat, to	**repetir**
pay, to	**pagar**	reply	**respuesta** (f.)
pencil	**lápiz** (m.)	reply, to	**responder**
people	**gente** (f.)	report	**informe** (m.)
people (of a nation)	**pueblo** (m.)	research	**investigación** (f.)
		reservation	**reservación** (f.)
person	**persona** (f.)	reserve	**reservar**
person in charge	**encargado** (m.)	restaurant	**restaurante** (m.)
petrol	**gasolina** (f.)		
place	**lugar** (m.)	return (trip, journey)	**ida y vuelta** (f.)
place, to	**colocar**		
please	**por favor**	return, to	**volver**
pleased to meet you	**encantado**	right	**derecha; verdad** (f.)
police, policeman, policewoman	**policía** (f., m., f.)	robbery	**robo** (m.)
		room	**habitación** (f.)
police station	**comisaría** (f.)	rum	**ron** (m.)
poor (in money)	**pobre;**	rushed	**apurado** (Sp. **apresurado**)
poor (in quality)	**malo**		
possible	**posible**	sad	**triste**
post office	**correo** (m.)	salad	**ensalada** (f.)
postcard	**postal** (f.)	Saturday	**sábado** (m.)
potato	**papa** (f.) (Sp. **patata**)	say, to	**decir**
		school	**colegio** (m.)
poverty	**pobreza** (f.)	sea	**mar** (m.)
prefer, to	**preferir**	season	**estación** (f.)
price	**precio** (m.)	seat	**asiento** (m.)
probable	**probable**	second	**segundo**
problem	**problema** (m.)	see, to	**ver**
product	**producto** (m.)	see you later	**hasta luego**
publication	**publicación** (f.)	sell, to	**vender**

send, to	**mandar**	sort	**tipo** (m.)
September	**setiembre, septiembre** (m.)	south	**sur** (m.)
		Spanish (language)	**castellano** (Sp. **español**)
seventh	**sétimo, séptimo**		
she	**ella**	speak, to	**hablar**
shirt	**camisa** (f.)	spend, to (money)	**gastar**
shoe	**zapato** (m.)		
short (length)	**corto**	spring (season)	**primavera** (f.)
short (height)	**bajo**	square	**plaza** (f.)
shoulder	**hombro** (m.)	stairs	**escalera** (f.)
shuttle service	**puente aéreo** (m.)	start, to	**comenzar; empezar**
side	**lado** (m.)	station	**estación** (f.)
sign, to	**firmar**	stay	**estadía** (f.) (Sp. **estancia**)
signature	**firma** (f.)		
silver	**plata** (f.)	stocking	**media** (f.)
since (as)	**como**	stomach	**estómago** (m.)
since (time)	**desde**	stop, to	**parar**
single (trip, journey)	**ida** (f.)	street	**calle** (f.)
		strong	**fuerte**
sister	**hermana** (f.)	student	**estudiante** (m., f.)
size	**tamaño** (m.)		
size (clothes)	**talla** (fm.)	study, to	**estudiar**
skin	**piel** (f.)	subway	**metro**
skirt	**falda** (f.)	sugar	**azúcar** (m.)
sleep, to	**dormir**	suite of furniture	**juego de muebles** (m.)
slow	**lento**		
slowly	**despacio**	suitcase	**maleta** (f.)
small	**chiquito**	surf the Net, to	**navegar en Internet**
small	**pequeño; chico; chiquito**		
		summer	**verano** (m.)
so, thus	**así**	Sunday	**domingo** (m.)
soap	**jabón** (m.)	supermarket	**supermercado** (m.)
sock	**media** (f.)		
some	**alguien**	surname	**apellido** (m.)
somebody	**alguien**	sweater	**suéter** (m.)
someone	**alguno**	swim, to	**nadar**
something	**algo**	swimming pool	**natatorio** (m.); **piscina** (f.)
son	**hijo** (m.)		
soon	**pronto**	T-shirt	**camiseta** (f.)
sorry!	**¡perdón!; lo siento**	table	**mesa** (f.)
		take, to	**tomar**

tall	**alto**	tidy up, to	**ordenar**
tax	**impuesto** (m.)	time	**tiempo** (m.)
tea	**té** (m.)	time (occasion)	**vez** (f.)
teacher	**profesor** (m.)	tired	**cansado**
telegram	**telegrama** (m.)	to	**para**
telephone	**teléfono** (m.)	tobacco	**tabaco** (m.)
telephone call	**llamada** (f.)	today	**hoy**
television	**televisión** (f.)	toilet	**baño** (m.) (Sp.
temperature	**temperatura** (f.)		**servico, aseo**)
than	**que**	tomorrow	**mañana** (m.)
thanks, thank	**gracias**	tongue	**lengua** (f.)
you		too much/many;	**demasiado**
that (m.)	**aquel, ese**	too	
that (f.)	**aquella, esa**	tooth	**muela** (f.)
that one (m.)	**aquél, ése**	tourist	**turista** (m., f.)
that one (f.)	**aquella, ésa**	town	**pueblo** (m.)
the	**el** (m. sing.), **la**	train	**tren** (m.)
	(f. sing.), **las**	traveler's check	**cheque de**
	(f. pl.), **los**		**viaje/viajero**
	(m. pl.)		(m.)
then	**entonces**	trip	**viaje** (m.)
then (later)	**luego**	trousers	**pantalón** (m.),
there	**allá; ahí; allí**		**pantalones**
there is/are	**hay**		(m. pl.)
these (m.)	**estos**	truth	**verdad** (f.)
these ones (m.)	**éstos**	Tuesday	**martes** (m.)
they	**ellos** (m.), **ellas**	turn off, to	**apagar**
	(f.)	turn on, to	**encender**
thing	**cosa** (f.)	type	**tipo** (m.)
thirst	**sed** (f.)	uncomfortable	**incómodo**
thirsty, to be	**tener sed**	underground	**metro** (m.)
this (m.)	**este**	underneath	**debajo**
this one (m.)	**éste**	understand, to	**comprender**
those(m.)	**aquel, ese**	United States	**Estados Unidos**
those (f.)	**aquellas, esas**	(m. pl.)	
those ones (m.)	**aquellos, ésos**	(North)	**estadounidense**
those ones (f.)	**aquellas, ésas**	American	
thousand	**mil**	until	**hasta**
throat	**garganta** (f.)	urgent	**urgente**
Thursday	**jueves** (m.)	useful	**útil, útiles**
ticket	**boleto** (m.)	vegetable	**verdura** (f.)
tie	**corbata** (f.)	very	**muy**

vest	**camiseta** (f.)	which?; which	**¿cuál?; cuál**
village	**pueblo** (m.)	whichever	**cualquiera**
visit, to	**visitar**	white	**blanco**
voice mail	**casilla de**	who?; who	**¿quién?; quien**
	mensajes (f.)	whole	**todo**
wait, to	**esperar**	wife	**esposa** (f.);
Wales	**Gales** (m.)		**mujer** (f.)
walk, to	**caminar; andar**	wind	**viento** (m.)
walk, to go for a	**pasear**	window (at a	**ventanilla** (f.)
wallet	**billetera** (f.);	bank)	
	cartera (f.)	wine	**vino** (m.)
want, to	**querer**	winter	**invierno** (m.)
warm	**templado**	with	**con**
warn, to	**avisar**	withdraw, to	**retirar**
wash, to	**lavar**	with me	**conmigo**
watch	**reloj** (m.)	with you	**contigo**
watch, to	**ver**	without	**sin**
water	**agua** (f.)	woman	**mujer** (f.)
we	**nosotros**	wool	**lana** (f.)
weather	**tiempo** (m.)	word	**palabra** (f.)
weather forecast	**pronóstico del**	work, to	**trabajar**
	tiempo (m.)	worth, to be	**valer**
web page	**Página Web**	write, to	**escribir**
	(f.)	year	**año** (m.)
Wednesday	**miércoles** (m.)	yellow	**amarillo**
week	**semana** (f.)	yes	**sí**
weekend	**fin de semana**	yesterday	**ayer**
	(m.)	you	**tú** (inf.), **usted**
weight	**peso** (m.)		(for.), **ustedes**
welcome	**bienvenido**		(for. and
well	**bien**		inf. pl.) (Sp.
Welsh	**galés**		**vosotros** = inf.)
west	**oeste** (m.)	young	**joven**
what?	**¿qué?**	young lady	**señorita** (f.)
what's happen-	**¿qué pasa?**	your	**tu, tus** (inf.): **su**
ing?, what's			(for.)
the matter?		you're welcome	**de nada**
when?; when	**¿cuándo?;**	(in response	
	cuando	to **gracias**)	
where?; where	**¿dónde?; donde**	zone	**zona** (f.)

Index of language points

The numbers refer to the lessons in the book.